PLAYS OF THE YEAR
Volume 41
1971–72

PLAYS OF THE YEAR

EDITED BY
J. C. TREWIN

HOME
David Storey

THE PATRICK PEARSE MOTEL
Hugh Leonard

TRELAWNY
Aubrey Woods, Julian Slade,
George Rowell
(from Pinero's *Trelawny of the 'Wells'*)

VOLUME 41
1971–2

PAUL ELEK LTD
LONDON

© PLAYS OF THE YEAR COMPANY
AND PAUL ELEK BOOKS LTD 1972

P.C. 10/72.

Published by
PAUL ELEK BOOKS LTD
54–58 Caledonian Road, N.1

HOME
© David Storey

THE PATRICK PEARSE MOTEL
© Hugh Leonard

TRELAWNY
© Aubrey Woods, Julian Slade,
George Rowell

*Printed in Great Britain by
Clarke, Doble & Brendon Ltd.,
Plymouth*

FOR WENDY
Looking from Fiesole

CONTENTS

INTRODUCTION

I

Our forty-first volume begins with David Storey's HOME, the fourth play by this extraordinary dramatist that we have so far published.* The Royal Court Theatre's programme, at the première, gave no indication either of place or the characters' relationships. We knew simply that Act One was before lunch, and Act Two after it; the people were named Harry, Jack, Marjorie, Kathleen, and Alfred. Photographs gave nothing away; and we could make what we wished of the cover design.

The play began and remained upon a terrace suggested by a portion of a balustrade, a flagpole without flag, and a small round table with two garden chairs. Presently two men were seated there, dressed well, apparently leisured. Fairly new acquaintances, they continued what we presumed to have been an on-and-off conversation over some days, an odd, fragmentary, stream-of-consciousness affair with its civilized bromides and its non-sequiturs.

* Others have been *The Restoration of Arnold Middleton* (Vol. 35), *In Celebration* (Vol. 38), and *The Contractor* (Vol. 40).

One of the men, acted by Sir John Gielgud, was mild and deprecating; his thoughts seemed often to be elsewhere. His friend, acted by Sir Ralph Richardson, was jauntier, more man-of-the-world, ready with an inconsequential progress of anecdotes about his aunt or a cousin on the mother's side. But no subject, no strange accident, detained them for long. They could not concentrate. The talk fluttered on, and we were increasingly aware of the strain, a sense of something awry.

Clearly, it was not an ordinary terrace, not altogether a routine walk and talk. Sir John and Sir Ralph acted with an uncanny, relaxed subtlety, every word and movement calculated. Slowly we understood what kind of home this was, what lay behind the small talk, the courtesies, the casual revelations; and we remembered another dramatist, 'Canst thou not minister to a mind diseased?'

The play that night was startling in its sympathy and curious rhythm. Its dramatist did not use shock tactics; nothing was cheap or melodramatic. The five unhappy people we met before and after lunch were shown to us as they saw each other. Though their lives were helpless, they had their own defences and put them up in their own fashion. Only now and again the mask dropped and the tears flowed: I had never known anybody weep more movingly and quietly than Sir John Gielgud did.

We wondered at first about the two middle-aged women patients (played by Mona Washbourne and Dandy Nichols). They could be tiresome, for their giggling and grumbling, surliness and facile invective, could jar upon the quietness of the sadly courteous men. But this contrast, we found, did not harm David Storey's play: a most

8

delicate and telling invention, especially at the last when the two men, once more alone and now with nothing to say, peered into the darkening sky and at their darkened lives. Sir John and Sir Ralph, in a production by Lindsay Anderson, gave performances, beautifully timed and judged, that did honour to the stage, and were seen again in a West End run at the Apollo; at the Morosco in New York (November 1970); and on English television. The text shows how sensitively David Storey, in his elliptical dialogue, established his people and their scene.

II

THE PATRICK PEARSE MOTEL, staged at the Queen's in London (with Norman Rodway) during 1971, after its success at the Dublin Theatre Festival, is by Hugh Leonard. Expert Irish author of many plays for stage and television, he is known particularly for Stephen D and The Poker Session (see Plays of the Year: 38). The new piece is an Irish farce—the scene of its first act is 'a suburb in Dublin's vodka-and-bitter-lemon-belt'—and Mr Leonard has a programme note: 'I owe a tribute and an acknowledgement to Georges Feydeau. THE PATRICK PEARSE MOTEL owes some of its construction to the principles embodied in the Feydeau farces of more than half a century ago, which established for all time that some matters are too serious to be turned into tragedies.'

Next the production that in January 1972 so splendidly re-opened the Theatre Royal at Bristol. The famous auditorium, dating from 1766, is untouched; but everything behind the proscenium is expanded, and in front of the house there

9

are new foyers that make use of the eighteenth-century Coopers' Hall.

TRELAWNY, of which we print the libretto, can now partner Sixty Thousand Nights *(Volume 36), devised for the theatre bicentenary. At that time I quoted Val May, the Bristol director, who said: 'Almost every great performer of the last two centuries has appeared on the Royal stage, and during these last two hundred years the theatre has witnessed many changes of style in acting, writing, and stage technique.' We can observe how appropriate TRELAWNY was as a re-opening play. Its adapters (Julian Slade is also the composer) have handled Pinero with affection; the main differences are the inclusion of the 'Wells' pantomime, a switching of scene, and some neat cuts. Bagnigge Wells is now called, frankly, Sadler's Wells.* (The dramatist himself did so in the 1925 revival of his play at the Old Vic.)*

Arthur Wing Pinero (1855–1934) loved the traditions of the theatre he served, first as an actor, then—and far more valuably—as dramatist. Trelawny of the 'Wells', *from his mid-career, was both a salute to the profession and a piece of theatrical history, disguised as one of the gentlest and most assured comedies of its age. Pinero set it in the early Sixties. What it celebrates is an event that was not much more than three decades distant when* Trelawny *arrived on the stage of the*

---

* In a note (January 1898) on the first Royal Court programme of his 'original comedietta,' Pinero said : 'Bagnigge (locally pronounced Bagnidge) Wells—formerly a popular mineral spring in Islington, London, situated not far from the better remembered Sadler's Wells. The gardens of Bagnigge Wells were much resorted to; but, as a matter of fact, unlike Sadler's Wells. it never possessed a playhouse. Sadler's Wells Theatre, however—always familiarly known as the 'Wells'—still exists. It was rebuilt in 1876–77.'

Court Theatre in January 1898. The event was a rebellion in English drama, the coming of naturalism, the success of T.W. (Tom) Robertson, Madge Kendal's brother—he was the eldest of twenty-two children, she the youngest—who created the 'teacup-and-saucer comedy' in a mid-Victorian theatre of hollow artifice. In Trelawny of the 'Wells' *he is disguised as Tom Wrench, an actor struggling with General Utility in the unshakeably hieratic organization of 'Bagnigge Wells'. His play is called* Life, *and an old hand says sadly that it has 'not a speech in it—not a real* speech; *nothing to dig your teeth into'. This can stand if we wish, and as Pinero clearly intended, for Robertson's* Society, *staged at the old Prince of Wales, off Tottenham Court Road, in November 1865. (Until 1971 the portico of the old theatre was still in service at the stage-door of the Scala; it disappeared in the Scala demolition.)*

The coming of naturalism is one theme of Trelawny of the 'Wells': *the other is an actor's pride in his calling. Set in a world of crinolines and peg-top trousers, of the 'weeper' and the flounced skirt, of mahogany and horsehair, the comedy shows how a wave from the sea-coast of Bohemia washes up, and over, a rigidly conventional household. Players, pomping folk, in the middle Sixties were regarded as 'gypsies,' dissolute and garish. In the circumstances, it is a social crime for the grandson of the terrifying Vice-Chancellor, Sir William Gower, of Cavendish Square, to woo a stock company actress of nineteen, even though (as Pinero says) she does look divine in washed muslin. But Rose Trelawny conquers. Sir William learns that her mother had acted with Edmund Kean, and his mood changes, for Kean was 'a splendid gypsy'. When Rose*

11

exhibits a chain and an Order, a sword-belt and sword—'very theatrical and tawdry'—and a gold fillet, the old man puts the chain over his shoulders handles the belt and sword, and for a moment re-lives a famous night. Always this comes through in performance. Pinero, man of the theatre, communicates his own loyalty and excitement.

If Rose has her victory then, Tom Wrench (or Robertson) has his at the end. Originally, much of the act was given to Life, a shrewd pastiche of what Archer defined as the new pre-Raphaelitism of the stage. There is pathos here, for two veteran players, a husband and wife of the older school, are reduced to minor duties, he as a small-part actor, she as wardrobe mistress. Before the rehearsal they talk together in some of Pinero's most often-quoted speeches: 'And so this new-fangled stuff, and these dandified people, are to push us, and such as us, from our stools!'—'Yes, James, just as some other new fashion will, in course of time, push them from their stools.' (Nobody who works in the theatre can afford to forget this.)

The comedy, tale of two conquests, has its under-current of defeat: Tom Wrench loses what he would have most wished to gain. Not that it saddens the night. Trelawny of the 'Wells' (and TRELAWNY) can be strangely wistful—I hope nobody will say 'nostalgic'—but we remember the warmth and spirit, the evocation of a period, the moments when Miss Trafalgar Gower realizes that troubadours in Cavendish Square are quite out of place, or Ferdinand Gadd finds that even a pantomime Demon of Discontent has some promising lines: 'I'm Discontent! From Orkney's isle to Dover/To make men's bile bile-over I endover.'

For the record, Trelawny of the 'Wells' had its

12

first revival in 1910, at the Duke of York's. There have been half-a-dozen other London productions, and one at the Malvern Festival of 1935. Irene Vanbrugh played Rose (of Cornish descent I would like to think) in 1898, 1910 and 1917, and the part has also been acted in London by Marie Ney, Margaret Bannerman, Sophie Stewart, Barbara Jefford, Louise Purnell (Chichester and the National), and at Malvern by Curigwen Lewis. Dion Boucicault created the Vice-Chancellor; Paul Arthur was the first Tom Wrench, and Gerald du Maurier the first Ferdinand Gadd. Bernard Shaw said in 1898 that Trelawny of the 'Wells' *had touched him more than anything Pinero had written. Shavians will recall the parenthesis: 'It is significant of the difference between my temperament and Mr Pinero's that when he, as a little boy, first heard "Ever of thee I'm fondly dreaming," he wept; whereas, at the same tender age, I simply noted with scorn the obvious plagiarism from "Cheer, Boys, Cheer."'*

In the Bristol TRELAWNY, *lovingly directed by Val May, Ian Richardson (his first stage part after a brilliant Stratford decade) was Tom Wrench; Hayley Mills, Rose; and Timothy West, the Vice-Chancellor.*

J. C. TREWIN

Hampstead
May 1972

I have as ever, and with deep gratitude, to thank my colleague, Mrs Judith Rayner (Miss Judith Farmer) for her expertise and tolerance during the preparation of this volume.

NOTE

Home was staged first at the Royal Court Theatre. Previous plays from the Court in this series have been :

HOME

by
DAVID STOREY

TO KAREL REISZ

who first brought these ends together

The English Stage Company presented *Home* at the Royal Court Theatre, London, on 17 June 1970, with the following cast:

HARRY	*John Gielgud*
JACK	*Ralph Richardson*
MARJORIE	*Dandy Nichols*
KATHLEEN	*Mona Washbourne*
ALFRED	*Warren Clarke*

Directed by Lindsay Anderson

Designed by Jocelyn Herbert

Music by Alan Price

Lighting by Andy Phillips

On 28 July 1970, it was staged at the Apollo Theatre, London. It has also been performed in New York and on English television.

CHARACTERS

HARRY

JACK

MARJORIE

KATHLEEN

ALFRED

ACT ONE

Scene 1

*The stage is bare but for a round metalwork table, set slightly off-centre, stage left, and two metalwork chairs.**

Harry comes on, stage right, a middle-aged man in his forties. He wears a casual suit, perhaps tweed, with a suitable hat which, after glancing pleasurably around, he takes off and puts on the table beside him, along with a pair of well-used leather gloves and a folded newspaper.

Presses his shoulders back, eases neck, etc., making himself comfortable. Settles down. Glances at his watch, shakes it, makes sure it's going: winds it slowly, looking round.

Stretches neck again. Leans down, wafts cotton from his turn-ups. Examines shoes, without stooping.

Clears his throat. Clasps his hands in his lap, gazes out, abstracted, head nodding slightly, half-smiling.

JACK : Harry !

(Jack has come on from the other side, stage left. He's dressed in a similar fashion, but with a slightly more dandyish flavour: handkerchief hanging from top pocket, a rakish trilby. Also has a simple though rather elegant cane.)

* In the Royal Court production the indications of a setting were provided : a white flag-pole, stage right, and upstage a low terrace with a single step down, centre, and balustrade, stage left.

19

HARRY : Jack.

JACK : Been here long?

HARRY : No. No.

JACK : Mind?

HARRY : Not at all.

(*Jack sits down. He stretches, shows great relief at being off his feet, etc.*)

JACK : Nice to see the sun again.

HARRY : Very.

JACK : Been laid up for a few days.

HARRY : Oh dear.

JACK : Chill. In bed.

HARRY : Oh dear. Still . . . Appreciate the comforts.

JACK : What? . . . You're right. Still . . . Nice to be out.

HARRY : 'Tis.

JACK : Mind?

HARRY : All yours.

(*Jack picks up the paper; gazes at it without unfolding it.*)

JACK : Damn bad news.

HARRY : Yes.

JACK : Not surprising.

HARRY : Gets worse before it gets better.

JACK : 'S right . . . Still . . . Not to grumble.

HARRY : No. No.

JACK : Put on a bold front. (*Turns paper over.*)

HARRY : That's right.

JACK : Pretty. (*Indicates paper.*)

HARRY : Very.

JACK : By jove . . . (*Reads intently a moment.*) Oh, well.

HARRY : That the one? (*Glances over.*)

JACK (*nods*) : Yes . . . (*Clicks his tongue.*)

HARRY (*shakes his head*) : Ah, well.

JACK : Yes . . . Still . . .

HARRY : Clouds . . . Watch their different shapes.

JACK : Yes? (*Looks up at the sky at which Harry is gazing.*)

HARRY : See how they drift over?

JACK : By jove.

HARRY : First sight . . . nothing. Then . . . just watch the edges . . . See.

JACK : Amazing.

HARRY : Never notice when you're just walking.

JACK : No . . . Still . . . Best time of the year.

HARRY : What?

JACK : Always think this is the best time.

HARRY : Oh, yes.

JACK : Not too hot. Not too cold.

HARRY : Seen that? (*Points at the paper.*)

JACK (*reads. Then*) : By jove . . . (*Reads again briefly.*) Well . . . you get some surprises . . . Hello . . . (*Reads farther down, turning edge of paper over.*) Good God.

HARRY : What I felt.

JACK : The human mind. (*Shakes his head.*)

HARRY : Oh dear, yes.

JACK : One of these days . . .

HARRY : Ah, yes.

JACK : Then where will they be?

HARRY : Oh, yes.

JACK : Never give it a thought.

HARRY : No . . . Never.

JACK (*reads again*) : By jove . . . (*Shakes his head.*)

(*Harry leans over; removes something casually from Jack's sleeve.*)

21

Oh . . .

HARRY : Cotton.

JACK : Oh . . . Picked it up . . . (*Glances round at his other sleeve, then down at his trousers.*)

HARRY : See you've come prepared.

JACK : What . . . ? Oh.

(*Harry indicates Jack's coat pocket. Jack takes out a folded plastic mac, no larger, folded, than his hand.*)

Best to make sure

HARRY : Took a risk. Myself.

JACK : Oh, yes . . . What's life worth . . .

HARRY : Oh, yes.

JACK : I say. That was a shock.

HARRY : Yesterday . . . ?

JACK : Bolt from the blue, and no mistake.

HARRY : I'd been half-prepared . . . even then.

JACK : Still a shock.

HARRY : Absolutely.

JACK : My wife . . . you've met? . . . Was that last week?

HARRY : Ah, yes . . .

JACK : Well. A very delicate woman.

HARRY : Still. Very sturdy.

JACK : Oh, well. Physically, nothing to complain of.

HARRY : Oh, no.

JACK : Temperament, however . . . inclined to the sensitive side.

HARRY : Really.

JACK : Two years ago . . . (*Glances off.*) By jove. Isn't that Saxton?

HARRY : Believe it is.

JACK : He's a sharp dresser, and no mistake.

HARRY : Very.
JACK : They tell me . . . Well, I never.
HARRY : Didn't see that, did he?

(They laugh, looking off.)

Eyes in the back of your head these days.
JACK : You have. That's right.
HARRY : Won't do that again in a hurry. What?
(Laughs.)
JACK : I had an uncle once who bred horses.
HARRY : Really.
JACK : Used to go down there when I was a boy.
HARRY : The country.
JACK : Nothing like it. What? Fresh air.
HARRY : Clouds. *(Gestures up.)*
JACK : I'd say so.
HARRY : *My* wife was coming up this morning.
JACK : Really?
HARRY : Slight headache. Thought might be better . . .
JACK : Indoors. Well. Best make sure.
HARRY : When I was in the army . . .
JACK : Really? What regiment?
HARRY : Fusiliers.
JACK : Really? How extraordinary.
HARRY : You?
JACK : No. No. A cousin.
HARRY : Well . . .
JACK : Different time, of course.
HARRY : Ah.
JACK : Used to bring his rifle . . . No. That was Arthur. Got them muddled. *(Laughs.)*
HARRY : Still.
JACK : Never leaves you.
HARRY. No. No.

JACK : In good stead.

HARRY : Oh, yes.

JACK : All your life.

HARRY : Oh, yes.

JACK : I was—for a very short while—in the Royal Air Force.

HARRY : Really?

JACK : Nothing to boast about.

HARRY : Oh, now. Flying?

JACK : On the ground.

HARRY : Chrysanthemums is my wife's hobby.

JACK : Really.

HARRY : Thirty-seven species round the house.

JACK : Beautiful flower.

HARRY : Do you know there are over a hundred?

JACK : Really?

HARRY : Different species.

JACK : Suppose you can mix them up.

HARRY : Oh. Very.

JACK : He's coming back . . .

HARRY : . . .?

JACK : Swanson.

HARRY : Saxton.

JACK : Saxton! Always did get those two mixed up. Two boys at school : one called Saxton, the other Swanson. Curious thing was, they both looked alike.

HARRY : Really?

JACK : Both had a curious skin disease. Here. Just at the side of the nose.

HARRY : Eczema.

JACK : Really?

HARRY : Could have been.

JACK : Never thought of that . . . When I was young I had an ambition to be a priest, you know.

HARRY : Really?

24

JACK : Thought about it a great deal.

HARRY : Ah, yes. A great decision.

JACK : Oh, yes.

HARRY : Catholic or Anglican?

JACK : Well . . . Couldn't really make up my mind.

HARRY : Both got a great deal to offer.

JACK : Great deal? My word.

HARRY : Advantages one way. And then . . . in another.

JACK : Oh, yes.

HARRY : One of my first ambitions . . .

JACK : Yes.

HARRY : Oh, now. You'll laugh.

JACK : No. No . . . No. Really.

HARRY : Well . . . I would have liked to have been a dancer.

JACK : Dancer . . . Tap or 'balley'?

HARRY : Oh, well. Probably a bit of both.

JACK : A fine thing. Grace.

HARRY : Ah, yes.

JACK : Physical momentum.

HARRY : Oh, yes.

JACK : Swanson might have appreciated that! (*Laughs.*)

HARRY : Saxton.

JACK : Saxton! By jove . . . At school we had a boy called Ramsbottom.

HARRY : Really.

JACK : Now I wouldn't have envied that boy's life.

HARRY : No.

JACK : The euphemisms to which a name . . . well. One doesn't have to think very far.

HARRY : No.

JACK : A name can be a great embarrassment in life.

25

HARRY : It can . . . We had—let me think—a boy called Fish.

JACK : Fish !

HARRY : And another called Parsons !

JACK : Parsons !

HARRY : Nicknamed 'Nosey'.

JACK : By jove ! (*Laughs; rises.*) Some of these nicknames are very clever.

HARRY : Yes.

JACK (*moves away stage right*) : I remember, when I was young, I had a very tall friend . . . extremely tall as a matter of fact. He was called 'Lolly'.

HARRY : Lolly !

JACK : It fitted him very well. He . . . (*Abstracted. Pause.*) Yes. Had very large teeth as well.

HARRY : The past. It conjures up some images.

JACK : It does. You're right.

HARRY : You wonder how there was ever time for it all.

JACK : Time . . . Oh . . . Don't mention it.

HARRY : A fine cane.

JACK : What? Oh, that.

HARRY : Father had a cane. Walked for miles.

JACK : A habit that's fast dying out.

HARRY : Oh, yes.

JACK : Knew a man, related to a friend of mine, who used to walk twenty miles a day.

HARRY : Twenty !

JACK : Each morning.

HARRY : That really shows some spirit.

JACK : If you keep up a steady pace, you can manage four miles in the hour.

HARRY : Goodness.

JACK : Five hours. Set off at eight each morning. Back for lunch at one.

HARRY : Must have had a great appetite.

JACK : Oh. Absolutely. Ate like a horse.

HARRY : Stand him in good stead later on.

JACK : Ah, yes . . . Killed, you know. In the war.

HARRY : Oh dear.

JACK : Funny thing to work out.

HARRY : Oh, yes.

(*Pause*).

JACK (*sits*) : You do any fighting?

HARRY : What?

JACK : Army.

HARRY : Oh, well, then . . . modest amount.

JACK : Nasty business.

HARRY : Oh! Doesn't bear thinking about.

JACK : Two relatives of mine killed in the war.

HARRY : Oh dear.

JACK : You have to give thanks, I must say.

HARRY : Oh, yes.

JACK : Mother's father . . . a military man.

HARRY : Yes.

JACK : All his life.

HARRY : He must have seen some sights.

JACK : Oh, yes.

HARRY : Must have all had meaning then.

JACK : Oh, yes. India. Africa. He's buried as a matter of fact in Hong Kong.

HARRY : Really?

JACK : So they tell me. Never been there myself.

HARRY : No.

JACK : Hot climates, I think, can be the very devil if you haven't the temperament.

HARRY : Huh! You don't have to tell me.

JACK : Been there?

HARRY : No, no. Just what one reads.

JACK : Dysentery.

27

HARRY : Beriberi.

JACK : Yellow fever.

HARRY : Oh dear.

JACK : As well, of course, as all the other contingencies.

HARRY : Oh, yes.

JACK : At times one's glad simply to live on an island.

HARRY : Yes.

JACK : Strange that.

HARRY : Yes.

JACK : Without the sea—all around—civilization would never have been the same.

HARRY : Oh, no.

JACK : The ideals of life, liberty, freedom, could never have been the same—democracy—well, if we'd been living on the Continent, for example.

HARRY : Absolutely.

JACK : Those your gloves?

HARRY : Yes.

JACK : Got a pair like that at home.

HARRY : Yes?

JACK : Very nearly. The seam goes the other way, I think. (*Picks one up to look.*) Yes. It does.

HARRY : A present.

JACK : Really?

HARRY : My wife. At Christmas.

JACK : Season of good cheer.

HARRY : Less and less, of course, these days.

JACK : Oh, my dear man. The whole thing has been ruined. The moment money intrudes . . . all feeling goes straight out of the window.

HARRY : Oh, yes.

JACK : I had an aunt once who owned a little shop.

HARRY : Yes?

28

JACK : Made almost her entire income during the few weeks before Christmas.

HARRY : Really.

JACK : Never seemed to occur to her that there might be some ethical consideration.

HARRY : Oh dear.

JACK : Ah, well.

HARRY : Still . . .

JACK : Apart from that, she was a very wonderful person.

HARRY : It's very hard to judge.

JACK : It is.

HARRY : I have a car, for instance.

JACK : Yes?

HARRY : One day, in December, I happened to knock a pedestrian over in the street.

JACK : Oh dear.

HARRY : It was extremely crowded.

JACK : You don't have to tell me. I've seen them.

HARRY : Happened to see something they wanted the other side. Dashed across. Before you know where you are . . .

JACK : Not serious, I hope?

HARRY : No. No. No. Fractured arm.

JACK : From that, you know, they might learn a certain lesson.

HARRY : Oh, yes.

JACK : Experience is a stern master.

HARRY : Ah, yes. But then . . .

JACK : Perhaps the only one.

HARRY : It is.

JACK : I had a cousin, on my mother's side, who once fell off a cliff.

HARRY : Really.

JACK : Quite a considerable height.

HARRY : Ah, yes.

JACK : Fell into the sea, fortunately. Dazed. Apart from that, quite quickly recovered.

HARRY : Very fortunate.

JACK : Did it for a dare. Only twelve years old at the time.

HARRY : I remember I fell off a cliff, one time.

JACK : Oh dear.

HARRY : Not very high. And there was someone there to catch me. (*Laughs.*)

JACK : They can be very exciting places.

HARRY : Oh, very.

JACK : I remember I once owned a little boat.

HARRY : Really.

JACK : For fishing. Nothing very grand.

HARRY : A fishing man.

JACK : Not really. More an occasional pursuit.

HARRY : I've always been curious about that.

JACK : Yes?

HARRY : 'A solitary figure crouched upon a bank.'

JACK : Never stirring.

HARRY : No. No.

JACK : Can be very tedious, I know.

HARRY : Still. A boat is more interesting.

JACK : Oh, yes. A sort of tradition, really.

HARRY : In the family.

JACK : No. No. More in the . . . island you know.

HARRY : Ah, yes.

JACK : Drake.

HARRY : Yes!

JACK : Nelson.

HARRY : Beatty.

JACK : Sir Walter Raleigh.

HARRY : There was a very fine man . . . poet.

JACK : Lost his head, you know.

HARRY : It's surprising the amount of dust that

collects in so short a space of time. (*Runs hand lightly over table.*)

JACK: It is. (*Looks round.*) Spot like this, perhaps, attracts it.

HARRY: Yes . . . (*Pause.*) You never became a priest, then?

JACK: No . . . No.

HARRY: Splendid to have a vocation.

JACK: 'Tis . . . Something you believe in.

HARRY: Oh, yes.

JACK: I could never . . . resolve certain difficulties, myself.

HARRY: Yes?

JACK: The hows and the wherefores I could understand. How we came to be, and His presence, lurking everywhere, you know. But as to the 'why' . . . I could never understand. Seemed a terrible waste of time to me.

HARRY: Oh, yes.

JACK: Thought it better to leave it to those who didn't mind.

HARRY: Ah, yes.

JACK: I suppose the same was true about dancing.

HARRY: Oh, yes. I remember turning up for instance, to my first class, only to discover that all the rest of them were girls.

JACK: Really?

HARRY: Well . . . there are men dancers, I know. Still . . . Took up football after that.

JACK: To professional standard, I imagine.

HARRY: Oh, no. Just the odd kick around. Joined a team that played in the park on Sunday mornings.

JACK: The athletic life has many attractions.

HARRY: It has. It has.

(*Pause.*)

JACK : How long have you been here, then?

HARRY : Oh, a couple of er.

JACK : Strange—meeting the other day.

HARRY : Yes.

JACK : On the way back, thought to myself, 'What a chance encounter.'

HARRY : Yes.

JACK : So rare, these days, to meet someone to whom one can actually talk.

HARRY : I know what you mean.

JACK : One works. One looks around. One meets people. But very little communication actually takes place.

HARRY : Very.

JACK : None at all in most cases ! (*Laughs.*)

HARRY : Oh, absolutely.

JACK : The agonies and frustrations. I can assure you. In the end one gives up in absolute despair.

HARRY : Oh, yes. (*Laughs, rising looking off.*)

JACK : Isn't that Parker? (*Looking off.*)

HARRY : No . . . N-no . . . Believe his name is Fielding.

JACK : Could have sworn it was Parker.

HARRY : No. Don't think so . . . Parker walks with a limp. Very slight.

JACK : That's Marshall.

HARRY : Really. Then I've got Parker mixed up again. (*Laughs.*)

JACK : Did you see the one who came in yesterday?

HARRY : Hendricks.

JACK : Is that his name?

HARRY : I believe that's what I heard.

JACK : He looked a very suspicious character to me. And his wife . . .

HARRY: I would have thought his girl-friend.

JACK: Really? Then that makes far more sense . . . I mean. I have great faith in the institution of marriage as such.

HARRY: Oh, yes.

JACK: But one thing I've always noticed. When you find a married couple who display their affection in public, then that's an infallible sign that their marriage is breaking up.

HARRY: Really?

JACK: It's a very curious thing. I'm sure there must be some psychological explanation for it.

HARRY: Insecurity.

JACK: Oh, yes.

HARRY: Quite frequently one can judge people entirely by their behaviour.

JACK: You can. I believe you're right.

HARRY: Take my father, for instance.

JACK: Oh, yes.

HARRY: An extraordinary man by any standard. And yet, throughout his life, he could never put out a light.

JACK: Really.

HARRY: Superstition. If he had to turn off a switch, he'd ask someone else to do it.

JACK: How extraordinary.

HARRY: Quite casually. One never noticed. Over the years one got quite used to it, of course. As a man he was extremely polite.

JACK: Ah, yes

HARRY (sits): Mother, now. She was quite the reverse.

JACK: Oh, yes.

HARRY: Great appetite for life.

JACK: Really?

HARRY: Three.

JACK : Three?

HARRY : Children.

JACK : Ah, yes.

HARRY : Youngest.

JACK : You were?

HARRY : Oh, yes.

JACK : One of seven.

HARRY : Seven!

JACK : Large families in those days.

HARRY : Oh, yes.

JACK : Family life.

HARRY : Oh, yes.

JACK : Society, well, without it, wouldn't be what it's like today.

HARRY : Oh, no.

JACK : Still.

HARRY : Ah, yes.

JACK : We have a wonderful example.

HARRY : Oh. My word.

JACK : At times I don't know where some of us would be without it.

HARRY : No. Not at all.

JACK : A friend of mine—actually, more of an acquaintance, really—was introduced to George VI at Waterloo.

HARRY : Waterloo?

JACK : The station.

HARRY : By jove.

JACK : He was an assistant to the station-master at the time, in a lowly capacity, of course. His Majesty was making a week-end trip into the country.

HARRY : Probably to Windsor.

(*Pause.*)

34

JACK : Can you get to Windsor from Waterloo?

HARRY : I'm ... No. I'm not sure.

JACK : Sandringham, of course, is in the country.

HARRY : The other way.

JACK : The other way.

HARRY : Balmoral in the Highlands.

JACK : I had an aunt once who, for a short while, lived near Gloucester.

HARRY : That's a remarkable stretch of the country.

JACK : Vale of Evesham.

HARRY : Vale of Evesham.

JACK : Local legend has it that Adam and Eve originated there.

HARRY : Really?

JACK : Has very wide currency, I believe, in the district. For instance. You may have read that portion in the Bible ...

HARRY : I have.

JACK : The profusion of vegetation, for example, would indicate that it couldn't, for instance, be anywhere in the Middle East.

HARRY : No. No.

JACK : On the other hand, for the profusion of animals ... snakes, for example ... would indicate that it might easily be a more tropical environment, as opposed, that is, to one which is merely temperate.

HARRY : Yes ... I see.

JACK : Then again, there is ample evidence to suggest that during the period in question equatorial conditions prevailed in the very region in which we are now sitting.

HARRY : Really? (*Looks around.*)

JACK : Discoveries have been made that would indicate that lions and tigers, elephants, wolves, rhinoceros, and so forth, actually inhabited these parts.

HARRY : My word.

JACK : In those circumstances, it wouldn't be unreasonable to suppose that the Vale of Evesham was such a place itself. The very cradle, as it were, of . . .

HARRY : Close to where your aunt lived.

JACK : That's right.

HARRY : Mind if I have a look?

JACK : Not at all.

(*Harry takes the cane.*)

HARRY : You seldom see canes of this quality these days.

JACK : No. No. That's right.

HARRY : I believe they've gone out of fashion.

JACK : They have.

HARRY : Like beards.

JACK : Beards!

HARRY : My father had a small moustache.

JACK : A moustache I've always thought became a man.

HARRY : Chamberlain.

JACK : Roosevelt.

HARRY : Schweitzer.

JACK : Chaplin.

HARRY : Hitler . . .

JACK : Travel, I've always felt, was a great broadener of the mind.

HARRY : My word.

JACK : Travelled a great deal—when I was young.

HARRY : Far?

JACK : Oh. All over.

HARRY : A great thing.

36

JACK : Sets its mark upon a man.

HARRY : Like the army.

JACK : Like the army. I suppose the fighting you do has very much the same effect.

HARRY : Oh, yes.

JACK : Bayonet?

HARRY : What?

JACK : The er.

HARRY : Oh, bayonet . . . ball and flame. The old three, as we used to call them.

JACK : Ah, yes.

HARRY : A great welder of character.

JACK : By jove.

HARRY : The youth of today : might have done some good.

JACK : Oh. My word, yes.

HARRY : In the Royal Air Force, of course . . .

JACK : Bombs.

HARRY : Really.

JACK : Cannon.

HARRY : Ah, yes . . . Couldn't have got far, in our job, I can tell you, without the Royal Air Force.

JACK : No. No.

HARRY : Britannia rules the waves . . . and rules the skies, too. I shouldn't wonder.

JACK : Oh, yes.

HARRY : Nowadays, of course . . .

JACK : Rockets.

HARRY : Ah, yes.

JACK : They say . . .

HARRY : Yes?

JACK : When the next catastrophe occurs . . .

HARRY : Oh, yes.

JACK : That the island itself might very well be flooded.

HARRY : Really.

37

JACK: Except for the more prominent peaks, of course.

HARRY: Oh, yes.

JACK: While we're sitting here waiting to be buried . . .

HARRY: Oh, yes.

JACK (*laughing*): We'll end up being drowned.

HARRY: Extraordinary! (*Laughs.*) No Vale of Evesham then.

JACK: Oh, no.

HARRY: Nor your aunt at Gloucester!

JACK: She died a little while ago, you know.

HARRY: Oh. I am sorry.

JACK: We weren't very attached.

HARRY: Oh, no.

JACK: Still. She was a very remarkable woman.

HARRY: Ah, yes.

JACK: In her own particular way. So few characters around these days. So few interesting people.

HARRY: Oh, yes.

JACK: Uniformity.

HARRY: Mrs Washington. (*Looking off.*)

JACK: Really? I've been keeping an eye open for her.

HARRY: Striking woman.

JACK: Her husband was related to a distant cousin of mine, on my father's side.

HARRY: My word.

JACK: I shouldn't be surprised if she recognizes me . . . No . . .

HARRY: Scarcely glanced. Her mind on other things.

JACK: Oh, yes.

HARRY: Parker. (*Looking off.*)

JACK: Oh, yes.

38

HARRY: You're right. He's not the man with the limp.

JACK: That's Marshall.

HARRY: That's right. Parker is the one who has something the matter with his arm. I knew it was something like that.

JACK: Polio.

HARRY: Yes?

JACK: I had a sister who contracted polio. Younger than me. Died within a matter of hours.

HARRY: Oh. Goodness.

JACK: Only a few months old at the time. Scarcely learnt to speak.

HARRY: What a terrible experience.

JACK: I had another sister die. She was how old? Eleven.

HARRY: Oh dear.

JACK: Large families do have their catastrophes.

HARRY: They do.

JACK: I remember a neighbour of ours, when we lived in the country, died one morning by falling down the stairs.

HARRY: Goodness.

JACK: The extraordinary thing was, the following day they were due to move into a bungalow.

HARRY: Goodness. (*Shakes his head.*)

JACK: One of the great things, of course, about my aunt's house.

HARRY: Yes?

JACK: In Gloucester. Was that it had an orchard.

HARRY: Now they *are* lovely things.

JACK: Particularly in the spring.

HARRY: In the spring especially.

JACK: And the autumn, of course.

HARRY: 'Boughs laden'.

JACK: Apple a day.

HARRY : Oh, yes.

JACK : I had a niece once who was a vegetarian.

HARRY : Really.

JACK : Ate nut rissoles.

HARRY : I tried once to give up meat.

JACK : Goes back, you know.

HARRY : Oh, yes.

JACK : Proctor. The young woman with him is Mrs Jefferies.

HARRY : Really.

JACK : Interesting people to talk to. He's been a missionary, you know.

HARRY : Yes?

JACK : Spent most of his time, he said, taking out people's teeth.

HARRY : Goodness.

JACK : Trained for it, of course. Mrs Jefferies, on the other hand.

HARRY : Yes.

JACK : Was a lady gymnast. Apparently very famous in her day.

HARRY : My word.

JACK : Developed arthritis in two of her er.

HARRY : Oh dear.

JACK : Did you know it was caused by a virus?

HARRY : No.

JACK : Apparently. I had a maiden aunt who suffered from it a great deal. She was a flautist. Played in an orchestra of some distinction. Never married. I thought that very strange.

HARRY : Yes.

JACK : Musicians, of course, are a strange breed altogether.

HARRY : Oh, yes.

JACK : Have you noticed how the best of them have very curly hair?

HARRY : Really.

JACK : My maiden aunt, of course, has died now.

HARRY : Ah, yes.

JACK : Spot of cloud there.

HARRY : Soon passes.

JACK : Ever seen this? (*Takes out a coin.*) There. Nothing up my sleeve. Ready? One, two, three . . . Gone.

HARRY : My word.

JACK : Here . . . (*Takes out three cards.*) Pick out the Queen of Hearts.

HARRY : This one.

JACK : That's right . . . Now . . . Queen of Hearts.

HARRY : This one.

JACK : No !

HARRY : Oh !

(*They laugh.*)

JACK : Try again . . . There she is. (*Shuffles them round on the table.*) Where is she?

HARRY : Er . . .

JACK : Take your time.

HARRY : This one . . . Oh !

(*They laugh.*)

JACK : That one !

HARRY : Well. I'll have to study those.

JACK : Easy when you know how. I have some more back there. One of my favourite tricks is to take the Ace of Spades out of someone's top pocket.

HARRY : Oh . . . (*Looks.*)

JACK : No. No. No. (*Laughs.*) It needs some preparation . . . Sometimes in a lady's handbag. That goes down very well.

41

HARRY : Goodness.

JACK : I knew a man at one time—a friend of the family, on my father's side—who could put a lighted cigarette into his mouth, take one half from one ear, and the other half from the other.

HARRY : Goodness.

JACK : Still lighted.

HARRY : How did he do that?

JACK : I don't know.

HARRY : I suppose—physiologically—it's possible, then.

JACK : Shouldn't think so.

HARRY : No.

JACK : One of the advantages, of course, of sitting here.

HARRY : Oh, yes.

JACK : You can see everyone walking past.

HARRY : Oh, yes.

JACK : Jennings isn't a man I'm awfully fond of.

HARRY : No.

JACK : You've probably noticed yourself.

HARRY : I have. In the army, I met a man . . . Private . . . er.

JACK : The equivalent rank, of course, in the air force, is aircraftsman.

HARRY : Or able seaman. In the navy.

JACK : Able seaman.

(*They laugh.*)

HARRY : Goodness.

JACK : Funny name. (*Laughs.*) Able seaman. I don't think I'd like to be called that.

HARRY : Yes ! (*Laughs.*)

JACK : Able seaman ! (*Snorts.*)

HARRY : Fraser. Have you noticed him?

42

JACK : Don't think I have.

HARRY : A thin moustache.

JACK : Black.

HARRY : That's right.

JACK : My word.

HARRY : Steer clear, probably, might be better.

JACK : Some people you can sum up at a glance.

HARRY : Oh, yes.

JACK : My mother was like that. Delicate. Not unlike my wife.

HARRY : Nevertheless, very sturdy.

JACK : Oh, yes. Physically, nothing to complain about. My mother, on the other hand, was actually as delicate as she looked. Whereas my wife looks . . .

HARRY : Robust.

JACK : Robust. My mother actually looked extremely delicate.

HARRY : Still. Seven children.

JACK : Oh, yes.

HARRY : My father was a very . . . emotional man. Of great feeling.

JACK : Like mine.

HARRY : Oh, very much like yours.

JACK : But dominated somewhat.

HARRY : Yes?

JACK : By your mother.

HARRY : Oh. I suppose he was. Passionate but . . .

JACK : Dominated. One of the great things, of course, about the war was its feeling of camaraderie.

HARRY : Friendship.

JACK : You found that, too? On the airfield where I was stationed it was really like one great big happy family. My word. The things one did for one another.

43

HARRY : Oh, yes.

JACK : The way one worked.

HARRY : Soon passed.

JACK : Oh, yes it did. It did.

HARRY : Ah, yes.

JACK : No sooner was the fighting over than back it came. Back-biting. Complaints. Getting what you can. I sometimes think if the war had been prolonged another thirty years we'd have all felt the benefit.

HARRY : Oh, yes

JACK : One's children would have grown up far different. That's for sure.

HARRY : Really? How many have you got?

JACK : Two.

HARRY : Oh, that's very nice.

JACK : Boy married. Girl likewise. They seem to rush into things so early these days.

HARRY : Oh, yes.

JACK : And you?

HARRY : Oh. No. No. Never had the privilege.

JACK : Ah, yes. Responsibility. At times you wonder if it's worth it. I had a cousin, on my father's side, who threw herself from a railway carriage.

HARRY : Oh dear. How awful.

JACK : Yes.

HARRY : Killed outright.

JACK : Well, fortunately, it had just pulled into a station.

HARRY : I see.

JACK : Daughter's married to a salesman. Refrigerators : he sells appliances of that nature.

HARRY : Oh. Opposite to me.

JACK : Yes?

HARRY : Heating engineer.

44

JACK : Really. I'd never have guessed. How extra-ordinary.

HARRY : And yourself.

JACK : Oh, I've tinkered with one or two things.

HARRY : Ah, yes.

JACK : What I like about my present job is the scope that it leaves you for initiative.

HARRY : Rather. Same with mine.

JACK : Distribution of food-stuffs in a wholesale store.

HARRY : Really.

JACK : Thinking out new ideas. Constant speculation.

HARRY : Oh, yes.

JACK : Did you know if you put jam into small cardboard containers it will sell far better than if you put it into large glass jars?

HARRY : Really?

JACK : Psychological. When you buy it in a jar you're wondering what on earth—subconsciously—you're going to do with the glass bottle. But with a cardboard box that anxiety is instantly removed. Result : improved sales : improved production; lower prices; improved distribution.

HARRY : That's a fascinating job.

JACK : Oh, yes. If you use your brains there's absolutely nothing there to stop you.

HARRY : I can see.

JACK : Heating must be a very similar problem.

HARRY : Oh, yes.

JACK : The different ways of warming up a house.

HARRY : Yes.

JACK : Or not warming it up, as the case may be.

HARRY : Yes !

(*They laugh.*)

JACK : I don't think I've met your wife.

HARRY : No. No . . . As a matter of fact. We've been separated for a little while.

JACK : Oh dear.

HARRY : One of those misfortunes.

JACK : Happens a great deal.

HARRY : Oh, yes.

JACK : Each have our cross.

HARRY : Oh, yes.

JACK : Well. Soon be time for lunch.

HARRY : Will. And I haven't had my walk.

JACK : No. Still.

HARRY : Probably do as much good.

JACK : Oh, yes.

HARRY : Well, then . . . (*Stretches. Gets up.*)

JACK : Yours or mine?

HARRY : Mine . . . I believe. (*Picks up the newspaper.*)

JACK : Ah, yes.

HARRY : Very fine gloves.

JACK : Yes.

HARRY : Pacamac.

JACK : All correct.

HARRY : Cane.

JACK : Cane.

HARRY : Well, then. Off we go.

JACK : Off we go.

(*Harry breathes in deeply; breathes out.*)

HARRY : Beautiful corner.

JACK : 'Tis.

(*Pause; last look round.*)

HARRY : Work up an appetite.

46

JACK : Right, then. Best foot forward.
HARRY : Best foot forward.
JACK : Best foot forward, and off we go.

(They stroll off, taking the air, stage left.)

Scene 2

Kathleen and Marjorie come on, stage right.

Kathleen is a stout middle-aged lady; she wears a coat, which is unbuttoned, a headscarf, and strap shoes. She is limping, her arm supported by Marjorie.

Marjorie is also middle-aged. She is dressed in a skirt and cardigan. She carries an umbrella and a large, well-used bag.

KATHLEEN : Cor . . . *blimey* !
MARJORIE : Going to rain, ask me.
KATHLEEN : Rain all it wants, ask me. Cor . . . *blimey* ! Going to kill me is this. (*Limps to a chair, sits down and holds her foot.*)
MARJORIE : Going to rain and catch us out here. That's what it's going to do. (*Puts umbrella up: worn, but not excessively so.*)
KATHLEEN : Going to rain all right, i'n't? Going to rain all right . . . Put your umbrella up—sun's still shining. Cor blimey. Invite rain that will. Commonsense, girl . . . Cor *blimey* . . . My bleedin' feet . . . (*Rubs one foot without removing shoe.*)
MARJORIE : Out here and no shelter. Be all right

47

if it starts. (*Moves umbrella one way then another, looking up.*)

KATHLEEN: Cor *blimey* . . . 'Surprise me they don't drop off . . . Cut clean through, these will.

MARJORIE (*looking skywards, however*): Clouds all over. Told you we shouldn't have come out.

KATHLEEN: Get nothing if you don't try, girl . . . Cor *blimey*! (*Winces.*)

MARJORIE: I don't know.

KATHLEEN: Here. You'll be all right, won't you?

MARJORIE: . . . ?

KATHLEEN: Holes there is. See right through, you can.

MARJORIE: What?

KATHLEEN: Here. Rain come straight through that. Won't get much shelter under that. What d'I tell you? Might as well sit under a shower. (*Laughs.*) Cor blimey. You'll be all right, won't you?

MARJORIE: Be all right with you in any case. Walk no faster than a snail.

KATHLEEN: Not surprised. Don't want me to escape. That's my trouble, girl.

MARJORIE: Here . . .

(*Jack and Harry slowly pass upstage, taking the air, chatting. Marjorie and Kathleen wait for them to pass.*)

KATHLEEN: What've we got for lunch?

MARJORIE: Sprouts.

KATHLEEN (*massaging foot*): Seen them, have you?

MARJORIE: Smelled 'em!

KATHLEEN: What's today, then?

MARJORIE: Friday.

KATHLEEN: End of week.

MARJORIE: Corn' beef hash.

48

KATHLEEN : That's Wednesday.

MARJORIE : Sausage roll.

KATHLEEN : Think you're right . . . Cor *blimey.*
(*Groans, holding her foot.*)

MARJORIE : Know what you ought to do, don't
you?

(*Kathleen groans holding her foot.*)

Ask for another pair of shoes, girl, you ask me.

KATHLEEN : Took me laced ones, haven't they?
Only ones that fitted. Thought I'd hang myself,
didn't they? Only five inches long.

MARJORIE : What they think you are?

KATHLEEN : Bleedin' mouse, more likely.

MARJORIE : Here. Not like the last one I was in.

KATHLEEN : No?

MARJORIE : Let you paint on the walls, they did.
Do anyfing. Just muck around . . . Here . . . I won't
tell you what some of them did.

KATHLEEN : What?

(*Marjorie leans over, whispers.*)

Never.

MARJORIE : Cross me heart.

KATHLEEN : Glad I wasn't there. This place is bad
enough. You seen Henderson, have you?

MARJORIE : Ought to lock him up, you ask me.

KATHLEEN : What d'you do, then?

MARJORIE : Here?

KATHLEEN : At this other place.

MARJORIE : Noffing. Mucked around . . .

KATHLEEN : Here . . .

(*Jack and Harry stroll back again, slowly, upstage,
in conversation; head back, deep breathing,*

49

bracing arms . . . Marjorie and Kathleen wait till they pass.)

MARJORIE : My dentist comes from Pakistan.

KATHLEEN : Yours?

MARJORIE : Took out all me teeth.

KATHLEEN : Those not your own, then?

MARJORIE : All went rotten when I had my little girl. There she is, waitress at the seaside.

KATHLEEN : And you stuck here . . .

MARJORIE : No teeth . . .

KATHLEEN : Don't appreciate it.

MARJORIE : They don't.

KATHLEEN : Never.

MARJORIE : Might take this down if it doesn't rain.

KATHLEEN : Cor blimey . . . take these off if I thought I could get 'em on again . . . (*Groans.*) Tried catching a serious disease.

MARJORIE : When was that?

KATHLEEN : Only had me in two days. Said, nothing the matter with you, my girl.

MARJORIE : Don't believe you.

KATHLEEN : Next thing : got home; smashed everything in sight.

MARJORIE : No?

KATHLEEN : Winders. Cooker . . . Nearly broke me back . . . Thought I'd save the telly. Still owed eighteen months. Thought : 'Everything or nothing, girl.'

MARJORIE : Rotten programmes.

KATHLEEN : Didn't half give it a good old conk.

MARJORIE (*looking round*) : There's one thing. You get a good night's sleep.

KATHLEEN : Like being with a steam engine, where I come from. Cor blimey, that much whistling and groaning; think you're going to take off.

MARJORIE: More like a boa constrictor, ask me. Here . . .

(*Jack and Harry stroll back, still taking the air, upstage; bracing, head back . . .*)

Started crying everywhere I went . . . Started off on Christmas Eve.

KATLEEN: S'happy time, Christmas.

MARJORIE: Didn't stop till Boxing Day.

KATHLEEN: If He ever comes again I hope He comes on Whit Tuesday. For me that's the best time of the year.

MARJORIE: Why's that?

KATHLEEN: Dunno. Whit Tuesday's always been a lucky day for me. First party I ever went to was on a Whit Tuesday. First feller I went with. Can't be the date. Different every year.

MARJORIE: My lucky day's the last Friday in any month with an 'r' in it when the next month doesn't begin later than the following Monday.

KATHLEEN: How do you make that out?

MARJORIE: Dunno. I was telling the doctor that the other day . . . There's that man with the binoculars watching you.

KATHLEEN: Where?

MARJORIE: Lift up your dress.

KATHLEEN: No.

MARJORIE: Go on . . . (*Leans over; does it for her.*) Told you . . .

KATHLEEN: Looks like he's got diarrhoea!

(*They laugh.*)

See that chap the other day? Showed his slides of a trip up the Amazon River.

MARJORIE : See that one with no clothes on? Supposed to be cooking his dinner.

KATHLEEN : Won't have him here again . . .

MARJORIE : Showing all his p's and q's.

KATHLEEN : Oooooh! (*Laughs, covering her mouth.*)

MARJORIE : Here . . .

(*Jack and Harry stroll back across, a little farther downstage glancing over now at Marjorie and Kathleen.*)

KATHLEEN : Lord and Lady used to live here at one time.

MARJORIE : Who's that?

KATHLEEN : Dunno.

MARJORIE : Probably still inside, ask me . . . (*Glances after Jack and Harry as they stroll off.*) See that woman with dyed hair? Told me she'd been in films. 'What films?' I said. 'Blue films?'

KATHLEEN : What she say?

MARJORIE : 'The ones I was in was not in colour.'

(*They laugh.*)

I s'll lose me teeth one of these days . . . oooh!

KATHLEEN : Better'n losing something else . . .

MARJORIE : Ooooh!

(*They laugh again.*)

KATHLEEN : Here . . .

(*Jack and Harry have strolled back on.*)

JACK (*removing hat*) : Good day, ladies.

KATHLEEN : Good day yourself, your lordships.

JACK : Oh, now. I wouldn't go as far as that. (*Laughs politely and looks at Harry.*)

HARRY : No. No. Still a bit of the common touch.

JACK : Least, so I'd hope.

HARRY : Oh, yes.

MARJORIE : And how have you been keeping, professor?

JACK : Professor? I can see we're a little elevated today.

MARJORIE : Don't know about elevated. But *we*'re sitting down.

(*Kathleen and Marjorie laugh.*)

KATHLEEN : Been standing up, we have, for hours.

HARRY : Hours?

MARJORIE : When you were sitting down.

JACK : Oh dear . . . I wasn't aware . . .

KATHLEEN : 'Course you were. My bleedin' feet. Just look at them. (*Holds them again.*)

MARJORIE : Pull your skirt down, girl.

KATHLEEN : Oh Gawd . . .

JACK : My friend here, Harry, is a specialist in house-warming, and I myself am a retailer in preserves.

MARJORIE : Oooooh! (*Screeches; laughs—covering her mouth—to Kathleen.*) What did I tell you?

KATHLEEN : No atomic bombs today?

JACK (*looks up at the sky behind him. Then*) : No, no. Shouldn't think so.

MARJORIE : And how's your mongol sister?

HARRY : Mongol . . . ? I'm afraid you must have the wrong person, Ma'm.

KATHLEEN : Ooooh! (*Screeches; laughs.*)

JACK : My friend, I'm afraid, is separated from his

wife. As a consequence, I can assure you, of many
hardships . . .

MARJORIE : Of course . . .

JACK : And I myself, though happily married in
some respects, would not pretend that my situation
is all it should be . . .

KATHLEEN : Ooooh !

JACK : One endeavours . . . but it is in the nature
of things, I believe, that, on the whole, one fails.

KATHLEEN : Ooooh !

HARRY : My friend . . . Jack . . . has invented
several new methods of retailing jam.

KATHLEEN : Ooooh !

MARJORIE : Jam. I like that.

JACK : Really?

MARJORIE (*to Kathleen*) : Strawberry. My favourite.

KATHLEEN : Raspberry, mine.

MARJORIE : Ooooh !

(*Kathleen and Marjorie laugh.*)

JACK : A friend of mine, on my father's side, once
owned a small factory which was given over,
exclusively, to its manufacture.

KATHLEEN : Ooooh !

JACK : In very large vats.

KATHLEEN : Ooooh !

MARJORIE : I like treacle myself.

JACK : Treacle, now, is a very different matter.

MARJORIE : Comes from Malaya.

HARRY : That's rubber I believe.

MARJORIE : In tins.

HARRY : The rubber comes from Malaya, I believe.

MARJORIE : I eat it, don't I? I ought to know.

KATHLEEN : She has treacle on her bread.

JACK : I believe it comes, as a matter of fact, from the West Indies.

KATHLEEN : West Indies? Where's that?

MARJORIE : Near Hong Kong.

HARRY : That's the East Indies, I believe.

MARJORIE : You ever been to the North Indies?

HARRY : I don't believe . . .

MARJORIE : Well, that's where treacle comes from.

HARRY : I see . . .

(Pause. The tone has suddenly become serious.)

JACK : We were just remarking, as a matter of fact, that Mrs Glover isn't looking her usual self.

KATHLEEN : Who's she?

HARRY : She's . . .

JACK : The lady with the rather embarrassing disfigurement . . .

MARJORIE : Her with one ear?

KATHLEEN : The one who's only half a nose.

MARJORIE : She snores.

KATHLEEN : You'd snore as well, wouldn't you, if you only had half a nose.

MARJORIE : Eaten away.

KATHLEEN : What?

MARJORIE : Her husband ate it one night when she was sleeping.

KATHLEEN : Silly to fall asleep with any man, I say. These days they get up to anything. Read it in the papers an' next thing they want to try it themselves.

HARRY : The weather's been particularly mild today.

KATHLEEN : Not like my flaming feet. Oooh . . .

JACK : As one grows older these little things are sent to try us.

KATHLEEN : Little? Cor blimey; I take size seven.

HARRY : My word.

JACK : My friend, of course, in the heating business, has a wide knowledge of the ways and means whereby we may, as we go along, acquire these little additional comforts.

MARJORIE : He wishes he was sitting in this chair, doesn't he?

HARRY : What . . .

JACK : It's extraordinary that more facilities of this nature aren't supplied, in my view.

KATHLEEN : Only bit of garden with any flowers. Half a dozen daisies . . .

HARRY : Tulips . . .

JACK : Roses . . .

KATHLEEN : I know daisies, don't I? Those are daisies. Grow three feet tall.

HARRY : Really?

MARJORIE : Rest of it's all covered in muck.

JACK : Oh, now. Not as bad as that.

MARJORIE : What? I call that muck. What's it supposed to be?

HARRY : A rockery, I believe.

KATHLEEN : Rockery? More like a rubbish tip, ask me.

JACK : Probably the flowers haven't grown yet.

MARJORIE : Flowers? How do you grow flowers on old bricks and bits of plaster?

HARRY : Certain categories, of course . . .

JACK : Oh, yes.

HARRY : Can be trained to grow in these conditions.

KATHLEEN : You're round the bend, you are. Ought to have you up there, they did.

HARRY (to Jack) : They tell me the flowers are just as bad at that end, too.

(Harry and Jack laugh at their private joke.)

MARJORIE : If you ask me, all this is just typical.

JACK : Typical?

MARJORIE : One table. Two chairs . . . Between one thousand people.

KATHLEEN : Two, they tell me.

MARJORIE : Two thousand. One thousand for this chair, and one thousand for that.

HARRY : There are, of course, the various benches.

KATHLEEN : Benches? Seen better sold for firewood.

MARJORIE : Make red marks they do across your bum.

KATHLEEN : Ooooh ! *(Screeches, covering her mouth.)*

HARRY : Clouding slightly.

JACK : Slightly. *(Looking up.)*

MARJORIE : Pull your skirt down, girl.

KATHLEEN : Oooh !

HARRY : Of course, one alternative would be to bring, say, a couple of more chairs out with us.

JACK : Oh, yes. Now that would be a solution.

HARRY : Four chairs. One each. I don't believe, say, for an afternoon they'd be missed from the lecture hall.

MARJORIE : Here, you see *Up the Amazon* last night?

JACK : Tuesday . . .

HARRY : Tuesday.

JACK : Believe I did, now you mention it.

MARJORIE : See that feller with a loincloth?

KATHLEEN : Ooooh ! *(Laughs, covering her mouth.)*

JACK : I must admit, there are certain attractions in the primitive life.

KATHLEEN : Ooooh !

JACK : Air, space . . .

MARJORIE : Seen all he's got, that's all you seen.

JACK : I believe there was a moment when the eye . . .

KATHLEEN : Moment . . . Ooooh!

HARRY : I thought his pancakes looked rather nice.

KATHLEEN : Oooooh!

HARRY : On the little log . . .

KATHLEEN : Ooooh!

MARJORIE : Not his pancakes he's seen, my girl.

KATHLEEN : Ooooh!

JACK : The canoe, now, was not unlike my own little boat.

KATHLEEN : Ooooh!

HARRY : Fishing there somewhat more than a mere pastime.

JACK : Oh, yes.

HARRY : Life and death.

JACK : Oh, yes.

MARJORIE : Were you the feller they caught climbing out of a window here last week?

JACK : Me?

MARJORIE : Him.

HARRY : Don't think so . . . Don't recollect that.

JACK : Where, if you don't mind me asking, did you acquire that information?

MARJORIE : Where? (*To Kathleen.*) Here, I thought you told me it was him.

KATHLEEN : Not me. Mrs Heller.

MARJORIE : You sure?

KATHLEEN : Not me, anyway.

JACK : I had a relative-nephew, as a matter of fact —who started a window-cleaning business . . . let me see. Three years ago now.

HARRY : Really?

JACK : Great scope there for an adventurous man.

MARJORIE : In bathroom windows 'specially.

KATHLEEN : Ooooh !

JACK : Heights . . . distances . . .

HARRY : On very tall buildings, of course, they lower them from the roof.

JACK : Oh, yes.

HARRY : Don't have the ladders long enough, you know.

KATHLEEN : Ooooh !

JACK : Your friend seems in a very jovial frame of mind.

HARRY : Like to see that.

JACK : Oh, yes. Gloom : one sees it far too much in this place. Mr Metcalf, now : I don't think he's spoken to anyone since the day that he arrived.

MARJORIE : What's he, then?

HARRY : He's the gentleman who's constantly pacing up and down.

JACK : One says hello, of course. He scarcely seems to notice.

KATHLEEN : Hear you were asking if they'd let you out.

JACK : Who?

MARJORIE : Your friend.

HARRY : Oh. Nothing as dramatic . . . Made certain inquiries . . . temporary visit . . . Domestic problems, you know. Without a man very little, I'm afraid, gets done.

MARJORIE : It gets too much done, if you ask me. That's half the trouble.

KATHLEEN : Ooooooh !

HARRY : However . . . It seems that certain aspects of it can be cleared up by correspondence. One doesn't wish, after all, to impose unduly . . .

JACK : Oh, no.

HARRY : Events have their own momentum. Take their time.

MARJORIE : You married to me, they would. I can tell you.

KATHLEEN : Oooooh !

HARRY : Oh, now . . . Missis . . . er . . .

MARJORIE : Madam.

KATHLEEN : Oooooh !

HARRY : Well . . . er . . . that might be a situation that could well be beneficial to us both, in different circumstances, in different places . . .

JACK : Quite . . .

MARJORIE : Listen to him !

HARRY : We all have our little foibles, our little failings.

JACK : Oh, indeed.

HARRY : Hardly be human without.

JACK : Oh, no.

HARRY : The essence of true friendship, in my view, is to make allowances for one another's little lapses.

MARJORIE : Heard all about your little lapses, haven't we?

KATHLEEN : Ooooooh !

JACK : All have our little falls from grace.

MARJORIE : Pull your skirt down, girl !

KATHLEEN : Oooooh !

MARJORIE : Burn down the whole bleedin' building, he will. Given up smoking because they won't let him have any matches.

KATHLEEN : Oooh !

JACK : The rumours that drift around a place like this . . . hardly worth the trouble . . .

HARRY : Absolutely.

JACK : If one believed everything one heard . . .

HARRY : Oh, yes.

JACK : I was remarking to my friend earlier this morning : if one can't enjoy life as it takes one, what's the point of living it at all? One can't, after all, spend the whole of one's life inside a shell.

HARRY : Oh, no.

MARJORIE : Know what he'd spend it inside if he had half a chance.

KATHLEEN : Ooooooh !

MARJORIE : Tell my husband of you, I shall.

KATHLEEN : Bus-driver.

JACK : Really? I've taken a lifelong interest in public transport.

KATHLEEN : Oooh !

MARJORIE : Taken a lifelong interest in something else more'n likely.

KATHLEEN : Oooooh !

MARJORIE : Pull your skirt down, girl !

KATHLEEN : Oooooh !

MARJORIE : Know his kind.

KATHLEEN : Oooooh !

JACK : Respect for the gentler sex, I must say, is a fast diminishing concept in the modern world.

HARRY : Oh, yes.

JACK : I recollect the time when one stood for a lady as a matter of course.

HARRY : Oh, yes.

MARJORIE : Know the kind of standing he's on about.

KATHLEEN : Oooooh !

JACK : Each becomes hardened to his ways.

KATHLEEN : Oooooh !

JACK : No regard for anyone else's.

MARJORIE : Be missing your dinner, you will.

JACK : Yes. So it seems.

HARRY : Late . . .

JACK : Nevertheless, one breaks occasionally one's usual . . . Normally it's of benefit to all concerned . . .

MARJORIE : Here. Are you all right?

JACK : Slight moment of discomposure . . .

(*Jack has begun to cry, vaguely. Takes out a handkerchief to wipe his eyes.*)

HARRY : My friend is a man—he won't mind me saying this . . .

JACK : No . . . no . . .

HARRY : Of great sensibility and feeling.

KATHLEEN : Here. You having us on?

JACK : I assure you, madam . . . I regret any anxiety or concern which I may, unwittingly, have caused. In fact—I'm sure my friend will concur— perhaps you'll allow us to accompany you to the dining-hall. I have noticed, in the past, that though one has to queue, to leave it any later is to run the risk of being served with a cold plate; the food cold, and the manners of the cook—at times, I must confess . . . appalling.

KATHLEEN (*to Marjorie*): We'll have to go. There'll be nothing left.

MARJORIE : It's this seat he's after.

HARRY : I assure you, madam . . . we are on our way.

KATHLEEN : Here : you mind if I lean on your arm?

MARJORIE : Kathleen !

HARRY : Oh, now. That's a very pretty name.

KATHLEEN : Got straps : makes your ankles swell. (*Rising.*)

HARRY : Allow me.

KATHLEEN : Oh. Thank you.

HARRY : Harry.

KATHLEEN: Harry.

HARRY: And this is my friend—Jack.

KATHLEEN: Jack . . . and this is my friend Marjorie.

JACK: Marjorie . . . Delightful.

MARJORIE (*to Kathleen*): Here. You all right?

KATHLEEN: You carrying it with you, or are you coming?

JACK: Allow me . . . Marjorie. (*Holds her seat.*)

MARJORIE: Here . . . (*Gets up, suspicious.*)

HARRY: Perhaps after lunch we might meet here again.

JACK: A little chat . . . Time passes very slowly.

MARJORIE: Here, where's my bag?

KATHLEEN: Need carrying out, I will.

(*Harry has taken Kathleen's arm.*)

HARRY: Now then. All right?

KATHLEEN: Have you all the time, I shall.

HARRY: Ready? . . . All aboard then, are we?

MARJORIE: Well, then. All right . . . (*Takes Jack's arm.*)

JACK: Right, then . . . Dining-hall: here we come!

(*They start off, Harry and Kathleen in front; slowly.*)

HARRY: Sausages today, if I'm not mistaken.

KATHLEEN: Oooh!

MARJORIE: Corned beef hash.

KATHLEEN: Oooh!

JACK: One as good as another, I always say.

KATHLEEN: Oooooh!

HARRY: Turned out better.

63

JACK : Turned out better.
HARRY : Altogether.
JACK : Altogether.
HARRY : Well, then. Here we go.

(*They go.*)

ACT TWO

Alfred comes in: a well-made young man, about thirty. His jacket's unbuttoned; he has no tie.

He sees the table; walks past it, slowly, eyeing it.

Pauses. Glances back at it.

Comes back, watching the table rather furtively, sideways.

He pauses, hands behind his back, regarding it.

Suddenly he moves towards it, grasps it; struggles with it as if it had a life of its own.

Groans. Struggles. Lifts the table finally above his head.

Struggles with it . . .

Marjorie comes on, as before, her umbrella furled.

MARJORIE : Here. You all right?
ALFRED : What?
MARJORIE : Alfred, i'n'it?
ALFRED : Yeh. (*Still holds the table above his head.*)
MARJORIE : You'll break that, you will.
ALFRED : Yeh . . . (*Looks up at it.*)

(*Marjorie however, isn't much interested; she's already looking round.*)

MARJORIE : You seen my mate?
ALFRED : . . . ?
MARJORIE : Woman that limps.
ALFRED : No. (*He pauses before all his answers.*)
MARJORIE : One day you get seconds and they go off without you. You like treacle pud?

ALFRED : Yeh.

MARJORIE : Get seconds?

ALFRED : No.

MARJORIE : Shoulda waited.

ALFRED : Yeh.

MARJORIE : Said they'd be out here after 'Remedials'.

ALFRED : ... ?

MARJORIE : You do remedials?

ALFRED : Yeh.

MARJORIE : What 'you do?

ALFRED : Baskets.

MARJORIE : Baskets. Shoulda known.

ALFRED : You got sixpence?

MARJORIE : No.

(Alfred lifts the table up and down ceremoniously above his head.)

Better go find her. Let anybody turn them round her hand, she will.

ALFRED. Yeh.

(She goes.

Alfred lowers the table slowly, almost like a ritual.

Crouches; picks up one chair by the foot of one leg and lifts it, slowly, exaggerating the effort, etc.

Stands, slowly, as he gets it up.

Bends arm slowly; lifts the chair above his head.

Puts it down.

Stands a moment, gazing down at the two chairs and the table, sideways.

Walks round them.

Walks round a little farther. Then:

Grabs the second chair and lifts it, one-handed, like the first chair, but more quickly.

Lifts it above his head; begins to wrestle with it as if it too possessed a life of its own, his grip, however, still one-handed.

Marjorie crosses upstage, pauses, looks, walks on.

She goes off; Alfred doesn't see her.

Alfred struggles; overcomes the chair.

Almost absent-mindedly lowers it, looks left, looks right, casually; puts the chair beneath his arm and goes.)

KATHLEEN (*off*): Oh Gawd . . . Oh . . . Nah, this side's better . . . Oh.

(*Comes on limping, her arm in Harry's. Harry carries a wicker chair under his other arm.*)

HARRY: Oh. Look at that.
KATHLEEN: Where's the other one gone, then?
HARRY: Well, that's a damned nuisance.
KATHLEEN: Still only two. Don't know what they'll say.
HARRY: Oh dear.
KATHLEEN: Pinch anything round here. Can't turn your back. Gawd . . . !

(Sinks down in the metal chair as Harry holds it for her.)

HARRY : There, now.

KATHLEEN *(sighs)* : Good to get off your feet . . .

HARRY : Yes, well . . .

(Sets his own chair to get the sun, fussing.)

KATHLEEN : Better sit on it. No good standing about. Don't know where she's got to. Where's your friend looking?

HARRY : Went to 'Remedials', I believe.

KATHLEEN : Get you in there won't let you out again. Here . . .

(Harry looks across.)

He really what he says he is?

HARRY : How do you mean?

KATHLEEN : Told us he was a doctor. Another time he said he'd been a sanitary inspector.

HARRY : Really? Hadn't heard of that.

KATHLEEN : Go on. Know what inspecting he'll do. You the same.

HARRY : Oh, now. Certain discriminations can be . . .

KATHLEEN : I've heard about you.

HARRY : Oh, well, you er.

KATHLEEN : Making up things.

HARRY : Oh, well. One . . . embodies . . . of course.

KATHLEEN : What's that, then?

HARRY : Fancies . . . What's life for if you can't . . . *(Flutters his fingers.)*

KATHLEEN : We've heard about that an' all. *(Imitates his action.)*

68

HARRY : Well. I'm sure you and I have, in reality, a great deal in common. After all, one looks around; what does one see?

KATHLEEN : Gawd . . . (*Groans, feeling her feet.*)

HARRY : A little this. A little that.

KATHLEEN : Here. Everything you know is little.

HARRY : Well . . . I er . . . Yes . . . No great role for this actor, I'm afraid. A little stage, a tiny part.

KATHLEEN : You an actor, then?

HARRY : Well, I did, as a matter of fact, at one time . . . actually, a little . . .

KATHLEEN : Here, little again. You notice?

HARRY : Oh . . . You're right.

KATHLEEN : What parts you play, then?

HARRY : Well, as a matter of fact . . . not your Hamlets, of course, your Ophelias; more the little bystander who passes by the . . .

KATHLEEN : Here. Little.

HARRY : Oh . . . yes ! (*Laughs.*)

KATHLEEN : Play anything romantic?

HARRY : Oh, romance, now, was . . . never very far away.

KATHLEEN : Here . . .

HARRY : One was cast, of course . . .

KATHLEEN : Think I could have been romantic.

HARRY : Oh, yes.

KATHLEEN : Had the chance . . . Got it here.

HARRY : Oh, yes . . .

KATHLEEN : Had different shoes than this . . .

HARRY : Oh, yes . . . everything, of course, provided.

KATHLEEN : Going to be a commotion, you ask me . . .

HARRY : Commotion . . . ?

KATHLEEN : When they get here.

(Indicates chairs.)

Three chairs—if he brings one as well . . . He'll have to stand. *(Laughs.)*

HARRY : Could have been confiscated, you know.

KATHLEEN : Confiscated?

HARRY : Often happens. See a little pleasure and down they come.

KATHLEEN : Here . . . little.

HARRY : Goodness . . . Yes.

(Pause.)

One of the advantages of this spot, you know, is that it catches the sun so nicely.

KATHLEEN : What bit there is of it.

HARRY : Bit?

KATHLEEN : All that soot. Cuts it down. 'Stead of browning you turns you black.

HARRY : Black?

KATHLEEN : All over.

HARRY : An industrial nation . . .

KATHLEEN : Gawd . . . *(Eases her feet.)*

HARRY : Can't have the benefit of both. Nature as well as er . . . The one is incurred at the expense of the other.

KATHLEEN : Your friend come in for following little girls?

HARRY : What . . .

KATHLEEN : Go on. You can tell me. Cross me heart and hope to die.

HARRY : Well . . . that's . . .

KATHLEEN : Well, then.

HARRY : I believe there were . . . er . . . certain proclivities, shall we say?

KATHLEEN : Proclivities? What's them?

HARRY : Nothing criminal, of course.

KATHLEEN : Oh, no . . .

HARRY : No prosecution . . .

KATHLEEN : Oh, no . . .

HARRY : Certain pressures, in the er . . . Revealed themselves.

KATHLEEN : In public?

HARRY : No. No . . . I . . . Not what I meant.

KATHLEEN : I don't know what you're saying half the time. You realize that?

HARRY : Communication is a difficult factor.

KATHLEEN : Say that again.

HARRY : I believe he was encouraged to come here for a little er.

KATHLEEN : Here. Little.

HARRY : Oh, yes . . . As it is, very few places left now where one can be at ease.

KATHLEEN : Could go on his holidays. Seaside.

HARRY : Beaches? . . . Crowded all the while.

KATHLEEN : Could go to the country.

HARRY : Spaces . . .

KATHLEEN : Sent me to the country once. All them trees. Worse'n people . . . Gawd. Take them off if I thought I could get them on again. Can't understand why they don't let me have me laces. Took me belt as well. Who they think I'm going to strangle? Improved my figure, it did, the belt. Drew it in a bit.

HARRY : Oh, now, I would say, myself, the proportions were in reasonable condition.

KATHLEEN : Oh, now . . .

HARRY : Without, of course, wishing to seem immodest . . .

KATHLEEN : Get little enough encouragement in my life. Gawd . . . My friend, you know, was always crying.

HARRY : Oh, now.

KATHLEEN : Everywhere she went . . . cigarettes . . . No sooner in the shop, opens her mouth, and out it comes. Same on buses.

HARRY : Oh dear, now.

KATHLEEN : Doesn't like sympathy.

HARRY : Ah, yes.

KATHLEEN : Get all I can, myself.

HARRY : Husband a bus-driver, I believe.

KATHLEEN : Hers. Not mine.

HARRY : Ah, yes.

KATHLEEN : Mine's a corporation employee.

HARRY : Ah, yes. One of the . . .

KATHLEEN : Cleans up muck. Whenever there's a pile of muck they send him to clean it up.

HARRY : I see.

KATHLEEN : You worked in a bank, then?

HARRY : Well, in a er.

KATHLEEN : Clean job. Don't know why he doesn't get a clean job. Doorman . . . Smells awful, he does. Gets bathed one night and the next day just the same.

HARRY : Ah, yes.

KATHLEEN : Puts you off your food.

HARRY : Yes.

KATHLEEN : 'They ought to fumigate you,' I said.

HARRY : Yes?

KATHLEEN : Know what he says?

HARRY : Yes?

KATHLEEN : 'Ought to fumigate you, my girl, and forget to switch it orf.'

HARRY : Goodness.

KATHLEEN : Going to be tea-time before they get here.

HARRY (*examines watch*) : No, no. Still a little time.

KATHLEEN : Your wife alive?

HARRY : Er.

KATHLEEN : Separated?

HARRY : Well, I . . .

KATHLEEN : Unsympathetic.

HARRY : Yes?

KATHLEEN : Your wife.

HARRY : Well . . . One can ask too much these days, I believe, of er.

KATHLEEN : Met once a fortnight wouldn't be any divorce. Ridiculous, living together. 'S not human.

HARRY : No . . .

KATHLEEN : Like animals . . . Even they run off when they're not feeling like it.

HARRY : Oh, yes.

KATHLEEN : Not natural . . . One man. One woman. Who's He think He is?

(Harry looks round.)

No . . . Him. *(Points up.)*

HARRY : Oh, yes . . .

KATHLEEN : Made Him a bachelor. Cor blimey : no wife for Him.

HARRY : No.

KATHLEEN : Saved somebody the trouble.

HARRY : Yes.

KATHLEEN : Does it all by telepathy.

HARRY : Yes.

KATHLEEN : Kids?

HARRY : What? . . . Oh . . . No.

KATHLEEN : Got married how old?

HARRY : Twenty er.

KATHLEEN : Man shouldn't marry till he's forty. Ridiculous. Don't know what they want till then. After that, too old to bother.

HARRY : Oh, yes.

73

KATHLEEN : Here . . .

(*Alfred comes in carrying the chair. Sees them, nods; then goes back the way he's come.*)

Here ! (*Calls after.*) That's where it's gone.
HARRY : Don't believe . . .
KATHLEEN : That's Alfred.
HARRY : Yes?
KATHLEEN : Wrestler.
HARRY : Yes.
KATHLEEN : Up here. (*Taps her head.*)
HARRY : Oh.
KATHLEEN : Where you going when you leave here?
HARRY : Well . . . I . . . er.
KATHLEEN : Lost your job?
HARRY : Well, I . . .
KATHLEEN : Wife not have you?
HARRY : Well, I . . .
KATHLEEN : Another man.
HARRY : Oh, now . . .
KATHLEEN : Still . . . Could be worse.
HARRY : Oh, yes.

(*Pause.*)

KATHLEEN : What's he want with that, then? Here . . . you were slow to ask.
HARRY : Yes . . .
KATHLEEN : You all right?
HARRY : Touch of the . . . (*Wipes his eyes, nose.*)
KATHLEEN : Here, couple of old cry-babies you are. Bad as my friend.
HARRY : Yes . . . Well . . .
KATHLEEN : Shoot my brains out if I had a chance. Gawd ! . . . (*Feels her feet.*) Tried to kill myself with gas.

74

HARRY : Yes . . . ?

KATHLEEN : Kiddies at my sister's. Head in oven. Knock on door, Milkman. Two weeks behind, he said. Broke everything I did.

HARRY : Yes?

KATHLEEN : Nearly killed him. Would, too, if I could have got hold. Won't tap on our door, I can tell you. Not again.

HARRY : Goodness.

KATHLEEN : You all right?

HARRY : Yes . . . I . . . er.

KATHLEEN : Here. Hold my hand if you like.

HARRY : Oh, now.

KATHLEEN : Go on. (*Puts her hand on the table*.) Not much to look at.

HARRY : Oh, now. I wouldn't say that.

KATHLEEN : Go on.

HARRY : Well, I . . . (*Takes her hand*.)

KATHLEEN : Our age : know what it's all about.

HARRY : Oh, well . . . A long road, you know.

KATHLEEN : Can't get to old age fast enough for me. Sooner they put me under . . .

HARRY : Oh, now . . .

KATHLEEN : Different for a man.

HARRY : Well, I . . .

KATHLEEN : I know. Have your troubles. Still. Woman's different.

HARRY : Oh, I . . .

KATHLEEN : Wouldn't be a woman. Not again . . . Here !

(*Alfred has entered. He goes past, upstage, carrying the chair. Glances at them. Goes off.*)

Been here years, you know. Do the work of ten men if they set him to it.

75

HARRY : I say . . . (*Looking off.*)
KATHLEEN : Dunno where they've been . . . (*Calls.*) Oi! . . . Deaf as a post. Here, no need to let go . . . Think you're shy.
HARRY : Oh, well . . .
KATHLEEN : Never mind. Too old to be disappointed.
HARRY : Oh, now . . .

(*Jack and Marjorie enter, the former carrying a wicker chair.*)

MARJORIE : Here you are, then. Been looking for you all over.
KATHLEEN : Been here, haven't we, all the time.

(*Harry stands.*)

JACK : Sun still strong.
HARRY : Oh, yes.
MARJORIE : Here. Where's the other chair?
KATHLEEN : He's taken it over there.
MARJORIE : What's he doing?
KATHLEEN : Dunno. Here, sit on his knee if you want to!
MARJORIE : Catch me. Who do you think I am? (*Sits.*)
KATHLEEN : Well, no good you both standing.
JACK (*to Harry*) : No, no. After you, old man.
HARRY : No, no. After you . . .
KATHLEEN : Be here all day, you ask me. Here, I'll stand . . . Gawd . . .
JACK : Oh, no . . .
HARRY : Ridiculous.
MARJORIE : Take it in turns.
JACK : Right, I'll er.
HARRY : Do. Do. Go ahead.

76

JACK : Very decent. Very. (*Sits; sighs.*)

MARJORIE : Been carrying that around, looking for you, he has.

KATHLEEN : Been here, we have, all the time.

MARJORIE : What you been up to, then?

KATHLEEN : Nothing you might mind.

MARJORIE (*to Harry*) : Want to watch her. Men all the time.

KATHLEEN : One who knows.

MARJORIE : Seen it with my own eyes.

KATHLEEN : Lot more besides.

JACK : Think it might look up. Clearing . . . (*Gazing up.*)

HARRY : Oh. Very. (*Gazes up.*)

MARJORIE : Fallen in love, she has.

JACK : Damn nuisance about the chair, what?

HARRY : Oh. Very.

MARJORIE : Has to see the doctor about it, she has.

KATHLEEN : See the doctor about you, girl.

MARJORIE : Can't let no tradesman near the house. Five kids. Milkman, window-cleaner . . .

KATHLEEN : Know your trouble, don't you?

MARJORIE : Nothing's bad as yours.

KATHLEEN : Can't go down the street without her trousers wetting.

JACK : Spot more sun, see those flowers out. Shouldn't wonder.

HARRY : Oh, yes.

JACK : By jove, Farrer, isn't it?

HARRY : Say he was a champion quarter-miler.

JACK : Shouldn't be surprised. Build of an athlete. Square shoulders.

HARRY : Deep chest.

JACK : Oh, yes.

KATHLEEN : You know what you should do with your mouth, girl.

MARJORIE : You know what you should do with something else.

KATHLEEN (*to Harry*): Take a little stroll if you don't mind . . . Gawd strewth . . . (*Gets up; Harry hastens to help.*)

MARJORIE : Mind she doesn't stroll you to the bushes.

KATHLEEN : Mind she doesn't splash.

MARJORIE : See the doctor about you, my girl!

KATHLEEN : See him all the time : your trouble. Not right in the head.

(*Kathleen has taken Harry's arm. They go off.*)

MARJORIE : Can't keep away from men.

JACK : Oh dear. (*Gazing after.*)

MARJORIE : Gardens.

JACK : Oh.

MARJORIE : Parks especially.

JACK : I have heard of such er.

MARJORIE : Complaints. Used to send the police in threes. Can't trust two and one was never enough.

JACK : My word.

MARJORIE : Oh, yes.

JACK : Can never tell a leopard . . .

MARJORIE : What? Should see her. Spots all over.

JACK : Oh dear.

MARJORIE : Never washes.

JACK : One of the advantages of a late lunch, of course, is that it leaves a shorter space to tea.

MARJORIE : What's your friend's name?

JACK : Harry . . .

MARJORIE : What's he do, then?

JACK : Temporary er . . . Thought a slight . . .

MARJORIE : Get one with her all right. Have another.

JACK : Oh, yes . . .

MARJORIE : Don't know what we're coming to.

JACK : Life . . . mystery . . . (*Gazes up.*)

(*Marjorie watches him. Then:*)

MARJORIE : What you put away for, then?

JACK : Oh . . . what?

MARJORIE : In here.

JACK : Oh . . . Little . . .

MARJORIE : Girl?

JACK : Girl?

MARJORIE : Girls.

JACK : Girls?

MARJORIE : In the street.

JACK : Really? (*Looks around.*)

MARJORIE : Here. . . What you in for?

JACK : A wholly voluntary basis, I assure you.

MARJORIE : Wife put you away?

JACK : Oh, no. No, no. Just a moment . . . needed . . . Thought I might . . .

MARJORIE : Ever been in the padded whatsit?

JACK : Don't believe . . . (*Looking around.*)

MARJORIE : Here . . . Don't tell my friend.

JACK : Oh, well . . .

MARJORIE : Lie there for hours, you can.

JACK : Oh, now.

MARJORIE : Been here twice before.

JACK : Really . . .

MARJORIE : Don't tell my friend.

JACK : Oh, no.

MARJORIE : Thinks it's my first.

JACK : Goodness . . .

MARJORIE : One of the regulars. Wouldn't know what to do without me.

JACK : Oh, yes. Familiar faces.

MARJORIE : Come for three months; out again. Back again at Christmas.

JACK : Oh, yes.

MARJORIE : Can't stand Christmas.

JACK : No. Well. Season of festivities . . . good cheer.

MARJORIE : Most people don't talk to you in here. You noticed?

JACK : Very rare. Well . . . find someone to communicate.

MARJORIE : 'Course. Privileged.

JACK : Yes?

MARJORIE : Being in the reception wing.

JACK : Oh, yes.

MARJORIE : Good as cured.

JACK : Oh, yes.

MARJORIE : Soon be out.

JACK : Oh, goodness . . . Hardly worth the trouble.

MARJORIE : No.

JACK : Here tomorrow!

MARJORIE : You been married long?

JACK : Oh, yes . . . What?

MARJORIE : You in love?

JACK : What?

MARJORIE : Your wife.

JACK : Clouds . . . This morning, my friend was remarking on the edges.

MARJORIE : Hardly worth the trouble.

JACK : Oh, yes.

MARJORIE : Going home.

JACK : Oh, well . . . one has one's . . . thought I might plant some seeds. Soil not too good, I notice . . .

MARJORIE : Tell you something?

JACK : Oh, yes.

MARJORIE : Set up here for good.

JACK : Oh, yes.

MARJORIE : Here, you listening? What you in for?

JACK : Oh . . .

MARJORIE : Here; you always crying.

JACK : Light . . . eye . . . (*Wipes his eye with his handkerchief.*)

MARJORIE : Tell you something.

JACK : Yes.

MARJORIE : Not leave here again.

JACK : Oh, no.

(*They are silent.*

Alfred comes on. He stands at the back, leaning on the chair.)

MARJORIE : You going to sit on that or something?

ALFRED : What?

MARJORIE : Sit.

ALFRED : Dunno.

MARJORIE : Give it to somebody who can, you do.

ALFRED : What?

MARJORIE : Give it to somebody who can.

ALFRED : Yeh.

MARJORIE : You know my friend?

ALFRED : No.

MARJORIE : This is Alfred.

JACK : Oh . . . Good . . . day. (*Stands formally.*)

ALFRED : Where you get your cane?

JACK : Oh . . . (*Looks down at it.*) Came with me.

ALFRED : I had a cane like that once.

JACK : Ah, yes.

ALFRED : Nicked it.

JACK : Oh, now.

MARJORIE : Had it when he came. Didn't you? Sit down.

JACK : Yes. (*Sits.*)

ALFRED : Wanna fight?

JACK : No . . .

ALFRED : You?

MARJORIE : No, thanks.

ALFRED : Got sixpence?

JACK : No.

MARJORIE : Here. You seen my friend?

ALFRED : No.

MARJORIE : What you in for?

ALFRED : In what?

MARJORIE : Thinks he's at home, he does. Doesn't know his own strength, do you?

ALFRED : No.

MARJORIE : Took a bit of his brain, haven't they?

ALFRED : Yeh.

MARJORIE : Feel better?

ALFRED : Yeh.

MARJORIE : His mother's eighty-four.

ALFRED : Seventy.

MARJORIE : Thought you said she was eighty-four.

ALFRED : Seventy.

MARJORIE : Won't know his own name soon.

ALFRED : You wanna fight?

MARJORIE : Knock you down one hand behind my back.

ALFRED : Garn.

MARJORIE : Half kill you, I will.

ALFRED : Go on.

MARJORIE : Wanna try? (*Stands.*)

(*Alfred backs off a couple of steps. Marjorie sits.*)

Take that chair off you, you don't look out.

JACK : Slight breeze. Takes the heat off the sun.

MARJORIE : Wanna jump on him if he bullies you.

JACK : Oh, yes.

MARJORIE (*to Alfred*): What you looking at then?

ALFRED: Sky. (*Looks up.*)

MARJORIE: They'll lock you up if you don't look out. How old's your father?

ALFRED: Twenty-two.

MARJORIE: Older than him, are you?

ALFRED: Yeh.

MARJORIE: Older than his dad he is. Don't know where that leaves him.

JACK: Hasn't been born, I shouldn't wonder.

MARJORIE: No! (*Laughs.*) Hasn't been born, he shouldn't wonder. (*Pause.*) Painted rude letters in the road.

ALFRED: Didn't.

MARJORIE: Did.

ALFRED: Didn't.

MARJORIE: Did. Right in the town centre. Took them three weeks to scrub it off.

ALFRED: Two.

MARJORIE: Three.

ALFRED: Two.

MARJORIE: Three. Apprentice painter and decorator. Didn't know what he was going to decorate. (*To Alfred.*) They'll apprentice you no more. (*To Jack.*) Doesn't know his own strength, he doesn't.

JACK (*looking round*): Wonder where . . .

MARJORIE: Send the police out for them, they will.

JACK: Clouds . . . (*Looking up.*)

MARJORIE: Seen it all, I have. Rape, intercourse. Physical pleasure.

JACK: I had a cousin once . . .

MARJORIE: Here, you got a big family, haven't you?

JACK: Seven brothers and sisters. Spreads around, you know.

MARJORIE: Here, you was an only child last week.

JACK : A niece of mine—I say niece . . . she was
only . . .

MARJORIE : What you do it for?

JACK : Oh, now . . .

MARJORIE (*to Alfred*) : Wanna watch him. Trained
as a doctor he has.

JACK : Wonder where . . . (*Gazing round.*)

MARJORIE (*to Alfred*) : What you paint in the road?

ALFRED : Nothing.

MARJORIE : Must have painted something. Can't
paint nothing. Must have painted something or
they couldn't have rubbed it off.

ALFRED : Paint you if you don't watch out.

MARJORIE : I'll knock your head off.

ALFRED : Won't

MARJORIE : Will.

ALFRED : Won't.

MARJORIE : Will.

ALFRED : Won't.

MARJORIE : What you doing with that chair?

ALFRED : Nothing. (*Spins it beneath his hand.*)

MARJORIE : Faster than a rocket he is. Wanna
watch him . . . Where you going?

(*Jack has got up.*)

JACK : Thought I might . . . Oh . . .

(*Harry and Kathleen have come on from the other
side, the latter leaning on Harry's arm.*)

KATHLEEN : Gawd . . . they're coming off. I'll have
nothing left . . . Oh . . .

(*Harry helps her to the chair.*)

MARJORIE : Here, where you been?

KATHLEEN : There and back.

MARJORIE : Know where you been, my girl.

KATHLEEN : Don't.

HARRY : Canteen. We've . . .

KATHLEEN : Don't tell her. Nose ten miles long she has. Trip over it one day she will. What's he doing? (*Indicating to Alfred.*)

MARJORIE : Won't give up his chair, he won't.

HARRY : Still got three, what?

JACK : Yes . . . what. Clouds . . .

HARRY : Ah . . . Rain.

JACK : Shouldn't wonder.

MARJORIE : Here. Put that chair down.

(*Alfred still stands there. Marjorie stands. Alfred releases the chair quickly.*)

(*To Jack*) You get it.

JACK : Er . . . right.

(*Goes and gets the chair. Alfred doesn't move.*)

MARJORIE : One each, then.

HARRY : Yes . . .

MARJORIE : Well . . . (*Indicates they sit.*)

KATHLEEN : Gawd . . . (*Holds her feet.*)

MARJORIE : Had a job once.

KATHLEEN : Gawd.

MARJORIE : Packing tins of food.

KATHLEEN (*to Alfred*) : What you looking at?

ALFRED : Nothing.

MARJORIE : Pull your skirt down, girl.

KATHLEEN : Got nothing up mine ain't got up yours.

MARJORIE : Put them in cardboard boxes.

JACK : Really? I had a . . .

MARJORIE : Done by machine now.

KATHLEEN : Nothing left for you to do, my girl. That's your trouble.

MARJORIE : 'Tis.

KATHLEEN : Cries everywhere, she does.

HARRY : Oh. One has one's . . .

KATHLEEN : 'Specially at Christmas. Cries at Christmas. Boxing Day. Sometimes to New Year.

JACK : Oh, well, one . . .

KATHLEEN (*indicating Alfred*) : What's he doing, then?

MARJORIE : Waiting to be born, he is.

KATHLEEN : What?

MARJORIE : Eight o'clock tomorrow morning. Better be there. (*Laughs. To Alfred.*) You better be there.

ALFRED : Yeh.

MARJORIE : Late for his own birthday, he is. (*To Alfred.*) Never catch up, you won't.

HARRY (*holding out hand; inspects it*) : Thought I . . . No.

JACK : Could be. (*Looks up.*)

HARRY : Lucky so far.

JACK : Oh, yes.

HARRY : Possibility . . . (*Looking up.*)

JACK : By jove . . .

MARJORIE : One thing you can say about this place . . .

KATHLEEN : Yes.

MARJORIE : 'S not like home.

KATHLEEN : Thank Gawd.

MARJORIE (*to Alfred*) : What you want?

ALFRED : Nothing.

KATHLEEN : Give you nothing if you come here . . . What you staring at?

ALFRED : Nothing.

MARJORIE : Taken off a bit of his brain they have.
KATHLEEN (*to Alfred*) : Where they put it then?
MARJORIE : Thrown it in the dustbin.
KATHLEEN : Could have done with that. (*Laughs.*)
Didn't cut a bit of something else off, did they?
MARJORIE : You know what your trouble is, my
girl.
JACK : Time for tea, I shouldn't wonder. (*Stands.*)
HARRY : Yes. Well . . . let me see. Very nearly.
JACK : Stretch the old legs . . .
HARRY : Oh, yes.
MARJORIE : Not your legs need stretching, ask me.
JACK : Ah, well . . . Trim. (*Bends arms; stretches.*)
MARJORIE : Fancies himself he does.
KATHLEEN : Don't blame him.
MARJORIE : Watch yourself, my girl.
KATHLEEN : No harm come from trying.
MARJORIE : Good job your feet like they are, ask
me.
KATHLEEN : Have them off in the morning. Not
stand this much longer.
MARJORIE : Slow her down; know what they're
doing.
KATHLEEN : Know what she is?
JACK : Well, I . . .
KATHLEEN : P.O.
JACK : P.O.
KATHLEEN : Persistent Offender.
MARJORIE : Ain't no such thing.
KATHLEEN : Is.
MARJORIE : Isn't.
KATHLEEN : Heard it in the office. Off Doctor . . .
what's his name.
MARJORIE : Never heard of that doctor, I haven't.
Must be a new one must that. Doctor what's his
name is a new one on me.

KATHLEEN : I know what I heard.
MARJORIE : Here. What's he crying about?

(*Harry is drying his eyes.*)

KATHLEEN : Always crying one of these two.
MARJORIE : Call them the water babies, you ask
me. (*To Alfred.*) You seen this?

(*Alfred gazes woodenly towards them.*)

KATHLEEN : He's another.
MARJORIE : Don't know what'll become of us, girl.
KATHLEEN : Thought you was the one to cry.
MARJORIE : So d'I.
KATHLEEN : My dad was always crying.
MARJORIE : Yeh?
KATHLEEN : Drank too much. Came out of his eyes.
MARJORIE : Ooh! (*Laughs, covering her mouth.*)
KATHLEEN : Here, what's the matter with you,
Harry?
HARRY : Oh, just a er.
JACK : Could have sworn . . . (*Holds out hand;
looks up.*)
KATHLEEN : 'S not rain. 'S him. Splashing it all
over, he is.
JACK : There, now . . .
MARJORIE : Here. Look at him : thinks it's raining.
KATHLEEN (*to Jack*) : Here. Your friend . . .

(*Jack breathes deeply: fresh-air exercises.*)

JACK : Freshening.
MARJORIE : I don't know. What they come out for?
KATHLEEN : Crying all over, they are.

MARJORIE (*to Jack*) : You going to help your friend, then, are you?

JACK : Oh. Comes and goes . . .

KATHLEEN (*to Harry*) : Wanna hold my hand?

(*Harry doesn't answer.*)

MARJORIE : Not seen so many tears. Haven't.

KATHLEEN : Not since Christmas.

MARJORIE : Not since Christmas, girl.

KATHLEEN : Ooooh!

MARJORIE (*to Jack*) : You all right?

(*Jack doesn't answer. Stands stiffly turned away, looking off.*)

Think you and I better be on our way, girl.

KATHLEEN : Think we had.

MARJORIE : Try and make something. What you get for it?

KATHLEEN : Get nothing if you don't try, girl.

MARJORIE : No.

KATHLEEN : Get nothing if you do, either.

MARJORIE : Ooooh! (*Laughs, covering her mouth; stands.*) Don't slow you down, do they? (*Indicates shoes.*)

KATHLEEN : Get my laces back or else, girl . . . Oh! (*Winces, standing. To Alfred.*) What you staring at?

ALFRED : Nothing.

KATHLEEN : Be dead this time tomorrow.

MARJORIE : No complaints then, my girl.

KATHLEEN : Not too soon for me.

MARJORIE : Going to say goodbye to your boyfriend?

KATHLEEN : Dunno that he wants to know . . .

MARJORIE : Give you a hand, girl?
KATHLEEN : Can't move without.
MARJORIE : There . . . on our way.
KATHLEEN : Gawd.
MARJORIE : Not stop here again.
KATHLEEN : Better get out of here, girl . . . Gawd !
Go mad here you don't watch out.

(*Groaning, Kathleen is led off by Marjorie. Pause. Alfred comes up. Holds table, waits, then lifts it. Raises it above his head. Turns. Walks off.*)

JACK : By jove.

(*Harry stirs.*)

Freshening . . . Surprised if it doesn't blow over by tomorrow.
HARRY :Oh, yes . . .
JACK : Saw Harrison yesterday.
HARRY : Yes?
JACK : Congestion.
HARRY : Soot.
JACK : Really?
HARRY : Oh, yes. (*Dries his eyes.*)
JACK : Shouldn't wonder if wind veers. North-west.
HARRY : East.
JACK : Really? Higher ground, of course, one notices.
HARRY : Found the er. (*Gestures after Marjorie and Kathleen.*)
JACK : Oh, yes.
HARRY : Extraordinary.
JACK : 'Straordinary.
HARRY : Get used to it after a while.

JACK : Oh, yes . . . I have a sister-in-law, for example, who wears dark glasses.

HARRY : Really?

JACK : Each evening before she goes to bed.

HARRY : Really.

JACK : Following morning : takes them off.

HARRY : Extraordinary.

JACK : Sunshine—never wears them.

HARRY : Well . . . I . . . (*Finally wipes his eyes and puts his handkerchief away.*) Extraordinary.

JACK : The older one grows, of course . . . the more one takes into account other people's foibles.

HARRY : Oh, yes.

JACK : If a person can't be what they are, what's the purpose of being anything at all?

HARRY : Oh, absolutely.

(*Alfred has returned. He pickes up one of the metalwork chairs; turns it one way then another, gazes at Jack and Harry, then slowly carries it off.*)

JACK : I suppose in the army, of course, one becomes quite used to foibles.

HARRY : Oh, yes.

JACK : Navy, too, I shouldn't wonder.

HARRY : Oh, yes.

JACK : A relative of mine rose to lieutenant-commander in a seagoing corvette.

HARRY : My word.

JACK : In the blood.

HARRY : Bound to be.

JACK : Oh, yes. Without the sea : well, hate to think.

HARRY : Oh, yes.

JACK : At no point is one more than seventy-five miles from the sea.

HARRY : Really.

JACK : That is the nature of this little island.

HARRY : Extraordinary when you think.

JACK : When you think what came from it.

HARRY : Oh, yes.

JACK : Radar.

HARRY : Oh, yes.

JACK : Jet propulsion.

HARRY : My word.

JACK : Television.

HARRY : Oh . . .

JACK : Steam-engine.

HARRY : Goodness.

JACK : Empire the like of which no one has ever seen.

HARRY : No. My word.

JACK : Light of the world.

HARRY : Oh, yes.

JACK : Penicillin.

HARRY : Penicillin.

JACK : Darwin.

HARRY : Darwin.

JACK : Newton.

HARRY : Newton.

JACK : Milton.

HARRY : My word.

JACK : Sir Walter Raleigh.

HARRY : Goodness. Sir . . .

JACK : Lost his head.

HARRY : Oh, yes.

JACK : This little island.

HARRY : Shan't see its like.

JACK : Oh, no.

HARRY : The sun has set.

JACK : Couple of hours . . .

HARRY : What?

JACK : One of the strange things, of course, about this place.

HARRY : Oh, yes.

JACK : Is its size.

HARRY : Yes.

JACK : Never meet the same people two days running.

HARRY : No.

JACK : Can't find room, of course.

HARRY : No.

JACK : See them at the gates.

HARRY : Oh, my word.

JACK : Of an evening, looking in. Unfortunately the money isn't there.

HARRY : No.

JACK : Exchequer. Diverting wealth to the proper . . .

HARRY : Oh, yes.

JACK : Witness : one metalwork table, two metalwork chairs; two thousand people.

HARRY : My word, yes.

JACK : While overhead . . .

HARRY : Oh, yes . . .

(*They both gaze up. Alfred comes in; he picks up the remaining white chair.*)

ALFRED : You finished?

JACK : What . . . ?

ALFRED : Take them back. (*Indicates their two wicker chairs.*)

HARRY : Oh, yes . . .

ALFRED : Don't take them back : get into trouble.

JACK : Oh, my word.

(*Alfred, watching them, lifts the metal chair with*

93

one hand, holding its leg; demonstrates his strength.

They watch in silence.

Alfred lifts the chair above his head; then, still watching them, turns and goes.)

Shadows.

HARRY : Yes.

JACK : Another day.

HARRY : Ah, yes.

JACK : Brother-in-law I had was an artist.

HARRY : Really?

JACK : Would have appreciated those flowers. Light fading ... Clouds.

HARRY : Wonderful thing.

JACK : Oh, yes.

HARRY : Would have liked to have been an artist myself. Musician.

JACK : Really?

HARRY : Flute.

JACK : Beautiful instrument.

HARRY : Oh, yes.

(They gaze at the view.)

HARRY : Shadows.

JACK : Choose any card ... (*Holds pack out from his pocket.*)

HARRY : Any?

JACK : Any one ...

HARRY (*takes one*) : Yes ... !

JACK : Eight of Diamonds.

HARRY : My word !

JACK : Right?

94

HARRY : Absolutely.

JACK : Intended to show the ladies.

HARRY : Another day.

JACK : Oh, yes. (*He reshuffles cards; holds them out.*)

HARRY : Again?

JACK : Any one.

HARRY : Er . . .

JACK : Three of Spades.

HARRY : Two of Hearts.

JACK : What? (*Inspects the cards briefly; puts them away.*)

HARRY : Amazing thing, of course, is the er.

JACK : Oh, yes.

HARRY : Still prevails.

JACK : Oh, my goodness.

HARRY : Hendricks I find is a . . .

JACK : Oh, yes.

HARRY : Moustache . . . Eye-brows.

JACK : Divorced.

HARRY : Oh, yes.

JACK : Moral fibre. Set to a task, never complete it. Find some way to back out.

HARRY : Oh, yes.

JACK : The sea is an extraordinary . . .

HARRY : Oh, yes.

JACK : Cousin of mine . . .

HARRY : See the church.

(*They gaze off.*)

JACK : Shouldn't wonder He's disappointed. (*Looks up.*)

HARRY : Oh, yes.

JACK : Heart-break.

HARRY : Oh, yes.

JACK : Same mistake . . . Won't make it twice.
HARRY : Oh, no.
JACK : Once over. Never again.

(*Alfred has come on.*)

ALFRED : You finished?
JACK : Well, I . . . er . . .
ALFRED : Take 'em back.
JACK : Oh, well. That's very . . .

(*Alfred grasps the two wicker chairs. Glances at Jack and Harry; picks up both the chairs.*

Glances at Jack and Harry again, holding the chairs. Takes them off.)

What I . . . er . . . yes.

Harry has begun to weep.

Jack gazes off.

A moment later Jack also wipes his eyes.

After a while the light slowly fades.

Curtain

THE PATRICK PEARSE MOTEL

by

HUGH LEONARD

D

© *Hugh Leonard, 1971*

H. M. Tennent, Ltd, by arrangement with Arthur Cantor, presented *The Patrick Pearse Motel* at the Queen's Theatre, London, on 17 June 1971, with the following cast:

DERMOD GIBBON	*Patrick Laffan*
GRAINNE GIBBON	*Moira Redmond*
FINTAN KINNORE	*Godfrey Quigley*
NIAMH KINNORE	*May Cluskey*
JAMES USHEEN	*Norman Rodway*
MISS MANNING	*Rosemary Martin*
HOOLIHAN	*Derry Power*

Directed by James Grout

Designed by Patrick Murray

Lighting by Joe Davis

Olympia Productions, in association with Gemini Productions, first presented the play at the Olympia Theatre, Dublin, during the Dublin Theatre Festival of 1971

CHARACTERS

DERMOD GIBBON

GRAINNE GIBBON

FINTAN KINNORE

NIAMH KINNORE

JAMES USHEEN

MISS MANNING

HOOLIHAN

ACT I

The living-room of Dermod and Grainne Gibbon in Foxrock—a suburb in Dublin's vodka-and-bitter-lemon belt. A winter's evening.

ACT II

<small>SCENE</small> 1. *The Motel. Fifteen minutes later.*

<small>SCENE</small> 2. *The same. A few minutes later. Time—the present.*

ACT ONE

The living-room of Dermod and Grainne Gibbon is an object lesson in gracious living. The rugs match the window-curtains, and the curtains harmonize with the covers and cushions. The coffee table is marble. There is a mini-chandelier. On the walls are a Yeats, a Keating and an O'Sullivan. A handsome antique cabinet houses the most expensive hi-fi system in Foxrock; huge loudspeakers stand at opposite ends of the room. There are two doors; one leads into the hall, the other into a small bar with high stools. The bar is a recent conversion: it is under the stairs, so that the ceiling slopes down sharply: the result being that no one who is more than 5' 2" in height can stand erect in it.

For ten seconds before the curtain rises we hear the amplified sound of a game of ping-pong in progress.

Curtain.

Dermod and Grainne and Niamh and her husband Fintan Kinnore are seated on the floor with their backs to the audience. They are listening to a stereo demonstration disc. The ping-pong ball seems to travel from one end of the room to the other. They turn their heads in perfect unison as if at a tennis match. The track comes to an end, and an American voice is heard from one of the speakers.

COMPERE: Anyone for ping . . . (*From the other speaker.*) pong?
FINTAN (*getting up*): What'll they think of next?

DERMOD : No, stay there—there's more.

GRAINNE : Isn't stereo wonderful; we're thinking of buying another record.

DERMOD : Ssh! This is fantastic. Can you guess what this is?

NIAMH : Is it someone throwing up?

DERMOD : It's sea-lions.

FINTAN : Certainly it's sea-lions. (To the others.) She hears them every day!

(*The recording ends. Dermod rises and switches off the power. The others get to their feet.*

A quick look at them. Dermod and Grainne are youngish and attractive. He is thirty-five or so, watches his weight, is go-ahead, wears horn-rims, which give him a deceptively earnest look. His clothes are well-cut; he wears a "dress" sweater and an ornate medallion. Grainne is petite. Her friendliness and beauty attract men; her poise and faintly goddess-like air tend to keep them at their distance. She speaks well. She and Dermod might have been born for affluent living; there is no trace of the parvenu about either of them. They hold hands and hug each other a great deal . . . always a dangerous sign. Fintan and Niamh are older; God knows they try hard, but prosperity sits on them both like a donkey on a thistle. Fintan is big, suspicious, inflammable. Niamh is the kind of woman on whom an expensive piece of haute couture would resemble a canvas awning. She does her best, but even her walk suggests a dignified gallop.)

NIAMH : That was beautiful, Dermod.

FINTAN : Highly impressive.

DERMOD (*modestly*) : It's not bad.

NIAMH : I love the gramophone.

FINTAN : How much did it run you?

DERMOD : Five seven-five.

FINTAN : That's not bad.

DERMOD : What about this, though?

(*He operates another switch. Fintan and Niamh listen intently. Utter silence.*)

FINTAN (*impressed*) : Will you listen to that!

(*Niamh looks at him, decides that she is in the wrong place, returns downstage and begins to sit on the floor.*)

Oh, leave it to the Japs.

DERMOD : It's on in the master bedroom.

FINTAN (*who is nobody's fool*) : Oh, I knew it was somewhere. (*He notices Niamh; an embarrassed whisper.*) Get up.

DERMOD (*another switch*) : Now it's on in the sauna.

FINTAN : By God, what?

NIAMH (*on her hands and knees*) : Such things as they invent. It's a great improvement on the old horny gramophones. (*As Fintan looks at her.*) Grainne, do you remember the old horny gramophones?

GRAINNE : No.

FINTAN : Will you get up.

NIAMH : Why? Is it off?

DERMOD : Yes.

FINTAN : Yes!

(*Niamh gets to her feet.*)

DERMOD : Who's for a drink?

FINTAN (*looking at his watch*) : Ummm . . .

GRAINNE : Shouldn't you and Mr Kinnore be off soon?

FINTAN } (*together*) : Fintan, Fintan!
NIAMH }

GRAINNE : Fintan. Shouldn't you?

DERMOD : No rush. If we leave at nine we'll still be in Cork by midnight.

GRAINNE (*a hint of alarm*) : Nine? You said you were leaving at eight-thirty.

DERMOD (*shrugging*) : Give or take. (*Putting his arms around her.*) She can't wait to be rid of me.

GRAINNE (*playing his game*) : You're right.

DERMOD : Got a boyfriend in the loft, haven't you?

GRAINNE (*shaking her head*) : In the hot press.

DERMOD (*nuzzling her*) : Hope he smothers.

GRAINNE (*reciprocating*) : Spoil-sport.

NIAMH (*watching their display of affection*) : It's like an advertisement for glue.

(*Fintan who is easily moved to passion, strokes her bottom.*)

Stop that.

FINTAN : Some people might do well to show a quarter as much affection.

NIAMH : If you mean me, I don't have to. You've got enough in you for an orgy.

GRAINNE (*to Dermod*) : Love, I hate to think of you drinking and then driving all that distance.

DERMOD : We'll be careful.

GRAINNE : And the weather is so awful.

FINTAN : Is it still raining?

NIAMH : I'll see. (*She walks with dignity to the window, pulls the curtain aside and looks out.*)

FINTAN : Well?

NIAMH : It's urinating.

GRAINNE : There !

NIAMH (*to Finton, who is glaring at her*) : You told me not to use the other word.

DERMOD : We have time for just the one. If you'll all step into the consulting room . . . !

(*They all go into the bar. The height of the ceiling obliges them to remain half-crouching while they are in there. Dermod goes behind the bar and begins to open a bottle of champagne.*)

GRAINNE : Wouldn't we be more comfortable in the living-room?

DERMOD : What's the point of having a bar put in if we don't drink in it?

NIAMH : Oh, this is very snug.

DERMOD : It's not bad, is it?

FINTAN : How much?

DERMOD : Twelve-fifty, with fittings.

NIAMH : It's so original. I love sunken ceilings.

GRAINNE : Believe it or not, that part of it was accidental.

NIAMH : Go 'way !

DERMOD : Absolutely.

FINTAN : By God.

(*Niamh begins to climb up on a barstool, facing it as if it were a ladder. She is trying to avoid hitting her head.*)

GRAINNE (*pointing upwards*) : It's the stairs, you

see. We thought of having them raised slightly, but ....

NIAMH (*straining*): Don't do that, you'll spoil it.

(*She is trying to turn into a sitting position on the stool. Fintan takes hold of her by the thighs.*)

FINTAN: Do you want a hand?

NIAMH (*a mite tetchy*): I'm all right, I'm all right. (*To Grainne.*) Don't touch it, it's perfect.

(*A 'pop' is heard from behind the bar as Dermod uncorks the champagne. The bottle comes into sight. Niamh sees it.*)

Oh, Jay, looka . . . (*As Fintan glares at her.*) Champagne . . . how lovely.

DERMOD: Well, it's an occasion. Fintan, here's to a long partnership and a successful day in Cork.

GRAINNE: And prosperity.

DERMOD: Same thing, love.

FINTAN: No, here's to friendship . . . friends, through and through, and to hell with money. (*He drinks.*) Good stuff. How much?

DERMOD: Ten-ten a half-doz.

FINTAN: That's with discount?

DERMOD: Sure.

FINTAN: I'll buy a gross.

GRAINNE: Darling, must you go to Cork?

DERMOD (*fondly*): Now, now . . .

GRAINNE: Don't. Stay home with me.

DERMOD: Can't.

GRAINNE: Yes!

FINTAN (*tolerantly*): Women, women! I'll have him back to you this time tomorrow night, with the deeds to a brand new motel.

108

DERMOD : What'll we call this one?

FINTAN : It's in Cork. Who's the most famous patriot from there?

DERMOD : Michael Collins.

FINTAN : The 'Michael Collins'!

NIAMH : Gorgeous.

DERMOD (*refilling Fintan's glass*) : Fintan, you're a genius.

FINTAN (*crowing*) : Our second motel . . . and the first one not even open yet!

DERMOD : Only one week to go!

GRAINNE : Stay here tonight.

DERMOD : I can't. We . . .

GRAINNE : I'll be all on my own.

DERMOD : No, you won't, you'll be staying with Niamh.

GRAINNE : It's not the same thing. I want to be *here*, with you.

DERMOD : Fintan, tell her . . .

GRAINNE : I don't care. You're mean. Where are my cigarettes? (*She goes into the living-room. Her peevishness at once disappears. She makes a dive for her handbag, fishes out her spectacles and peers myopically at her wristwatch.*)

FINTAN : By God, that girl is mad about you.

NIAMH : Can't bear to let him out of her sight.

DERMOD (*modestly*) : I know, I know.

NIAMH : Lovebirds!

GRAINNE (*a howl of anguish*) : Half-past eight . . . is the rotten pig going to stay here all night? (*Hissing towards the bar.*) Get out, get out, go to Cork, go to Cork! Oh, God : will you make the stupid, useless maggot go to C . . .

(*She breaks off, suddenly noticing the presence of us, the audience. She holds her glasses to her eyes,*

*just to make sure, then hastily puts them back in
her handbag. She smiles at us charmingly, now the
perfect hostess.)*

Welcome, welcome to our home. I do wish you
could see all of it. You'd adore my kitchen : it's
eighteenth-century English and all-electric. And
the master bedroom is a dream : in white, everything built-in, and the carpet so deep, if you lost
an ear-ring you'd need a safari to find it. (*She
laughs at her little joke.*) And there's a sunken bath
—Dermod got the idea from *Spartacus*—all done
in tiles inspired by the graffiti at Pompeii : daring,
but nice. And I can just see you all sitting in our
sauna.

*(She looks at us for a moment, imagining this.
Then, anxious for our good opinion.)*

I hope I don't seem to boast? Dermod and I
couldn't always afford little extras. But he worked
so hard . . . well, I won't bore you, but we were
in this teeny flat, and there was this government
contract, because the Department of Defence had
sold their aeroplane. *You know* . . . the jet. But
they shouldn't have, because the Department of
Agriculture had nothing to spray crops with.
A-a-nnnd, they wanted it back, and there was
this purchasing contract. A-a-nnnd there was this
man who seemed certain to get it, only some awful
person reported him for diddling the income tax,
so he didn't get it; and it turned out that the
poor man hadn't been—diddling, I mean, but by
then Dermod had the contract, and that was the
beginning. And now we have all this, and we're
so happy and grateful and sincerely humble. Be-

cause we're still simple people who sit home and look at colour television, just like you do. *Some* things are different: we swopped our old parish priest for a Jesuit; and *he* told us that the bit about the rich man, and the camel going through the eye of a needle doesn't apply in areas where poverty has been eradicated . . . such as Foxrock. Does money bring happiness? Well, I have my ring and my brooch (*Showing them.*) and nice clothes—you'll see my coat later—and my car, and, of course, Dermod; and I can assure you . . . (*Her voice quavers as she descends further into abject misery with each word.*) that I'm the most . . . content and the happiest . . . girl in the whole . . . wide . . . world.

(*She dissolves into tears and gropes for her handkerchief as Dermod comes from the bar. He heads for the telephone and dials a number.*)

(*Coldly.*) Who are you 'phoning?
DERMOD (*his joke*) : My girlfriend.
GRAINNE (*a snort of derision*) : Huh !
DERMOD : No, that's one thing that'll never come between us, love. You'll always be the only girl for me.

(*He blows her a kiss. She blows him one back, then turns away and, in utter disgust,*)

GRAINNE : Yeccch !
DERMOD : Fintan reminded me that our new manageress is due in town. I don't want her ringing here and getting no answer, with us in Cork and you staying with Niamh. (*Into telephone.*) Come on, come on . . .

111

NIAMH (*in the bar*) : Fintan, help me down, I'm getting a nose-bleed. (*As he assists her.*) and will you stop feeling me . . . you've been at it all night.

FINTAN : I can't help it.

NIAMH : Yes, you can.

FINTAN : You're so lovely.

NIAMH : You must be as blind as a bat.

FINTAN : Fifteen years, and everytime I look at you I go mad inside. I don't know what I'm going to do in Cork without you.

NIAMH : I know what I'm going to do tonight . . . sleep ! Oh, just to lie in an empty bed, to be able to roll over without a voice roaring in me ear, 'Good girl, good girl, here I am' !

FINTAN (*sure of himself*) : Not at all : you'll cry yourself to sleep without me. Ah, don't fret, girl, I'll make it up to you tomorrow night on the double.

NIAMH (*hollowly*) : Oh, God.

DERMOD (*into telephone*) : Hello . . . Royal Shamrock Hotel? You might answer your switchboard, do you call this efficiency? . . . I want no lip, thank you . . . has Miss Manning checked in yet? . . . Yes, she is : I myself made the reservation . . . But she must be; she was due in at six from London . . . You did what? That was damned officious of you . . . Oh, yes? Well, will you kindly tell your manager he'll be hearing from me. The name is Gibbon . . . Dermod Gibbon of Mother Ireland Motels, Limited. (*He hangs up.*) Bloody nerve.

GRAINNE : What is?

DERMOD : She hasn't turned up, so they've cancelled her room.

GRAINNE : So?

DERMOD (*angry*) : I made that reservation.

GRAINNE (*feigning horror*): And they cancelled it?
Oh, the fools.

DERMOD: Not funny, love. I'll ring the airport.

GRAINNE (*agitated*): You haven't time. I'll do it,
you go to Cork.

DERMOD (*mildly amused*): Haven't time? What's
the matter with you? (*He dials. Through the
following he gets his number and talks into the
phone.*)

NIAMH (*in the bar*): I'll tell you what's the matter
with you. You're so randy that you can't even look
at a wasp without imagining it with its stripes off.

FINTAN: 'Randy' . . . that's exquisite language
from a woman's mouth.

NIAMH: And what's more, you're twisted.

FINTAN: Me?

NIAMH: Anyone who likes ugly women *must* be
twisted.

FINTAN: What ugly woman? (*Pointing out of the
bar.*) Do you mean her? That ugly article out
there?

(*Grainne, who looks anything but ugly, is idly
smoothing her dress over her thighs, head thrown
back. The effect is definitely erotic.*)

Sure a man would be mad to look at her twice!

NIAMH (*half to herself*): It's true, I knew it: he's
woman-blind.

FINTAN: I know what your game is; you're trying
to get me confused. There's another man.

NIAMH (*stunned*): A what?

FINTAN: I'm not enough for you. You want to use
that body of yours to drag other poor unfortunates
to their destruction.

NIAMH: What body?

113

FINTAN : And that face. Beside you, Cleopatra was an oul' ratbag.

(*Niamh stares towards the audience, her face numb with stupefaction.*)

Well, you're not going to get the chance to exercise your lust while I'm in Cork. That ugly article out there is going to stay with you—that was *my* idea. And if I ever catch you looking crossways at a man I'll crucify you and I'll tear him to bits . . . Do you hear me?

NIAMH (*frightened by his towering rage*) : Yes, Fintan.

DERMOD (*on the telephone*) : . . . Closed down completely? Nothing getting off at all?

(*Niamh, drink in hand, makes to move out of the bar.*)

FINTAN : Come back here. You mind your manners, because that bugger is putting me up for the country club, and men of substance who get into the country club do not have wives who at the first sight of a bottle of champagne, say, 'Ah, *Jay* . . . looka !'

NIAMH : You're always telling me to be myself.

FINTAN : At home—not when you're out. Go on, now.

(*They move out of the bar as Dermod hangs up.*)

NIAMH (*emerging at a half-stoop*) : We thought we'd come out before we were left this way.

FINTAN (*glaring at her, to Dermod*) : What's the news of your Miss Manning?

114

GRAINNE (*to Niamh, an urgent whisper*): I've got to talk to you.

DERMOD: London Airport is closed for the night. Fog.

FINTAN: Well, there's no rush: she'll . . . (*Seeing that Niamh has not straightened up.*) You're out now, pet. (*To Dermod.*) She'll be here tomorrow.

DERMOD: I promise you she's a jewel. I met her at a cocktail party in London. Grainne's old boy-friend was there . . . James Usheen.

NIAMH (*excited*): Oh, you don't mean the one on the television? (*To Grainne.*) You don't know *him*?

GRAINNE (*a tight smile*): I used to.

DERMOD: Before he was famous. Her first love, yes?

GRAINNE: Something like that.

NIAMH: You and him? Oh, Jay . . . mes Usheen, how interesting for you.

GRAINNE (*wishing the subject had not come up*): It was twelve years ago. I haven't seen him since . . . except on the box.

NIAMH: I watch him every Sunday. I love him when he's insulting people.

FINTAN: Is he in colour?

NIAMH: Yes.

FINTAN: I'd have seen him, so.

NIAMH: He's here now.

GRAINNE (*whirling around, hand on throat*): Where?

NIAMH: Here in town. He's opening a supermarket. I saw it in the *News of the World* . . . (*As Fintan looks at her.*) *The Times.* Do you remember how he got famous? When he made that remark on the television . . . 'Homosexuality is only a pain in the a - -' . . .

FINTAN: That'll do!

115

NIAMH : I'm only saying what he . . . .

FINTAN : Well, don't . . . (*For the benefit of the others.*) pet. Yes, I know him now. Didn't some husband get costs off him in a divorce case? And he's on every Sunday, belittling his own country and running down the sacrament of marriage. Oh, a credit to us . . . if he was in black and white I'd switch him off.

GRAINNE : They say he's a horrid person; let's not talk about him. (*Feigning surprise.*) Look at the time ! . . . where *does* the evening go to? Now . . . coats! (*She goes out, humming to herself and trying not to hurry.*)

FINTAN : You've got a fine girl there.

DERMOD : I know.

FINTAN : She's a monument to your good taste. Not many men appreciate that beneath a plain exterior there often beats a heart of gold.

DERMOD (*at sea*) : Pardon?

NIAMH (*softly*) : You can take him nowhere.

FINTAN : It was a very beautiful woman that first said that to me. Did you ever meet my ex-secretary Miss Shanahan? Oh, a smasher . . . she was the spitting image of that Robert Morley.

DERMOD : Is that so?

FINTAN : She went into a convent.

NIAMH : I wonder why.

FINTAN : A shocking waste. (*Businesslike.*) Partner, I'll be honest with you. There are women and women . . . man-eaters like this one (*Indicating Niamh.*) and decent plain creatures like your wife. But I don't like the sound of this new manageress of yours at all.

DERMOD : Miss Manning?

(*Grainne returns carrying overcoats and scarves.*)

GRAINNE : Here we are. Now both of you wrap up well.

DERMOD : Because she was at a cocktail party? Fintan, she is the dowdiest, dullest, most . . .

FINTAN : I accept that.

DERMOD : Then why?

GRAINNE : Let me help you.

(She assists them into their coats and scarves. The two men are too involved in their argument to notice. Niamh looks at her empty glass and goes into the bar for a refill.)

DERMOD : If it's her qualifications . . .

FINTAN : No, it's her nationality.

DERMOD *(disbelieving)* : Because she's English? Oh, Fintan . . . !

FINTAN : Don't misunderstand me : I'm not a bigot. Ordinarily, I wouldn't even care if she was a black. *(Second thoughts.)* Well, if she was a . . . Norwegian.

DERMOD : But . . .

FINTAN : We decided, you and I did, to run our motels on patriotic principles as a tribute to the men who died for Ireland. We owe it to them.

DERMOD : Absolutely. *(To Grainne.)* Thanks love. But I don't see . . .

FINTAN : Next week, five miles up those mountains *(Pointing out.)* we'll have our first grand opening. The motel will be named after the greatest patriot of all time. The Tricolor and the Plough and the Stars will float over the swimming pool, there will be an oil painting of a different patriot in every bedroom. Look . . . look at the menu. *(He produces a sheet of paper.)* 'Battle of the Boyne Salmon . . . Vinegar Hill Mayonnaise . . . Black

117

and Tan Pigs' feet . . . I.R.A. Bombe Surprise . . .'

DERMOD : Yes, and Remember Limerick Ham. But what has that to . . .

FINTAN : It has this to do with it. With all that patriotism, I wouldn't feel right having a manageress who was English.

DERMOD : I disagree. (*To Grainne, absently.*) Thanks, dear. (*To Fintan.*) I think we've more than done our bit. There's a night watchman out there now who served the 1916 Rising. He's too old to be efficient, but we hired him. We advertised here for a manageress, and you saw the applicants. Any one of them would have ruined us in a month. Ireland first, Fintan, and at all costs. But it is not patriotic to lose money. It is a betrayal of the economy.

FINTAN : My answer is still no.

DERMOD : Miss Manning has a contract . . . she could sue us.

FINTAN : Let her.

DERMOD : And she'll win.

FINTAN (*after a pause*) : I am a patriot. But I don't want to look like a fanatic . . . we'll give her a try.

DERMOD : Fintan, you have greatness in you.

GRAINNE : There ! . . . you're weather-proof. (*Kissing Dermod.*) Goodbye, my darling. Think of me, and drive carefully. I'll miss you.

FINTAN : But I'd like to see her references.

GRAINNE : And I wish you every success in Cork.

DERMOD : They're upstairs in my workroom. I'll get them.

FINTAN : I'll go with you, I need to use the amenities.

(*They go out. Grainne has been too intent on*

getting rid of them to pay heed to what has been said.)

GRAINNE (*calling musically*): Niamh . . . Fintan is go-ing! (*It dawns on her that they have merely gone upstairs.*) Dermod, Cork is *that* way! Oh, my God.

(*Niamh comes out of the bar.*)

(*Ashen-faced.*) They're still here.

NIAMH: I know. Before Fintan goes anywhere he always mauls me goodbye.

GRAINNE (*shoving her wrist-watch under Niamh's nose*): What time is it?

NIAMH: Quarter to.

GRAINNE: I'm done for. They're going to stay on and on, and when he comes they'll still be here.

NIAMH: When who comes?

GRAINNE: Who? Who? Who do you think? . . . James Usheen!

NIAMH: *Him?*

GRAINNE: Yes!

NIAMH: Shaggin' hell.

GRAINNE: Have you got the letter?

NIAMH: What?

GRAINNE: The *letter*!

NIAMH (*in a daze*): It came yesterday. (*She takes an envelope from her handbag and glances at the printed heading.*) The Royal Anna Liffey Hotel.

GRAINNE: That's the one.

NIAMH: He's . . . coming here?

GRAINNE: He's due now.

NIAMH: And Dermod doesn't . . .

GRAINNE: Ssssh! No.

NIAMH: Will I see him?

119

GRAINNE : You'll do much more than see him. I need your help.

NIAMH : What for . . . to jump on him? (*She laughs.*)

GRAINNE (*grimly*) : If there's any jumping to be done, I'll do it. (*As Niamh gapes at her, realizing that she is in earnest.*) If only they'd go to Cork! Niamh, do you know what it's like living in England? Over there women have affairs.

NIAMH : Do they?

GRAINNE : For God's sake, love, don't you read your 'Nova'? They have freedom. In a big city a woman is like a needle with a haystack to hide in, and she's never caught.

NIAMH : Some are.

GRAINNE : Not so many. The *News of the World* never goes more than thirty-two pages.

NIAMH (*nodding*) : And eight of those are sport.

GRAINNE : I have never looked at any man except Dermod. Where's the point? A man can take one look at a woman and love her for the rest of his life. But we women are different, we're realists.

NIAMH : I know. Just looking at a steak won't fill your stomach.

GRAINNE : You expressed that very well, Niamh.

NIAMH : Ta.

GRAINNE : I've tried to be a wife, not a vegetable. I take guitar lessons, I've studied early Irish art and I read Harold Robbins. But in this country women are bond-slaves. I love Ireland. I believe that whatever English women have, we owe it to our pride as a nation to let Irish women have some of it, too.

NIAMH : There's an awful lot of patriotism around here this evening.

GRAINNE : God has given me so very much. But

it's the little things we can't have that turns us into monsters. I want to spare Dermod that, Niamh.

NIAMH : Aren't you good to him !

GRAINNE (*with sudden passion*) : Apart from which, he is so bloody dull, and this house is dull, and I would love to have a man just once, just once before my throat gets wrinkles and people look at my brooch first and my ring, and then me, and I swear, I swear I will never ask another thing so long as I live . . . just one short fleeting night of harmless innocent adultery, oh God, is that too much to ask for ?

(*Pause.*)

NIAMH : Have you tried St Ann?

GRAINNE (*calm*) : I had almost given up hope, then Dermod met James Usheen at that party. He introduced himself as my husband. Next day, James rang me. He said he was coming over to open a supermarket, and could we meet? He sounded so affectionate.

NIAMH (*half-horror, half-awe*) : You wouldn't !

GRAINNE : When Dermod said that he and Fintan were going to Cork this evening, I knew it was a sign from heaven. I booked a double room in your name at the Royal Anna Liffey Hotel. (*Hugging the letter.*) That's why I had them send you the confirmation.

NIAMH : In my name?

GRAINNE : Yours and Fintan's.

NIAMH : He'll slaughter me.

GRAINNE : He won't know. I've planned every little detail, and if only they'll stop dithering upstairs and go to Cork, then nothing . . . positively nothing . . . can go wrong.

(*Grainne looks at the letter and emits a shriek of horror.*)

NIAMH : What is it?
GRAINNE : The hotel's full up.

(*Dermod returns.*)

NIAMH : Ah, no.
GRAINNE : They can't take us.
NIAMH : Well, isn't that the . . .
DERMOD : Who can't take you?

(*Grainne and Niamh swing around to stare at him. Grainne thrusts the letter behind her back.*)

GRAINNE : The hairdresser.
NIAMH (*simultaneously*) : The chiropodist.
DERMOD : Both full up, are they? . . . hard luck. Say goodbye, love. We're off.

(*He moves towards Grainne to kiss her goodbye. She backs away, comes up against the table on which is Niamh's handbag, and—operating by touch—shoves the letter blindly into it. Niamh does not see this: she is looking apprehensively at Fintan, who has now come in and is about to say his goodbyes.*)

DERMOD : Take care, darling. I'll miss you.
GRAINNE : I'll miss you, too. Now be good.
DERMOD (*fondly*) : *You* be good.
GRAINNE (*lovingly, groping for the handbag*) : What do *you* think?
NIAMH (*as Fintan advances on her*) : Keep away from me.

122

FINTAN : I want to say goodbye.

NIAMH : The only thing worse than you saying goodbye is you saying hello. (*As he closes with her.*) Now get off!

FINTAN (*struggling with her, to the others*): It's our little game, isn't she great?

GRAINNE : Don't go.

DERMOD : Must. (*A last kiss.*) 'Bye. Fintan . . . ?

NIAMH : Oh, you messer.

FINTAN (*thickly*): Right. (*He manages to plant a kiss on Niamh's face.*) Now remember what I said.

NIAMH : Yes!

FINTAN (*a threat*): And mind yourself . . . pet. Goodbye, Mrs Gibbon.

GRAINNE : Grainne.

DERMOD : 'Bye, Niamh.

(*Dermod and Fintan go out. Grainne sees them to the front door, off. Niamh, exhausted by her battle with Fintan, sags into a chair.*)

DERMOD (*off*): Don't come out in the rain, love. 'Bye!

GRAINNE (*off*): Drive carefully! (*She comes back into the living-room.*)

NIAMH : In bed or out of it, he's the same. He comes at me like a threshing machine.

GRAINNE : Shhh!

(*She listens. Car doors are slammed, off. There is the sound of the engine starting up, then the noise of wheels on gravel.*)

Gone. (*A broad smile.*)

NIAMH : What are you looking so happy about? If the hotel is full up . . .

GRAINNE : There's one other place we can go to.

NIAMH : At this hour?

GRAINNE : It came to me while I was kissing Dermod goodbye. What does 'P.P.' stand for?

NIAMH : The parish priest's house? You wouldn't!

GRAINNE : I mean the Patrick Pearse.

NIAMH : The motel?

GRAINNE : Why not? It's furnished, the heating's on, and there are eighty-four bedrooms, all empty. There's even a swimming pool, in case James turns out to be kinky.

NIAMH : But the night watchman . . .

GRAINNE : He doesn't know me by sight; Dermod engaged him. And next week, when the motel is open, he'll be let go, he'll never see me again. It's perfect.

NIAMH : If men only knew what goes on inside women's heads while they're kissing them! But, Grainne, you can't . . . not in Dermod's motel.

GRAINNE : In a way, it's appropriate. When a ship is launched, it's always the owner's wife who christens it. Now I must go upstairs and change.

NIAMH : Out of *that* dress?

GRAINNE : For James—nothing but the best. Niamh, be a love and fetch me a drink, I'm shaking with nerves. Oh, when he finds out what I've got in store for him!

NIAMH (*stunned*) : He doesn't know?

GRAINNE : How could he? Do you take me for the kind of woman who would tell a man she intends to go to bed with him? . . . he'd think I was fast.

NIAMH : Yeah . . . I'm sorry.

GRAINNE (*beginning to unzip her dress*) : The drinks, love . . . and have one yourself. I'll .

(*Again, the sound of car wheels on gravel.*)

It's too late, he's here! (*Babbling.*) I left the door off the catch, I told him to come straight in. One never looks one's best on a doorstep. Niamh . . . I want the first thing he sees to be me, alone, waiting. So would you . . . ?

NIAMH : Would I what?

GRAINNE (*pointing to the bar*) : Please?

(*Niamh nods, crosses herself resignedly and goes into the bar. Grainne braces herself for the great moment. As footsteps are heard in the hall, she shuts her eyes dreamily and extends her arms towards the open door, ready to be embraced.*)

Darling . . .

(*But it is Fintan who appears.*)

. . . is it really you?

FINTAN : No, he's out in the car.

GRAINNE (*staring at him*) : Oh.

FINTAN : Niamh's Mini is blocking the drive. (*Yelling.*) Niamh !

NIAMH (*in the bar*) : What?

GRAINNE : I was just going upstairs to . . . pack a suitcase. (*She goes out.*)

NIAMH (*yelling from the bar*) : What do you want?

FINTAN : Your car is in our way. Where are the keys?

NIAMH : In my handbag.

(*She pours a drink for herself and for Grainne. Fintan finds her handbag, rummages inside it, takes out the letter, looks at it, puts it back, finds the key, shuts the handbag and starts for the door. Halfway across the room he comes to a shuddering*) *stop. He goes racing back to the handbag, takes the letter out again and reads it. Disbelief gives way to a convulsion of sheer, towering rage. He growls like an animal and raises his hands above his head, the letter crushed in his fist. Niamh comes from the bar, a glass of champagne in each hand.)*

NIAMH (*coldly*): Why don't you go to Cork . . . you're not wanted here. And leave my keys in the dashboard.

(He reaches for her as if about to strangle her.)

And don't paw me with my hands full. (*She goes out.*)

(Fintan sits brokenly and begins to sob. Dermod comes in.)

DERMOD: What's the delay for? (*Looking at him.*) Why are you laughing?

(Fintan holds out the letter. Dermod takes it.)

What is it? (*He smooths out the letter and reads it.*) So? You and Niamh tried to book into the Royal Anna Liffey tonight, and it's full up. What's so . . . (*He looks at the letter again.*) Tonight? But . . . (*A heartrending sob from Fintan.*) Fintan, stop that.
FINTAN: It was . . . in her handbag.
DERMOD: Yes?
FINTAN: Her and some bollix.
DERMOD: Good God.
FINTAN: Me in Cork, and her in her element.

126

DERMOD : Niamh? I don't believe it.

FINTAN (*a terrible roar*) : I'll kill her!

(*He lurches towards the door, blind with rage. Dermod grabs him.*)

DERMOD : Fintan, no.

FINTAN : Let go of me.

DERMOD : Not until you control yourself. The state you're in now, you might kill her.

FINTAN : I will, I will.

DERMOD : Yes, and then what?

FINTAN : What do you mean, then what? We'll have it hushed up, what do you think? Now get your hands off.

DERMOD : Fintan, listen to me. We're going to Cork . . .

FINTAN : To hell with Cork, I'm not going to Cork, I never liked Cork.

DERMOD (*quietly, in charge*) : We are going to Cork, because whatever Niamh was up to, it's fallen through . . . (*Showing Fintan the letter.*) The hotel is full up. Furthermore, Grainne will be with her tonight in your house, and there'll be no monkey business with her there. In Cork, you can think things over calmly, and tomorrow you can sort it all out with Niamh in a civilized manner.

FINTAN : You're right.

DERMOD : Good man.

FINTAN : I'll kill her tomorrow.

DERMOD : Have you her car keys? (*He sees that Fintan is holding the keys and takes them from him.*)

FINTAN : Maybe I ought to kill her now.

DERMOD : No!

FINTAN : I didn't get where I am today by putting

things off. Can you wait five minutes? (*He makes for the door.*)

DERMOD : Fintan.

FINTAN : Why did I have to marry a raving beauty? Do you know what I'm going to do? I'll choke her till there's just enough breath left in her gizzard to gasp out the name of the man. And when I find him . . . !

DERMOD (*shaking him violently*) : Fintan !

(*Fintan looks glassily at him.*)

Cork.

FINTAN (*childlike*) : Cork?

DERMOD : And money.

FINTAN : Money . . .

DERMOD : That's the man !

(*He leads the suddenly docile Fintan out by the hand. As they reach the door, Niamh passes them carrying her own glass of champagne. Fintan emits a terrible roar and is about to spring at her, but Dermod yanks him out into the hall. By the time Niamh turns around they are both gone.*)

NIAMH (*assuming that the roar was a sneeze*) : Bless you. (*Calling.*) Grainne . . . they've . . .

(*Grainne enters. She has changed into her newest most stunning dress, and carries the other glass of champagne.*)

. . . gone.

GRAINNE : I know, I saw them. Zip me up?

128

(*We hear the sound of the car moving off.*)

How do I look?

NIAMH: In that dress you won't have time to get to the motel . . . it'll happen in the middle of the road.

GRAINNE (*coolly*): No, it won't. It's all going to be beautiful.

NIAMH: But it's a sin.

(*Grainne laughs.*)

Yes, yes, it is.

GRAINNE: Father Semple—our Jesuit—said to me that if there was no sin there would be no need for priests, and if there were no priests everybody in the country would be committing adultery. Well, if we're going to turn into a race of degenerates it won't be my fault. That's why there's that bit in the Bible about a man laying down his wife for his friend. So it's . . .

NIAMH: No, stop. You've lost me. And if I'm confused, I won't sleep, and tonight I am going to sleep. (*Ecstatically.*) When I stretch out in that big bed it's going to be like lying in a field, and not a bull in sight.

GRAINNE: You poor thing.

NIAMH (*hastily*): I don't want you to think badly of Fintan. He's the kindest man in the world . . . yes, he is. And it's not even the night after night I object to. You'll think I'm too sensitive, but what I've come to dread, what turns me into a nervous wreck, is waiting for the very last minute, when he roars 'Up the rebels!' What the English did to the Irish for 700 years Fintan's been doing to me for the past fifteen. How is Dermod that way?

GRAINNE : Nothing.

NIAMH : Do you mean he doesn't roar?

GRAINNE : I mean nothing nothing.

NIAMH : But he's never done hugging you.

GRAINNE : That's for visitors.

NIAMH (*nodding*) : I *thought* you looked very fresh. But why?

GRAINNE (*shaking her head*) : I'm not a disobliging wife. I know my duty. Every night I lie on my bed with my face smothered in cream I wear to keep my pores open, just for him. And he sits in *his* bed totting up figures and looking at me as if I were the Man in the Iron Mask.

NIAMH : Twin beds. Oh, Jay.

GRAINNE : His new Jensen gets more affection than I do. At least *it* gets driven. But when James Usheen walks through that door ... !

NIAMH : I don't want to hear. What'll you do?

GRAINNE : Not a thing. He'll take one look and sweep me into his arms.

NIAMH : Oh, Jay, don't go on.

GRAINNE : Did you read what the judge called him in that divorce case? ... a dedicated philanderer ... And yet, when I knew him, he was all pimples and damp hands ... I used to want to scream whenever he touched me. But *now* ... oh, when I look at that man on television! So debonair, so beautifully dressed, and that low-pitched sexy voice!

(*The door bursts open and James Usheen staggers in. His overcoat and most of his face is caked with mud.*)

USHEEN (*croaking*) : Where's the fucking brandy?

GRAINNE ⎫ *(together, pointing)* : In the bar.
NIAMH ⎭

(Without pausing for a moment, Usheen goes into the bar, hitting his head on the ceiling.)

USHEEN : Shite!
GRAINNE : James!
NIAMH : It's him!

(They rush into the bar, where Usheen is nursing his head with one hand and pouring himself a drink with the other.)

GRAINNE : James, what's happened to you? You . . .
USHEEN : Belt up, will you . . . I think I may drop dead. *(They watch as he knocks back a brandy.)* That's better. Who owned this house before you did—pygmies?
GRAINNE : James, your clothes . . .
USHEEN : I'm lucky to be alive. Two raving maniacs in a Jensen nearly ran over me at your front gate.
NIAMH : But that must have been . . .
GRAINNE *(shutting her up)* : . . . terrible for you.
USHEEN : They ought to be locked up. Then I fell into a bloody great hole out there.
GRAINNE : That's going to be our swimming pool.
USHEEN *(coldly)* : Oh, yes?
GRAINNE : Heated.
NIAMH : You're lucky : next month you would have drowned.
USHEEN *(eyeing her bleakly)* : Have we met?
GRAINNE : Excuse me . . . this is Niamh Kinnore. Niamh is my very dearest friend . . . we've known each other a week.
USHEEN : Charmed.

131

NIAMH : I watch you every Sunday, Mr Usheen. I don't know how you think up all the . . .

USHEEN : Could we move out of here, or are we rehearsing for a Japanese wedding?

GRAINNE : Of course, James.

NIAMH (*lamely*) : . . . all those funny rude remarks you make.

(*They move back into the living-room. Usheen brings the brandy bottle with him.*)

USHEEN : Have you just had visitors?

GRAINNE : Why do you ask?

USHEEN : That Jensen was coming out of your drive.

GRAINNE : Was it? Sometimes cars use our gateway to turn in. Did you get the number?

USHEEN : No . . .

GRAINNE : What a pity.

USHEEN : . . . But just before I threw myself into your flowerbed I saw the ugly red face of the bastard who was driving. He was actually shouting at me. He said 'I'll kill her, I'll kill her' . . .

NIAMH : Why would Fintan want to . . .

GRAINNE : Heavens, look at your coat. Take it off. James. (*She assists him.*)

USHEEN : I suppose he mistook me for a woman. I never forget a face, and I won't forget that one.

NIAMH (*a golden-tongued flatterer*) : I would never mistake you for a woman, Mr Usheen.

USHEEN : You're a perceptive little thing, aren't you? Yes, I'll remember that git. And if I ever meet him . . . !

GRAINNE : My goodness, what a beautiful coat.

USHEEN : Think so? I bought it to spite Eamonn Andrews. Now it's ruined.

GRAINNE : No, it's only mud, it'll brush out. The important thing is, you got here.

USHEEN : Where's your husband?

GRAINNE : He . . . went to Cork.

USHEEN : Oh?

GRAINNE : Unexpectedly.

USHEEN : I'm sorry to have missed him.

GRAINNE : So I'm afraid we're all alone.

USHEEN : You and I?

GRAINNE : Yes.

USHEEN : What's *that* then?

(*They both look at Niamh, who has been drinking in every word.*)

GRAINNE : Niamh, why don't you take James's coat somewhere and see what you can do with it?

NIAMH : Will I hang on here until it's dry?

GRAINNE : No, dear.

NIAMH : Well, will I come straight back?

GRAINNE (*shaking her head slowly and deliberately*) : Of course come straight back.

(*Niamh reluctantly takes the coat and goes to the door.*)

(*To Usheen, smiling.*) Well!

USHEEN : Well!

NIAMH : Pssst!

GRAINNE (*to Usheen*) : Excuse me. (*Going to Niamh.*) What?

NIAMH : Be careful.

GRAINNE : Clean the coat.

NIAMH : I suppose coming from England, he's on the pill?

GRAINNE : The coat, Niamh.

133

NIAMH : Make sure.

(*She goes out unwillingly. Grainne comes down to Usheen. They face each other.*)

USHEEN : Well!
GRAINNE (*smiling*) : Well?

(*He starts towards her. She prepares herself for a blissful embrace, but he bypasses her. His destination is the brandy bottle.*)

GRAINNE : Do please help yourself.
USHEEN : Do you realize, this brandy has probably been in cask since the last time I saw you?
GRAINNE : Twelve years,
USHEEN : Is it? (*Sniffing the brandy.*) You're right you know!
GRAINNE : You've said hello to it twice—you might say hello to me. How do I look?
USHEEN : Superb.
GRAINNE (*pleased*) : Liar.
USHEEN : The prettiest brunette on our road. You still are.
GRAINNE : There's mud on your glasses.
USHEEN : Is there? (*Takes them off.*) Oh, my God.
GRAINNE (*touching her hair*) : I wouldn't have changed it but Dermod likes me in red.
USHEEN : Oh, yes?
GRAINNE : He says it'll remind us of the days when we had an overdraft. God has been so good to us since then.
USHEEN : I do congratulate Him.
GRAINNE : Do you, James? Some men might be disappointed. Some men might wish that a girl hadn't done quite so well for herself without him.

134

USHEEN : I couldn't be more thrilled.

GRAINNE : Thank you, James.

USHEEN : And that dress !

GRAINNE : This old thing? It's my newest.

USHEEN : It'll be a knockout when it's finished.

GRAINNE : I like your suit.

USHEEN : Good.

GRAINNE : One of dozens?

USHEEN : I have six . . .

GRAINNE : Dermod has ten.

USHEEN : Beige, that is.

GRAINNE : Speaking of hand-made shoes . . .

USHEEN (*looking at painting*) : That is beautiful.

GRAINNE : What? Oh, yes : we like that.

USHEEN : I love it.

GRAINNE : It's a Paul Henry. (*Or whatever.*)

USHEEN : I know. I have the original.

GRAINNE : Oh?

USHEEN : Somewhere.

GRAINNE : Well, we've both come a long way.

USHEEN : Would you say?

GRAINNE : You, especially.

USHEEN : Yes, I suppose I have.

GRAINNE : But then, of course, I didn't have nearly so far to travel.

USHEEN : You're beautiful when you smile.

GRAINNE : Am I, James?

USHEEN : Are those your own teeth?

GRAINNE : Seriously, James, Dermod and I are two of your most devoted fans. We've watched every programme of yours right from the very beginning.

USHEEN : All of them?

GRAINNE : I swear.

USHEEN : Good God.

GRAINNE : Except one.

135

USHEEN : How super.

GRAINNE : Yes.

USHEEN : Fantastic.

GRAINNE : Mmmm.

USHEEN : How come you missed one?

GRAINNE : We switched over to Eamonn Andrews. More brandy? (*She sails into bar.*) I got him, I got him! I got him!

USHEEN : Grainne!

GRAINNE : Com-ing!

USHEEN : I am going home.

GRAINNE : He's going home.

USHEEN : Goodbye.

GRAINNE : Good . . . bye!

(*He stomps out.*)

Goodbye? My God, I must have been mad. James, come back.

(*Usheen returns.*)

USHEEN : Where is my overcoat?

GRAINNE : I was joking.

USHEEN : You were not.

GRAINNE : I was.

USHEEN : There are two things one does not joke about . . . death and Eamonn Andrews.

GRAINNE : So it was a joke in poor taste.

USHEEN : Sick.

GRAINNE : The reason I missed your programme just that once was because the children had tonsillitis.

USHEEN : And that is your excuse?

GRAINNE : We thought they were dying.

USHEEN : That's better.

136

GRAINNE : Of course it is.

USHEEN : I'll buy that.

GRAINNE : So sit, have your drink and talk to me.

USHEEN : Yes, when I met your husband in London he mentioned you had children.

GRAINNE : Two. Emer and Ronan.

USHEEN : Where are the little bug . . . beggars?

GRAINNE : They're convalescing at the moment with friends of ours who have a house in Greece.

USHEEN : I like Greece.

GRAINNE : So do we.

USHEEN : For weekends.

(*A moment of strain.*)

GRAINNE : *Pax*, James.

USHEEN : *Pax*. Your husband seems a nice fellow.

GRAINNE : Yes, doesn't he !

USHEEN : I suppose you're mad about him.

GRAINNE : I adore him. But let's not talk about what's-his-name . . . Dermod . . . and me. Especially not me. All I am is a plain, dull, boring house-wife.

(*Usheen smiles to himself and nods his head. When she looks at him, the nod turns into a shake.*)

Tell me what you've been up to. (*Playfully.*) I've heard the most shocking stories.

USHEEN : About me?

GRAINNE : And women. I'm afraid you're a wicked man.

USHEEN : Ha-ha.

GRAINNE : And here I am alone in the house at your mercy.

USHEEN : Isn't your friend still here?

GRAINNE : She won't come in—not unless she heard
me screaming the place down.
USHEEN : Well, then!
GRAINNE (*eyeing him firmly*) : I never scream.

(*For a moment, Usheen is stunned by the implica-
tions of this. Then:*)

USHEEN : I see! What you mean is, there won't
be any need for you to scream, because you trust
me. Thank you . . . and yes, yes, you can!
GRAINNE : Can what?
USHEEN : Trust me.
GRAINNE : Yes?
USHEEN : You are the one woman I will always
respect.
GRAINNE : Oh, shit. (*She bursts into tears. Grainne
is a noisy weeper.*)
USHEEN : Why I'd sooner lose my Sunday-night
TAM ratings than harm a hair of your head. (*He
pats her head.*) There, there, there! No need to
snivel. To me, you'll always be the shy little girl
who used to shudder with virginal passion whenever I touched her. You're as safe with me as you
were then. Of course, I'm only human. The best
of men sometimes commit the most horrible deeds.

(*At this ray of hope, Grainne stops crying.*)

They kill the things they love—perhaps through
frailty, perhaps in a fit of drunkenness.

(*Grainne at once pours him a drink and puts it
firmly into his hand.*)

But if I were to utter one lustful word to you,

drunk or sober, I hope I should drop dead. Thanks. (*He drinks.*) I'm not a virtuous man. You may as well know that what they say about me is true. I have had women . . . in a way.

GRAINNE : How interesting. (*Delicately.*) Which way did you have them?

USHEEN : And yet, through the whole ugly, sordid mess, there was always one woman I truly loved.

GRAINNE (*overwhelmed*) : Do you mean . . . ?

USHEEN : One person who meant everything to me.

GRAINNE : Oh James.

USHEEN : A love that stayed fine throughout the years.

GRAINNE : Don't . . .

USHEEN : Her name was Venetia. (*He misinterprets Grainne's stunned reaction.*) And you're right— bloody stupid name for a woman. The silly cow liked to pretend she'd been conceived in a gondola. You read about that divorce case I was mixed up in? She was the woman. Afterwards, we lived together. Openly. Convention thrown to the winds, lost to all sense of shame, God no longer existed.

GRAINNE : Why didn't you marry her?

USHEEN : Are you mad? Marry a divorced woman —and be excommunicated? You're not paying attention, are you? Get the wax out, there's a good girl. Where was I?

GRAINNE : Venetia.

USHEEN : Don't mention that woman's name to me.

GRAINNE : But didn't you love her?

USHEEN : I curse the day I first laid hands on her. Three o'clock in the morning . . . 'James, do you love me?' I reply tenderly . . . (*Snarling.*) 'I'm in bed with you, amn't I?' Do you think that satisfies her? No, she wants more endearments, and then it's 'You don't love me, you don't. And I broke up my marriage for you.' Her marriage! Her husband was a fifty-three-year-old alcoholic who narrowly escaped prosecution on a charge of attempted misconduct with a pillar-box while under the impression that it was a Chinese street-walker. And that's the kind of anatomical education you pick up at Eton! Oh, those four words . . . 'You don't love me!'—the great digestive belch of a woman who's been feeding on your entrails. Then, after the recriminations, the threats. 'I'll give myself to the first man I meet.'

GRAINNE (*taking his now empty glass*): Did she?

USHEEN: She tried it once. Disappeared. Of course I knew where to find her. Seven a.m., and she was in Chiswick, walking up and down outside Eamonn Andrews' front gate. Silly cow, didn't even know he'd moved. And after the threats, the worst part.

GRAINNE: What was that? (*She begins to refill his glass.*)

USHEEN: She . . . (*His voice breaks.*)

GRAINNE: She tried to kill herself.

USHEEN: Worse. She did what was unforgivable.

GRAINNE: Tell me.

USHEEN: If you'll shut up for a minute, I will. She was rude to me.

GRAINNE: Oh.

USHEEN: Insults, sarcasm, nasty little jibes. She said I had a big head and a small . . . Oh, but some people have wicked tongues. Do you know what that woman did? She castrated me.

(*Grainne considers this, then regretfully begins to pour his brandy back into the bottle. Then:*)

Figuratively speaking.

140

(*Grainne pours the brandy back into the glass.*)

GRAINNE : Did you leave her?

USHEEN : Regularly. I took up with those other women you just now mentioned. I didn't need her, and I'd prove it. The trouble was, when it came right down to the nitty-gritty, I couldn't.

GRAINNE : You couldn't what?

USHEEN : I just . . . couldn't. Perhaps I'd had too much to drink at the time. Perhaps that was why,

(*Grainne sighs, looks at the brandy and once more pours it from the glass back into the bottle.*)

No . . . no, it wasn't.

(*Grainne gives him both bottle and glass and lets him do his own pouring.*)

At the moment of truth the same thing always happened. I kept seeing her mole.

GRAINNE : Her what?

USHEEN : She had a large mole right here . . . (*He prods his chest, then prods Grainne's.*) There. I beg your pardon.

GRAINNE : My pleasure.

USHEEN : I kept seeing that mole—her beauty spot, she called it. Ugly looking thing. It ruined my life. Three weeks ago, I made up my mind, left her for good. It's over now.

GRAINNE : Venetia and you?

USHEEN : Everything. Involvements, emotions, sex. I've finished with it all.

NIAMH (*off*) : Oh, Jay.

(*Usheen opens the door and reveals Niamh, kneeling at the keyhole.*)

141

NIAMH : Excuse me. The television set in the kitchen isn't working.

GRAINNE (*stunned, still looking at Usheen*) : Try the one in the loo.

(*Usheen closes the door.*)

USHEEN : I'm sorry—this must be distressing for you.

GRAINNE : You have no idea.

USHEEN : It's my own fault. I should have fallen in love with an Irish girl.

GRAINNE : An Irish girl might have had a mole, too.

USHEEN : Yes, but I'd never have seen it.

GRAINNE : If you believe that, you've been away for longer than you think.

USHEEN (*shaking his head*) : Some things never change. That's why I came to see you—my first love. The girl who longed to be a nun.

GRAINNE : Did I say that?

USHEEN : Have you forgotten? That was the reason you gave for not wanting to see me any more.

GRAINNE (*remembering*) : So it was.

USHEEN : If I'm going to embark upon a life of celibacy, I thought it should begin here, with the only truly pure girl I ever knew.

GRAINNE : Me?

(*Tongue-tied with emotion, he cocks a finger at her like a pistol and fires an imaginary shot by way of an affirmative.*)

Did you really love me, James?

USHEEN : I adored every black hair on your red head. I mean I . . .

GRAINNE (*swallowing this*) : And I was fond of *you*,

James. I still am, and I'm not going to stand by and watch you let a tiny mole ruin your life.

USHEEN : It was a brute of a mole. And what can you do?

GRAINNE : Supposing you were to slip on our imported Hong Kong marble bathroom floor and break your back? You'd expect me to help, wouldn't you? You'd expect me to . . . to do whatever it is you would do for a broken back.

USHEEN : Yes, but . . .

GRAINNE : This is the same thing. You're still moping over that awful woman, and I think what you need is a . . . love transplant. (*As he is about to speak.*) Don't argue . . . I am a woman, and that means I'm wonderfully wise, and I know that perfect love, and perfect love alone, casteth out moles, James, I have something to show you.

USHEEN (*nervously*) : Oh?

GRAINNE : Right now.

USHEEN (*his eyes on her bosom*) : I don't think I want to . . .

GRAINNE : You'll love it. It's the most beautiful mo . . .

USHEEN : I won't look.

GRAINNE : . . . motel in the world. Dermod owns it —at least he owns half of it. Let's go there.

USHEEN : To a motel? What for?

GRAINNE : I'll tell you on the way. It's only up the mountains.

USHEEN : Up the . . . ?

GRAINNE : The view is marvellous.

USHEEN : It's pitch dark out, it's pouring rain and there's a gale blowing.

GRAINNE : Irish weather, James—what they call a soft night. (*This strikes her as humorous, she giggles.*)

143

USHEEN : But what has you showing me a motel got to do with Venetia's mole?

GRAINNE : No questions. You must put yourself completely in my hands. Don't move, I'll get my coat.

USHEEN : Couldn't we just sit here and . . .

(*She has gone out. He remains seated, looking baffled.*)

A motel? Why does she want us to? (*The truth dawns.*) She wouldn't! (*Discarding the idea as preposterous.*) Don't be a fool, James, lad—she's an Irish Catholic wife and mother. The only thing she's got left is her virginity. (*He rises and takes a step towards the door, calling.*) Grainne, I . . .

(*He stops. A look of physical discomfort comes over his face. He touches his trouser-legs.*)

Damn.

(*Grainne swings back into the room, now wearing a mink coat. She remembers to model it for us briefly, humming 'A Pretty Girl is Like a Melody'. She passes the stricken Usheen on her way to the bar.*)

GRAINNE : I threw on just any old thing.

USHEEN : Grainne . . .

(*She resumes humming and goes into the bar, ducking expertly, picks up two bottles of brandy, and comes out at once, ducking again.*)

Grainne, I can't go.

GRAINNE : Yes, you can.

USHEEN : There's something you don't know.

GRAINNE : About Venetia?

USHEEN : About me. (*Indicating his upper leg.*) Touch me here.

GRAINNE : Later, James.

USHEEN : I mean I'm soaked to the skin.

GRAINNE : For heaven's sake, a little dampness . . . !

USHEEN : Oh, if ever I get my hands on that redfaced bastard in the Jensen . . . !

GRAINNE : Take off your trousers.

USHEEN : I beg your pardon?

GRAINNE : You can borrow a pair of Dermod's.

USHEEN : But . . .

GRAINNE : Or do you *want* to catch cold? (*She goes to the door and calls off.*) Niamh, is Mr Usheen's overcoat dry yet? (*To Usheen.*) Will you do as you're told? Take them *off*. (*She goes out.*)

(*Usheen broods for a moment, then reluctantly removes his trousers. He begins to empty the pockets. Niamh comes in with his overcoat. The sight of Usheen trouserless, stops her dead in her tracks.*)

NAIMH : *Already?*

USHEEN : My trousers got wet.

NIAMH (*a forced smile*) : Ah, sure why wouldn't they !

(*An embarrassed pause. Usheen toys with his drink. Niamh tries unsuccessfully to keep her eyes away from his shorts. Their eyes meet.*)

Terrible weather.

USHEEN (*shortly*) : Yes.
NIAMH : You'd need those on you this evening.
USHEEN : I'm sure.
NIAMH : I like blue.

(*Usheen contrives to hide his shorts from view.*)

Fintan won't wear them. He says they're unmanly.
So I'm always at him. (*As he looks at her.*) To
wear drawers, I mean. If you were him now and
I was another woman, there'd be a court case. Can
I ask you something, Mr Usheen?
USHEEN : No.
NIAMH : I might never get the chance again, so
just as a favour would you say something insulting?
USHEEN (*losing his temper*) : Bugger off.
NIAMH : Ah, thanks.

(*Grainne comes back with a pair of trousers.*)

GRAINNE : These are just back from the cleaners.
Put them on.
USHEEN : Grainne, perhaps we should give the
motel a miss for this evening. It's getting late,
and ...
GRAINNE : Late? The night is still a pup. Now put
them on. We won't look ... (*To Niamh.*) Will we?
NIAMH : Couldn't be bothered.

(*Grainne and Niamh retire to a position behind
Usheen and watch fascinated as he puts on the
trousers. Through the following, they keep their
eyes on him.*)

NIAMH : Grainne ...
GRAINNE : What?

146

NIAMH : Be good, will you?
GRAINNE : I'll be magnificent.

(*Niamh moans feebly.*)

Now, listen. Leave his wet trousers on the radiator
in the kitchen.
NIAMH : Right.
GRAINNE : And when we're gone, ring up the motel.
Tell the caretaker you're me. Say that two married
friends of yours are on their way there. They need
a room, and he's to let them in. Got that?
USHEEN : Blast.
GRAINNE : What's wrong?
USHEEN : The zip's stuck.
GRAINNE : That's what the dry cleaning does. Pull
it.
USHEEN : I am . . . it's stuck.
GRAINNE : Soap will fix it. Wait . . . (*She goes out.*)

(*Usheen pulls on the zip. Niamh kneels down in
front of him and peers closely at the zip.*)

USHEEN : What are you doing?
NIAMH : Let me have a go—I'm great with lids.
Hold still.

(*As she wrestles with the zip, still kneeling in front
of Usheen, Fintan appears outside the french windows. He clutches his face in horror at what he
thinks he sees, then bangs on the glass with his
fists.*)

NIAMH : Do you hear that for wind?
USHEEN : That doesn't sound like . . .
NIAMH : There, I've got it.

(*Fintan, grabbing his hair in fury, goes tearing off around the side of the house.*)

(*Yelling.*) Grainne, come back, I've got it!
USHEEN : Thank you, and bless your little frank-frurter fingers. My overcoat?
NIAMH : It's here.

(*She helps him on with it. Grainne returns.*)

GRAINNE : Is he fastened?
NIAMH : Yes.
GRAINNE (*picking up the brandy*) : Then let's go. Niamh, you know what to do?
NIAMH : Yes. No. I don't know the number of the ... (*Looking at Usheen.*) M—O—T—T—E—L.
USHEEN : Mottel?
GRAINNE : It's in Dermod's address book. In the study, across the hall. (*Taking Usheen's arm.*) 'Bye, now.
USHEEN : Are you sure this excursion is necessary?
GRAINNE : I'll be the judge of that, James. You just keep on repeating as we drive—'there are no moles on Grainne'.
USHEEN : Pardon?
GRAINNE : You heard.

(*She crosses herself and pushes him out ahead of her.*)

NIAMH : 'Bye, 'bye, now. Have a nice ... (*Getting on safer ground.*) 'Bye ... !

(*The front door slams. Niamh wavers for a moment, then:*)

Address book!

(*She goes out at the very moment when Fintan reappears at the window now brandishing a hatchet. He smashes the lock on the french windows with one blow, then bursts into the room waving the hatchet. His hair is flattened by the rain.*)

FINTAN (*triumphantly*) : Gotcha!

(*He realizes that the room is empty. Then his eyes focus on the bar. He emits a growling noise and rushes in. We expect him to bang his head, but he ducks just in time and stands inside the bar, crouching. Dermod comes in by the french windows, noting the shattered lock.*)

DERMOD (*sharply*) : Fintan!

(*Fintan jerks upright and bangs his head on the ceiling.*)

FINTAN : Jasus.
DERMOD : Come out here. Did you break that lock?
FINTAN (*dazed*) : What?
DERMOD : And where did you get that hatchet?
FINTAN : In your shed.
DERMOD : That shed was locked.
FINTAN : I broke the lock.
DERMOD : What for?
FINTAN : To get the hatchet to break *that* lock. (*He indicates the french windows.*) Why else do you think I broke the branch off the tree?
DERMOD : What tree?
FINTAN (*pointing out*) : *That* tree!

149

DERMOD : My cherry tree?

FINTAN : God, didn't I need the branch to break the lock of the shed to get the hatchet to break *that* lock? (*To the audience.*) He's so thick. And she's upstairs now.

DERMOD : Who is?

FINTAN : Niamh. I saw her through the window. She was . . .

DERMOD : She was what?

FINTAN : Kneeling down.

DERMOD : Praying?

FINTAN : If she was, it wasn't for a mild winter.

DERMOD : What was she doing?

FINTAN : I won't tell you. I wouldn't tell anyone. It's a mortal sin even to *know* what she was doing. There was this man . . .

DERMOD : What man?

FINTAN : And I know his face from somewhere. He . . .

DERMOD : Niamh and a man? You're raving.

FINTAN : I tell you they're upstairs. My God, if they'd do what I saw them doing in a living-room, what are they not perpetrating in the presence of a bed? I'll kill her.

DERMOD : Fintan, your wife is not in this house.

FINTAN : She's bouncing on your springs.

DERMOD : She's gone.

FINTAN : Get stitched.

DERMOD : While you were pulling up my good tree, Grainne's car went out the gate. She and Niamh have gone to your house for the night, as they were supposed to.

FINTAN (*hollowly*) : He's taken her off to some whorehouse!

DERMOD : There was no man here with Niamh.

FINTAN : I saw him.

150

DERMOD : You saw Grainne.

FINTAN : Your wife is ugly, but I wouldn't mistake her for a man.

DERMOD (*blinking*) : My wife is ugly?

FINTAN : I know, but don't dwell on it.

DERMOD (*losing his temper*) : That does it?

FINTAN : Does what?

DERMOD : I let you drag me back, all the way from Terenure, because it's either end up in bits on the motorway, or let you see for yourself that Niamh is here and up to no harm. So I wait in the car, and what's my thanks? You break my cherry tree, you smash the lock on my shed, you butcher my french windows, and now you insult my wife. And all because your brain is unhinged.

FINTAN : Say that again!

DERMOD : You're having hallucinations.

FINTAN : You pup, you.

DERMOD : There was no man in this room.

FINTAN (*almost dancing with fury*) : I saw him, I saw him, I saw him!

DERMOD : You saw your reflection in the glass.

FINTAN : I saw my . . .

(*He breaks off. It occurs to him that Dermod may be right.*)

DERMOD (*having won his point*) : And now I'm going to have a drink.

(*He goes into the bar. Fintan looks from the french windows to the spot where he saw Niamh and Usheen.*)

Do you want one?

FINTAN (*convinced*) : He was a handsome bugger,

151

right enough. Funny the way your mind plays tricks. I could have sworn that I saw her kneeling down . . .

(*He starts towards the bar, then sees Usheen's trousers on the back of a chair. He picks them up, discovers that they are wet and drops them with a gasp of revulsion. He heads into the bar.*)

So I'm imagining things, am I?

DERMOD (*wearily*): Oh, God.

FINTAN: Am I imagining a pair of trousers? A pair of *wet* trousers.

DERMOD: You're demented.

FINTAN: Is that so? Come out and look.

(*Niamh returns with the address book. She goes towards the telephone, then notices the trousers. She picks them up and goes out with them.*)

DERMOD: Look at what?

FINTAN: The trousers.

DERMOD: Whose?

FINTAN: His. They're in there, and they're sopping wet.

DERMOD: Trousers?

FINTAN: He couldn't even wait to drop them till he got upstairs.

DERMOD: Why are they wet?

FINTAN: Don't ask me. Will you come and look?

DERMOD: Damn sure I'll come and look.

(*Niamh disappears with the trousers a split second before they emerge from the bar.*)

FINTAN: Now we'll see who's demented. (*He points at the chair.*) There!

DERMOD : Where?

FINTAN : There . . . are you . . .

(*He stares at the empty chair. He goes on his knees and looks under it, then runs his hands over the chair, as if the trousers were still on it but had turned invisible.*)

They were here ten seconds ago.

DERMOD : Fintan, see a doctor.

FINTAN : I saw them, I touched them. They were wet. Feel my hand.

DERMOD (*doing so*) : Your hand is dry.

FINTAN : Of course it's bloody dry—I wiped it !

DERMOD : Fintan, go home, go to bed.

FINTAN (*jumping up and down, almost weeping with rage*) : I saw the bugger's trousers, I saw them, I saw them.

DERMOD : Fintan, stop that.

FINTAN : I did, I did, I did. (*Three more mighty jumps.*)

DERMOD : You'll upset all the thermostats.

FINTAN (*with sudden cunning*) : I know what it is. It's a plot to drive me mad.

DERMOD : Now look . . .

FINTAN : You're behind it—you and that ugly wife of yours. You want the Cork motel for yourself.

DERMOD (*coldly*) : I think we should forget about the Cork motel for the time being. Perhaps our partnership wasn't such a good idea after all.

FINTAN : There's no perhaps about it.

DERMOD : Seeing trousers that aren't there, I can understand. But *wet* trousers—that's sick.

FINTAN : You'll be sick in a minute.

(*He looks about him wildly for the hatchet.*

153

Dermod sees it at the same moment, and they both make a rush for it. Dermod gets there first.)

DERMOD (*loftily*) : My hatchet, I believe.

FINTAN : What else could I expect from a get who got where he is by informing on people to the Income Tax.

DERMOD : Earlier, you said you wished you'd thought of it first.

FINTAN (*massively*) : *That* was common politeness.

DERMOD (*dignified*) : Fintan, I wish you good night.

FINTAN : There's no harm in wishing.

DERMOD : I mean goodbye.

FINTAN : The only place I'm going is up your stairs. That's where my wife is, and there's a man with her with his trousers off.

DERMOD : If I go up and look, will that convince you?

FINTAN : I wouldn't believe you if you told me that Paisley was a Protestant. Give me that hatchet.

DERMOD : I'll keep the hatchet, Fintan.

(He goes out. Fintan is on the point of following him, but decides that he needs a weapon. He goes into the bar and picks up a bottle which he strikes viciously into the palm of his hand. He discards it in favour of a heavy decanter which he holds like a cudgel. Niamh comes in carrying the address book and humming loudly to herself. She goes to the telephone and dials. Fintan, hearing the humming, looks puzzled and rotates a finger in his ear to get rid of it.)

NIAMH (*shrilling*) : 'Let me call you sweetheart, I'm in love with you; let me hear you whisper that you love me too . . .' (*Into phone.*) Hello, is

154

that the Patrick Pearse Motel? Are you the care-taker? This is Mrs Dermod Gibbon speaking.

(*Fintan sticks his head around the door of the bar to look at Niamh.*)

I'm well, and how are you? Aren't you great. The thing is, there are two friends of mine who need a room for tonight, and I'm sending them up to the motel . . . Yes, so it's all right to let them in. A lady and a gentleman, yes. No, not a twin, I think they'd like a double. The main thing is, you'll be ready for them?

(*Fintan nods slowly, and with emphasis.*)

Thanks very much. Not at all. Goodbye.

(*She hangs up, looks heavenwards for forgiveness, and goes out, humming again. Fintan emerges from the bar.*)

FINTAN : Oh, the rip. Lust under the Plough and Stars . . . there's not a jury in the country will convict me. What are you talking about? You'll be made a papal count. But the rip !

(*Dermod returns.*)

DERMOD : There's no one upstairs, not a soul. Go and see for yourself.
FINTAN : Your word is good enough for me.
DERMOD : I'm not accustomed to being called a . . . pardon?
FINTAN (*elaborately casual*) : It seems I was mis-taken. I'll go home, so . . . home to bed.

155

DERMOD : Fintan, are you all right?

FINTAN : Me? How can I be all right? I imagine things, I'm demented, I'm sick.

DERMOD : If I said anything in haste ...

FINTAN (*airily*) : Don't give it a thought. I daresay we'll meet again. And if we don't, sure our solicitors will.

(*He gives Dermod a nod from a great height and goes out.*)

DERMOD : Solicitors? I always knew he had a slate loose. Failure has gone to his head.

(*He removes his coat, aware that he is plainly in for a solitary evening. He goes up to the hi-fi unit and sets about selecting a record. As he puts it on the turntable, Niamh comes in, dressed to go home. She is about to switch off the lights when she sees Dermod with his back to her. She emits a hoarse cry of shock, then goes haring out again. Dermod turns, just in time not to see her. He goes towards the door.*)

Who's that? Who is it, who's there? (*Looking into the hall.*) You? What are you doing here?

(*Miss Manning comes in, smiling the smile of modest achievement. She wears spectacles, her hair is drawn back severely into a bun. Her coat and galoshes are sensible. She has the habit of saying 'Ai' and 'mai' instead of 'I' and 'my'.*)

MISS MANNING : How nice to see you again, Mr Gibbon. Wasn't I expected?

DERMOD : Not tonight, Miss Manning. They told me London Airport was closed.

MISS MANNING : It is. I took a train to Manchester and an aeroplane from there. A good employee can always find a way.

DERMOD : I congratulate you.

MISS MANNING : Might I compliment you, Mr Gibbon, upon the vigour of your friends?

DERMOD : Pardon me?

MISS MANNING : I was almost bowled over in your driveway by a gentleman who was running like billy-o.

DERMOD : That would have been my partner, Mr Kinnore. Running, did you say?

MISS MANNING : And again in your hall by a lady in a tizz.

(*Dermod comes out of the bar with a bottle of scotch.*)

DERMOD : A lady?

MISS MANNING : I'm sure you know best, Mr Gibbon.

DERMOD : Do sit down, Miss Manning. Did you have a good journey?

MISS MANNING : Beastly. On the train, I had to move my seat three times. Men with roving eyes, you know. No roving eyes here, Mr Gibbon.

DERMOD (*a forced smile*) : Well, just a few.

(*She gives a genteel little laugh, which turns into a no less genteel cough.*)

MISS MANNING : Hem! Might I have a glass of water?

157

DERMOD : Of course. Perhaps something a little stronger?

MISS MANNING : Well . . . ?

DERMOD : Sherry?

MISS MANNING : Brandy?

DERMOD (*taken slightly aback*) : Certainly. (*He goes to the bar.*) Odd . . . (*Then.*) . . . the brandy seems to have disappeared, Miss Manning. There's only scotch.

MISS MANNING : I'm not fussy.

(*She looks at him appraisingly as he pours her drink.*)

I went directly to my hotel, but they seem to have cancelled my reservation. So I'm open to suggestions.

DERMOD : Well, I . . .

MISS MANNING : Such a charming home. Perhaps I might impose on Mrs Gibbon and you for the night?

DERMOD : My wife is staying with a friend.

MISS MANNING : Oh? (*Receiving her drink.*) 'Nk yow !

DERMOD : So it would hardly be proper if . . .

MISS MANNING : Quite. We must be proper, mustn't we? (*She knocks back half her drink in one go.*) I seem to be a little problem.

DERMOD : Not at all . . .

MISS MANNING : All I ask for is a bed. Then first thing in the morning, I can begin my duties.

DERMOD (*inspired*) : But of course !

MISS MANNING : Yes?

DERMOD : The motel ! You'll be staying there to-morrow anyway when the staff arrive. Why not tonight?

MISS MANNING : How super.

DERMOD : The only thing is, it's a little bit isolated.

MISS MANNING : I don't mind loneliness—I was married for five years.

DERMOD : Oh, yes?

MISS MANNING : Horrid man. I shall adore being at the motel. Tomorrow morning, I shall say to myself, 'Here you are in Ireland, the land of creamery butter, little boggy roads, and religious mania.' I've done my homework, you see !

DERMOD : Ha-ha.

MISS MANNING : Might we go now?

DERMOD : To the motel? Yes. Have you luggage?

MISS MANNING : I left it on the doorstep.

DERMOD : It'll get soaked there. I'll put it in the car. You finish your drink.

MISS MANNING : Too kind.

(*He takes his coat and goes out. Miss Manning knocks back her drink, then helps herself to a refill —hefty one. Carrying her glass, she drifts over to the hi-fi unit. She switches on the record player. The music is modern, sensuous.*)

Irish music . . . how super !

(*She continues her tour of the room, drinking as she goes. Gradually and apparently without realizing it, she begins to move in rhythm with the music. She opens a button of her coat, then shrugs one shoulder free, then the other. The coat falls to the floor and she steps out of it. She undoes the bow holding her hair in place, then shakes her head and lets her hair fall about her shoulders. Her mind seems to be a thousand miles away, but*) *her body is getting into the spirit of the music. She takes off her glasses. She begins to unbutton her blouse. Dermod comes in and stands stockstill. Swaying sinuously, Miss Manning now unzips her skirt. She sees Dermod and zips it up again, taking her time and not in the least embarrassed. She switches off the record player.)*

MISS MANNING: I find music ever so restful, don't you?

DERMOD (*croaking*): Yes.

MISS MANNING: Is something not right?

DERMOD: No. You don't seem quite the same as you did in London.

MISS MANNING: Gentlemen often say that about me—that I'm different. I don't know why. I hope I won't be a disappointment to you, Mr Gibbon.

DERMOD: I'm sure you won't.

MISS MANNING: And I know *I'm* going to enjoy working for *you*. I haven't had an interesting position since before my marriage, and it's so important to a girl as to whom she is under.

DERMOD: Oh, yes?

MISS MANNING: Will Mrs Gibbon be away *all* night?

DERMOD: Yes.

MISS MANNING: Oh, poor thing.

DERMOD: I'm supposed to be in Cork.

MISS MANNING: And amn't I glad you aren't!

DERMOD: Shall we go now?

MISS MANNING: Super. I can't wait. (*She gives him her coat to hold. She puts it on.*) 'Nk yow! Now I'm all yours.

(She turns so that she is very close to him. He is on the point of losing control, when she moves

*away from him abruptly and goes towards the
door.)*

MISS MANNING : Are you partial to animals, Mr
Gibbon?
DERMOD : Animals, Miss Manning?
MISS MANNING : Call me Venetia. I have the
prettiest mole you have ever seen.

She goes out as he takes a step to follow her.

Curtain

ACT TWO

Scene 1

The Motel.

We see two bedrooms and a section of corridor. Seen from above, the corridor would resemble a letter 'H' lying on its side. It runs from left to right upstage, and parallel to this downstage. A connecting length of corridor at stage centre cuts the stage in two and separates the two bedrooms. These are the Emmet room and the Parnell room. Each room is a mirror image of the other, except that one contains a large oil painting of Charles Stewart Parnell (right), and the other (left) of Robert Emmet. Each room contains a double bed built-in wardrobe—in the walls, left and right, an easy chair and a chest of drawers. Bathrooms are situated off, at downstage left and right.

The time is fifteen minutes after the end of Act One. Hoolihan, the night watchman, appears in the corridor, followed by Grainne and Usheen. He is in his late seventies.

HOOLIHAN: Now this, sir and missus, is what they call the Nineteenth Century wing. (*He indicates the doors at rear.*) There's a lovely room, the Isaac Butt room. And next to it, the Manchester Martyrs room, with three single beds. You don't want that.

USHEEN: He's made a mistake. Tell him we're not staying.

HOOLIHAN: Yes, sir, sure they're all lovely rooms. And this one—excuse me, sir and missus—is the Chief's room . . .

162

USHEEN: The old eejit thinks we're staying the night.

(*Hoolihan goes into the Parnell room, salutes the painting and stands before it at attention.*)

HOOLIHAN: Charles Stewart Parnell!
USHEEN: This isn't a motel, it's Madame Tussaud's.
GRAINNE: Be respectful, James. He was out in 1916.
USHEEN: By the look of him he hasn't come in yet. Let's get away from here now.
GRAINNE: James, it's time you and I had our little talk.
USHEEN: Right, we can have it back at your place —I've got to pick up my trousers anyway.
GRAINNE: But . . .

(*Hoolihan, having again saluted, comes out.*)

HOOLIHAN: Now I'll show you another lovely room. Named after bold Robert Emmet, sir, the darlin' of Erin. (*He goes into the Emmet room, salutes the portrait and stands before it in homage.*)
USHEEN: He's doing it again. My God, it's a political Stations of the Cross. How many rooms in his madhouse?
GRAINNE: Eighty-four.
USHEEN: We'll be here all bloody night.
GRAINNE (*a cat-like smile*): Mmm . . .
USHEEN: What does that mean?

(*Hoolihan comes out.*)

We're obliged to you for your trouble. This lady and I must be off now.

HOOLIHAN : It is, it is. The next room is the Wolfe
Tone room and the O'Donovan Rossa room . . .
USHEEN : He's senile.
GRAINNE : Well, he's old.
USHEEN : That's no excuse.
HOOLIHAN (*tottering forward*) : Hup, two, three,
four ! Hup, two, three, four !
GRAINNE : We'll give him the slip in a minute . . .
you just be ready.

(*As Hoolihan turns, waiting for them.*)

We're com-ing !
HOOLIHAN : Then there's the Thomas Davis room
and the Michael Davitt room . . .

(*He goes out of sight, followed by Usheen and
Grainne.*)

(*Off.*) All lovely snug rooms. Hup, two, three, four !

(*Pause.*)

GRAINNE (*off*) : *Now*, James !

(*Grainne comes back into view, pausing for a
moment, apparently leading an unseen Usheen by
the hand.*)

Don't hang back, he'll see us.

(*She pulls, not Usheen, but Hoolihan into view
and drags him after her at an agonized trot.*)

Any room will do us. In here . . . quickly.

(*She drags him after her into the Parnell room and shuts the door. Hoolihan looks dazedly at his hand.*)

There, we did it. (*She turns and sees him.*) Oh, my God.

HOOLIHAN : You squeezed me hand.

GRAINNE : I what?

HOOLIHAN : The modern girls is very rough.

(*Usheen comes into view looking for Grainne.*)

USHEEN (*calling*) : Grainne . . . ? (*He goes off, right.*)

HOOLIHAN : You'd no call to go pulling and hauling at an old man and giving him a squeeze hand. I'm seventy-eight, I have to be very careful.

GRAINNE : Yes, I'm sorry.

HOOLIHAN : I have to go to the lav now over you.

(*He shuffles into the bathroom. Grainne goes out and comes downstage.*)

GRAINNE : James, here I am. I made the silliest . . . (*She sees that he is gone.*) James, where are you? James?

(*She hesitates, then goes off left. Nimah appears at rear wandering along the corridor and carrying Usheen's trousers. She is looking for a sign of life.*)

NIAMH (*a timid whisper*) : Grainne . . . ? Mr Ushee-en? (*Then very loudly.*) Wooo-ooo !

(*She returns upstage and goes out of sight. Usheen*

*and Grainne come into view from downstage left
and right.)*

GRAINNE ⎱ *(together)* : *There* you are !
USHEEN ⎰

GRAINNE : Really, James, must you wander around?
(Going to him.) And if you want me, you know
my name. There's no need to go 'woo-ooo'.

USHEEN : I didn't go 'woo-ooo'.

GRAINNE : Come in here. *(She pushes him ahead
of her into the Robert Emmet room.)*

USHEEN : You're the one who went 'woo-ooo'.

GRAINNE : Who did?

USHEEN : You did.

GRAINNE : I did?

USHEEN : Just now, like a yak in labour.

GRAINNE *(bridling)* : Wives of Members of the
South Dublin Country Club, James, are not in the
habit of sounding like yaks in labour.

USHEEN : Then they must regard *you* as something
of a novelty.

GRAINNE *(losing her temper)* : James, I did not
go . . .

(Niamh appears upstage centre.)

NIAMH : Woo-ooo ! *(She goes off upstage left.)*

GRAINNE : Exactly. So . . .

*(She breaks off. They look in the direction whence
the cry came, then at each other.)*

USHEEN : Then what the hell was it?

GRAINNE : I don't know.

USHEEN *(looking into the bathroom)* : Perhaps it
was the wind whistling through the bidets.

166

GRAINNE : There aren't any bidets—Irish plumbers won't handle them.

USHEEN : In that case . . .

GRAINNE : Well?

USHEEN : Do you think it could have been a yak?

GRAINNE : James, there are no yaks in the Dublin Mountains.

USHEEN : There's *something* out there . . .

GRAINNE (*heatedly*) : It isn't a yak.

USHEEN : Listen to me. I am a city boy. Where the footpaths stop, so do I, and I now wish to return to civilization.

GRAINNE : James, we're fifteen minutes from Foxrock. You can't *get* more civilized than that.

USHEEN : Did you hear that 'woo-ooo'?

GRAINNE : The wind.

USHEEN : It was not the wind. What a way for James Usheen to finish up—in a concrete tomb high up in these God-forsaken mountains, torn limb from limb by some kind of Abominable Bogman!

GRAINNE (*becoming frightened*) : Now stop that.

USHEEN : It's out there now.

(*They hear a toilet flushing, then the sound of Hoolihan as he emerges from the bathroom and passes through the Parnell room, clearing his throat loudly. Then he marches upstage centre and off right.*)

HOOLIHAN : Hup, two, three, four . . . hup, two, three, four!

(*They breathe more easily.*)

GRAINNE : James, what's got into you?

USHEEN : I see it all with dreadful clarity. He hates me, he wants to kill me.

GRAINNE : Who does?

USHEEN : So he sends two of his henchmen to run me down with a Jensen. Then I fall into a carefully dug pit. I survive that, and then, for no apparent reason, you take me up the mountains in a storm to a deserted bunker guarded by a madman. You work for Eamonn Andrews, don't you?

GRAINNE : No!

USHEEN : Then why was I brought here?

GRAINNE (*decisively*) : I'll show you. (*She removes her coat and lies on the bed invitingly.*)

USHEEN (*through this, to himself*) : They all hate me.

GRAINNE : Look at me, James. *Now*, do you know why you were brought here?

(*He looks at her. Realization finally dawns.*)

USHEEN : You're having me on.

GRAINNE : Exactly.

USHEEN : You wouldn't.

GRAINNE : I meant what I said, James. You've seen your last mole.

USHEEN : You'd do that for me?

GRAINNE (*simply*) : What are friends for?

NIAMH (*baying in the distance*) : Wooo-ooo!

GRAINNE (*catching her breath*) : There it is again.

USHEEN : Ignore it. (*Looking at her.*) This is the nicest thing anyone ever offered to do for me.

GRAINNE : It's purely medicinal.

USHEEN : Even so . . . I couldn't.

GRAINNE : Why not?

USHEEN : You . . . who wanted to be a nun?

GRAINNE : I wouldn't dream of enjoying it.

USHEEN : I know that, love.

GRAINNE : I'm not immoral.

USHEEN : Sure.

GRAINNE : Don't you find me attractive?

USHEEN : I'm mad about you . . . I always have been, but how could I do such a thing in your husband's trousers?

GRAINNE : Silly . . . you won't be wearing them.

USHEEN : Besides, I've decided to return to my religion

GRAINNE : How soon?

USHEEN : Tomorrow.

GRAINNE : Well, that gives us all night.

USHEEN : That's true. You really mean this?

GRAINNE : Don't look so amazed. You'd do as much for me if I kept seeing moles on Dermod. Try thinking of it as laying a ghost.

USHEEN : When did you decide?

GRAINNE : Quite on the spur of the moment. In the car.

USHEEN : It's ridiculous. I haven't even a tooth-brush.

GRAINNE : I have two in my handbag.

USHEEN (*wiping his eyes*): What can I say, but that I accept gratefully, knowing that a refusal often gives offence.

GRAINNE (*kindly*): You need a drink. Where's the brandy?

USHEEN : You had it last.

GRAINNE : I left it in the car. You wait here . . . I'll go out the back way, it's shorter.

USHEEN : Run.

(*She hurries out, comes downstage and goes off right.*

169

*He picks up her handbag, opens it and takes out the
two toothbrushes. His eyes moisten with affection.
Then he sees something else in the handbag. He
pulls into view what looks like several yards of
rolled-up, see-through black nylon nightdress. He
holds it up, picturing Grainne in it.*

*Niamh, footsore by now, comes into view from
downstage left, still carrying Usheen's trousers. She
cups her hands over her mouth for another mighty
yell.*

*Usheen beats her to it. The sight of the nightdress
causes him to emit a cry of sheer anticipation.*

USHEEN : Woo-ooo !

*Niamh looks puzzled. Usheen gleefully rolls up
the nightdress and puts it back in the handbag.
He takes off his overcoat and hangs it on a hook
on the back of the half-open door.*

*Niamh decides to investigate the source of the yell.
She comes to the threshold of the Emmet room and
looks in. She and Usheen are hidden from each
other by the door. Seeing an apparently empty
room, she goes out again, closing the door behind
her. Usheen sees the door and his overcoat swing-
ing away from him.*

*Niamh turns her attention to the Parnell room.
She goes in, just as Usheen looks around the door
of the Emmet room and sees nothing. Niamh's
feet are killing her and she is dispirited. She sits
on the bed and takes her shoes off. Simultaneously,
in the other room, Usheen sits on the bed and*

removes his shoes. They emit independent sighs of relief and begin to massage their toes.

Fintan appears from upstage right and stations himself between the two rooms. He is in a murderous mood.

FINTAN (*hissing off, impatiently*): Come on, come on, come on! Will you hurry up. I'm not paying you to sleep on your feet.

(*Hoolihan comes into view carrying a lethal-looking shillelagh.*)

Is that the biggest shillelagh we have in the gift shop?

HOOLIHAN: It's crooked.

FINTAN: It's meant to be crooked. What room did you say she pulled you into?

HOOLIHAN: Funny-lookin' walkin' stick.

FINTAN: For God's sake man, can't you understand plain Irish? I'm talking about the woman.

(*Hoolihan looks at him blankly.*)

. . Who pulled you into a bedroom?

HOOLIHAN: She squeeze me hand.

FINTAN: The whore.

HOOLIHAN: Hard.

FINTAN: Describe her to me.

(*Hoolihan merely holds up his hand.*)

Would you call her a raving beauty?

HOOLIHAN: I had to go to the lav over her.

FINTAN: I know that feeling . . . it's her all right.

171

Which room did she go into? (*Grabbing him.*) Which room?

HOOLIHAN (*saluting*): Charles Stewart Parnell.

FINTAN: Parnell. Of course . . . where else for adultery. Oh, the slut.

(*Gripping the shillelagh, he advances on tiptoe towards the Emmet room, in which Usheen is now removing his tie and jacket.*)

HOOLIHAN: Bold Robert Emmet.

FINTAN: Shut up. (*Then he sees the nameplate on the door.*) Oh.

(*He changes course for the Parnell room. Niamh has put her shoes on again and now goes towards the bathroom, closing the door. Fintan pounces in.*)

Gotcha!

(*He stops in frustration. Hoolihan comes in behind him. Usheen goes into the bathroom.*)

Gone.

HOOLIHAN (*looking at the portrait of Parnell*): Gone . . . all of them gone.

FINTAN: Wait!

(*He sees Usheen's trousers lying on the bed, where Niamh has left them.*)

The same trousers I saw seven miles away . . . and they're still sopping wet! I don't know what it is, but there's a perverted act going on here somewhere.

(Grainne reappears with the brandy. She goes into the Emmet room and opens one of the bottles, humming to herself.)

I'll search every room in the place from Brian Boru up to Bernadette Devlin. And when I find them ... ! *(Raising his voice.)*

(Still holding the trousers, he hustles Hoolihan out ahead of him. In his anger he has left the shillelagh on the bed. Niamh, attracted by Fintan's final shout, comes out of the bathroom, dabbing at her face with a towel. By now, Fintan and Hoolihan have gone off downstage left.)

NIAMH : Mr Usheen ... ?

(She is about to return to the bathroom when she notices that Usheen's trousers have gone. She looks for them with mounting panic but can only find the shillelagh. In the Emmet room, Grainne taps on the bathroom door.)

GRAINNE : James, dear, are you in there?

USHEEN *(off)* : No.

GRAINNE : Well, really, haven't you ever heard of ladies first? Never mind, I'll use one of the other bathrooms.

(She takes her handbag and goes out. She enters the Parnell room, where Niamh is on her hands and knees looking for the lost trousers. Grainne goes into the bathroom without seeing her. Niamh gives up the search and returns to the bathroom. Niamh screams, off. Grainne comes out, dragging

173

Niamh after her with one hand and holding her nightdress in the other.)

Of all the mean things. How dare you come here and spy on us? Don't you know I'd have given you all the details tomorrow?

NIAMH : There's not going to be any details. Dermod's come home.

GRAINNE : He's what?

NIAMH : I saw him.

GRAINNE : The rotten thing.

NIAMH : And if he's at home, you may depend on it so is Fintan. There goes my night off.

GRAINNE : Men! You can't trust them out of your sight.

NIAMH : So since you're supposed to be staying at my place, I came to collect you and give Mr Usheen back his trousers. Where is he?

GRAINNE *(pointing)* : In there.

NIAMH : This will be a terrible let-down for him.

GRAINNE *(wincing)* : Don't.

NIAMH *(indicating the nightdress)* : What's that?

GRAINNE : My nightie.

NIAMH *(fascinated by it)* : A hell of a let-down.

GRAINNE : I've been saving it for a rainy night.

NIAMH *(examining it)* : I suppose it's the same as sunglasses, you can see everything through it, but it takes away the glare.

GRAINNE : I'm furious with Dermod—my first evening out in ages, and he has to go and spoil it. Well, I won't let him. I've been to too much trouble, and waste is sinful.

NIAMH : You can't stay the whole night here—not now.

GRAINNE : I'm aware of that. James will just have to put up with the abridged version.

NIAMH : Grainne, come home now.

GRAINNE : *You* go home.

NIAMH : Without you?

GRAINNE : Tell Fintan I'm following in my car. When I get there I'll say I had a puncture. Yes?

NIAMH (*fearing the worst*) : Oh, Jay.

GRAINNE : And to prove I'm grateful, you can have that (The nightdress) tomorrow as a present. You can wear it for Fintan.

NIAMH : I'd never see the sun come up.

GRAINNE : But please go *now*. Where are James's trousers?

NIAMH : They were here five minutes ago.

GRAINNE : Well?

NIAMH (*holding up the shillelagh*) : Now all I can find is this.

GRAINNE : The night watchman must have taken them—what a funny old man. I'll find them. You go home.

(*She leads Niamh, still holding the shillelagh, into the corridor.*)

NIAMH : How soon will you be after me?

GRAINNE : As soon as I decently can. Now go. (*She goes into the Emmet room.*)

NIAMH : The trousers might be under the bed . . .

(*Grainne closes the door. Niamh, left on her own, has no choice but to head for home. She comes down centre.*)

(*Decisively.*) Adultery can't be a sin—you go through so much suffering to commit it.

(*She goes off upstage right. Grainne pours herself a brandy. She goes to the bathroom door.*)

GRAINNE : James, are you still in there?

USHEEN (*off*) : The bloody zip is stuck again.

GRAINNE : Well, do hurry. There's been some bad news. We're not playing a full eighteen holes any more. It's been changed to pitch-and-putt. (*Then:*) Trousers . . .

(*She takes her glass of brandy into the Parnell room. She puts down her glass and looks under the bed. Niamh reappears in the corridor, now in a state of yammering terror.*)

NIAMH : Fintan's here, Fintan's here! (*She rushes into the Emmet room, assuming that Grainne is still there.*) Grainne, we're nackered, it's F . . .

(*She realizes that Grainne is no longer there. She tries the bathroom door. It is locked. By now, Fintan and Hoolihan have appeared in the corridor. Niamh hammers on the bathroom door.*)

Fintan's here . . . let me in.

FINTAN : The shillelagh was in your charge, do I have to see to everything myself? Shift your feet man . . . which room were we in?

NIAMH (*hearing this*) : He'll slaughter me.

FINTAN (*close at hand*) : It was this room. I know exactly where I left it.

(*Niamh assumes that he is about to enter the Emmet room. She utters a moan of 'Oh, Jay!' and begins to run around in circles like a decapitated hen, finally collapsing into the built-in wardrobe. At the same time, Fintan and Hoolihan go into the Parnell room, where Fintan looks wildly about him for his shillelagh, and Hoolihan comes to atten-*

*tion in front of the portrait of Parnell. In the
Emmet room, Usheen comes out of the bathroom,
his flies half undone.)*

USHEEN *(ranting)* : What kind of a Communist
country is this? Can't a man undo his fly in peace?
(Looking about him.) Grainne . . . ?
FINTAN : Gone . . . the shillelagh's gone. I'm going
mad. I left it here, you saw me. *(He turns and sees
Hoolihan.)* Stop saluting that adulterer! Wait . . .
I know where they are—*(Pointing to the bathroom.)* in there! Easy now, Fintan, he's got a
shillelagh.

*(Observed by Grainne, who by now is under the
bed, he charges into the bathroom. She reaches for
her nightdress, which is lying on the floor. She
draws it towards her. Hoolihan sees it moving. He
tries to jump on it and misses. He tries again and
succeeds. He picks it up. At first he does not know
what it is. Then dawn breaks.*

*Usheen is meanwhile attacking the stuck zip with
such fury that he is whirling around the room. He
begins to cry with childish rage. Hoolihan holds
the nightdress in front of himself and stands before
the mirror.)*

HOOLIHAN *(cackling)* : Hih, hih, hih, hih!
USHEEN : Bugger it, bugger it, bugger it!

*(Fintan comes out of the bathroom. He is holding
Grainne's fur coat.)*

FINTAN *(quietly; nothing else can happen)* : Now

177

I know. Now at last I know why she's doing it—
for a mangy piece of rabbit skin.

(*The bed rocks violently. Fintan sits on it heavily.*)

And for this she's willing to throw away a woman's
most precious possession—her husband's social
status. Well, I'll say this much in her favour, at
least she's not doing it for love.

HOOLIHAN (*still enjoying himself*): Hih, hih, hih,
hih!

FINTAN (*snarling*): What are you sniggering at?
(*He sees the nightdress.*) Show me that.

(*He snatches it from Hoolihan. In the Emmet
room, Usheen calms down.*)

USHEEN: Steady James love! You don't want to
use up all your strength on a zip. Treat it as you
would a studio audience. That's it . . . soap! (*He
goes into the bathroom.*)

(*Fintan is examining the nightdress.*)

FINTAN: My God, she'd wear this for *him*, but
I'm only let see her in her skin! It's so thin she
must have paid a fortune for it. The faggot . . .
spending my good money on clothes that are only
meant to be put on so as they can be ripped off.
(*To Hoolihan.*) Look at it. Jasus, what's wrong
with flannelette? (*He throws it over Hoolihan's
head.*)

(*Usheen comes hopping out of the bathroom, happily removing his trousers. Humming a snatch of*

'Does your Mother Come from Ireland?' he begins to fold them neatly.)

We'll wait here . . . she'll be back.

(He slumps down on the bed again, knocking the breath out of Grainne.)

USHEEN : What the hell am I doing? They're not *my* trousers.

(He opens the wardrobe door wide, rolls the trousers into a ball, throws them in and closes the door. He comes downstage, takes up the brandy bottle and the remaining glass and begins to pour himself a drink. Suddenly he realizes what he has seen in the wardrobe. The neck of the bottle beats a frenzied tattoo against the lip of the glass.)

(Almost a whisper.) Grainne? Grainne, there's a corpse in the wardrobe.

(The wardrobe door begins to creak open of its own accord. Usheen's nerve goes.)

(A loud cry.) Grainne . . . !

(Fintan leaps to his feet. Usheen grabs his shoes and overcoat and goes tearing out of the Emmet room and dashes off down the corridor, downstage left.)

(As he goes.) Grainne, where are you?
FINTAN : It came from outside. Follow me.
HOOLIHAN *(doing so)* : Hup, two, three, four !
FINTAN : Shut up or I'll kill you.

179

(They go into the Emmet room, just missing the sight of Usheen galloping down the corridor in his shorts. Fintan makes a quick reconnoitre, looking first into the bathroom. Grainne extricates herself from under the bed and goes cautiously into the corridor. In his lightning tour of the room, Fintan slams the wardrobe door shut.)

Someone's been in here. Look at this, a man's coat and tie, brandy and a shillelagh. This can only mean sex. Sit down, Hoolihan; they're gone now, but when they come back we'll be ready for them. Bring me that brandy.

(Grainne, now at the door of the Emmet room, mouths the word 'gone?' in puzzlement. She realizes that Usheen must be elsewhere. She tiptoes along the passage.)

GRAINNE *(a whispered shout)*: Jay-ames . . . where are you? . . . it's me-ee! *(She goes off upstage left. Softly.)* Woo-ooo . . . ?

(Fintan and Hoolihan sit on the bed. A silence, broken only by Fintan thudding the shillelagh into his hand. On the fourth thud the shillelagh breaks neatly in two. He looks at it. Pause.)

FINTAN : Effin' Japanese shillelaghs.

(He helps himself to Usheen's brandy. The door of the wardrobe opens and Niamh crawls out, bent double. She practically walks into Hoolihan, who is looking at her. He salutes her. She returns the salute, turns, and goes back into the wardrobe, closing the door.)

HOOLIHAN (*conversationally, after a pause*): Them is grand spacious wardrobes, sir.

(*Fintan grunts.*)

I was up here in nineteen-sixteen. No motor car hotels up here then. No houses up here then. Nothing up here then, except me. Shot through the lung.

(*Fintan looks at him.*)

Couldn't see the city with the smoke from the fires. Can't see it now with the rain.

FINTAN: You were shot?

HOOLIHAN: 'Is it rainin'?' some gobshite says to me in the South Dublin Union. So I look through the winda. Out in the yard there's a shagger in a tin helmet pointin' a gun at me. I seen the flash, but I didn't hear the bang. They say you don't, on account of the bullet gets to you before the bang does, and once the bullet gets to you you're not interested in listenin'. So I sit down on the floor. 'Is it rainin'?' says the same gobshite to me. 'No', says I, 'but I am'. Wasn't I quick, but?

FINTAN: How did you get up the mountains?

HOOLIHAN: Yis.

FINTAN: I said how did you . . .

HOOLIHAN: So they brung me up the mountains. This Volunteer puts me lyin' in a field and goes off to look for milk. Never cem back. 'The sunlight'll do you good,' he says. I have a bad chest ever since. He was another gobshite.

FINTAN: I'd offer you a drink, but there's only the one glass.

(Hoolihan unscrews the lens cap from his flashlight. He holds it out and Fintan pours brandy into it.)

HOOLIHAN: The brother got shot in nineteen-twenty, shot in the ankle. They gev him a pension, only he was in a motor bike accident in nineteen-thirty-six and he lost his leg. The ankle went with it, so they stopped the pension. *(He drinks.)* Thanks. Good job I didn't lose the lung. I do like walkin' around this wing, and I do like bein' in the restaurant with the big paintin's on the wall . . .

FINTAN *(with pride)*: The Famine Room . . . best steaks in Ireland.

HOOLIHAN: But I don't like the nineteen-sixteen wing. I don't like real things. But wasn't Mr Pearse full of oul' codology, wha'?

(Fintan, his glass half-raised, stares at him.)

The rubbidge he used to come out with. 'Never tell a lie. Strength in our hands, truth on our lips, and cleanness in our hearts.' Jasus, what sort of way is that to run a country?

FINTAN: Nice talk from a man who fought in nineteen-sixteen!

HOOLIHAN: Your lot has more sense. I do like to see the big motor cars and the women with all the rings, and to feel the heat comin' out of the doors of the hotels. I do like to see everybody buyin' things and sellin' things and batin' the lard out of the other fella. Money is great, though.

FINTAN: How dare you criticize Pearse to me? You don't deserve to have been shot in the lung.

HOOLIHAN: Decent man. 'Freedom!' says he. They wouldn't have shot him if they'd a known what

we were goin' to do with it when he got it for us.
They were gobshites, too.

FINTAN : You ought to be ashamed of . . .

HOOLIHAN (*with dignity*): I have to go to the lav
now. If I hadda had brains, I'd be rich, too, because it's the best nationality.

(*He goes into the bathroom. Fintan follows him
and stands in the doorway.*)

FINTAN : You wouldn't be in the cushy job you're
in today if it wasn't for men like Pearse, Emmet
and me. You're in a free country, and all you can
think of is money. And that carpet is new, and
you're splashing it!

(*He comes back into the room in disgust. Miss
Manning appears in the corridor upstage right,
followed by Dermod. She comes down to the
Parnell Room.*)

DERMOD : Miss Manning, you don't have to inspect
every room in the building.

MISS MANNING : But I do, it's my job. Besides, my
quarters, as charming as they are, really do quite
reek of paint . . .

DERMOD : I'm sorry about that . . .

MISS MANNING : . . . So we must find me another
little nest, hmm? Who is in this room?

DERMOD : Parnell.

(*She waits for him to open the door for her. He
does so. She goes in.*)

MISS MANNING : 'Nk yow!

DERMOD : The rooms are really all the same.

MISS MANNING : This one isn't. I spy with my little eye something beginning with 'n'.

DERMOD : 'N'?

MISS MANNING (*holding up Grainne's nightdress*) : For night attire.

DERMOD : How did that get there?

MISS MANNING : Oh, innocent Amy. As if you didn't know!

DERMOD : I don't.

MISS MANNING : You mean you haven't been entertaining young ladies here on the sly?

DERMOD : Miss Manning, what an idea!

MISS MANNING : Yes, isn't it! (*Examining the nightdress.*) I call this quite saucy.

DERMOD : If that night watchman has been letting couples in here for immoral purposes, I'll kick him the length of the building. That's funny . . .

MISS MANNING : What is?

DERMOD : I . . . once bought my wife a nightdress like this.

MISS MANNING : Silly man. Of course she didn't wear it.

DERMOD : How do you know?

MISS MANNING : Wives never do. They can't bear the disappointed look on a man's face when he realizes that underneath the mint sauce is the same old mutton. (*She coughs modestly.*)

DERMOD (*stiffly*) : As it happens, Miss Manning, my wife is an attractive woman.

MISS MANNING : Saddle of Lamb? How nice.

DERMOD : And the nightdress was accidentally set fire to.

MISS MANNING : You were there?

DERMOD : She showed me the ashes.

MISS MANNING (*dryly*) : There's no fooling you, is there, Mr Gibbon?

184

DERMOD : So if this room is to your liking . . . ?

MISS MANNING : I'm not sure. (*Pointing to the portrait.*) Who is he?

DERMOD : Charles Stewart Parnell. My partner didn't want a room named after him, but we ran short of patriots. He destroyed himself because of a woman—an English woman.

MISS MANNING : This room will do nicely.

DERMOD : Good. I'll get your suitcase from reception.

MISS MANNING : It's been such a day, I can't face the thought of unpacking. And all my pretties are at the bottom.

DERMOD : Oh, yes?

MISS MANNING : Of my suitcase, Mr Gibbon. (*Holding the nightdress.*) I know . . . why don't I wear this?

DERMOD : That?

MISS MANNING : Finders keepers, losers weepers. And, as you can see, I'm the kind of woman who will wear any old thing. Let's hope that this one won't go on fire.

DERMOD : Why? Do you smoke in bed?

MISS MANNING : I was thinking of spontaneous combustion. Mr Gibbon, would you be so kind as to fetch my little vanity case . . .

DERMOD : Certainly.

MISS MANNING : And then I hope you won't be in a hurry to be off.

DERMOD : Well, I . . .

MISS MANNING (*reclining on the bed*): Because it's lonelier here than I had imagined. Also, there is such a thing as loneliness of the soul. Did I mention that my gentleman friend has left me?

DERMOD : I'm sorry to hear it.

MISS MANNING : 'Nk yow! It happened after the

185

party—the night you and I met. Mr Gibbon, you see before you a woman scorned. I gave that man the best nights of my life—and of his, too—and he threw me aside like an old bedsock. In my bitterness, (*All in one breath.*) I even thought of yielding my body to the first man with whom I should happen to find myself alone in a bedroom in a deserted building on a mountainside at dead of night, but of course that would have been silly.

(*She looks at him enquiringly.*)

DERMOD (*his voice trembling*) : Not necessarily.

MISS MANNING (*kneeling up on the bed*) : No? Mr Gibbon, I hope you're not about to make an erotic proposal.

DERMOD (*retreating*) : I wasn't.

MISS MANNING : I mean, just because we happen to be alone in a bedroom in a deserted building on a mountainside at dead of night . . .

DERMOD : Are we?

MISS MANNING : Aren't we?

DERMOD (*hoarsely*) : Yes.

MISS MANNING (*seizing him*) : So kindly don't come any closer.

DERMOD : I won't.

MISS MANNING (*pulling him on to the bed*) : You aren't listening, are you? I mean it—not another step. (*She is now as close to him as she can get. She puts her arms around him, as if on the point of fainting.*) There now. I knew I shouldn't be safe with you. Mr Gibbon, this is madness. Think what Mrs Gibbon would say.

DERMOD : I am.

MISS MANNING : . . . If you were silly enough to tell her.

(Dermod attempts to return her embrace. At once she breaks away.)

(Firmly.) No, it's too soon. The wounds go too deep. I shall need time.

DERMOD *(crestfallen)* : Of course.

MISS MANNING : Five minutes?

DERMOD : I'll get your vanity case.

(He goes out and hurries off upstage right, to-wards reception. Miss Manning heads for the bath-room. On the way, she sees the fur coat, which is on the floor where Fintan dropped it and has been hitherto hidden by the bed. She picks it up.)

MISS MANNING *(casually)* : Oh . . . nice. *(Carrying it into the bathroom.)* James Usheen, I will be revenged on you this night !

(She goes off. Fintan has meanwhile been sitting on the bed waiting for Hoolihan, who now emerges from the bathroom.)

HOOLIHAN : I enjoyed that.

FINTAN : You've been in there long enough to float a rowboat. In future use the staff lavatory down the hill.

HOOLIHAN : Yis. *(He starts out.)*

FINTAN : Not now . . . you've just been. Listen to me. I want you to go to the souvenir shop. *(Care-fully, gripping Hoolihan by the lapels.)* Get me another shillelagh. One that won't break. Do it now.

HOOLIHAN *(saluting Emmet)* : Gone . . . all of them gone.

FINTAN : I said get out. And remember about that

187

lavatory. I didn't lay out ten quid for corrugated iron for my own amusement.

(*Hoolihan goes out. Grainne reappears from downstage left with Usheen, still trouserless, in tow.*)

GRAINNE : Dead women in wardrobes . . . I never heard such nonsense.
USHEEN : I tell you she . . .
GRAINNE : Quiet !

(*She starts violently as she comes face to face with Hoolihan.*)

Oh. (*Standing in front of Usheen.*) Hello . . . we were just . . .
HOOLIHAN : Gone.
GRAINNE : Pardon me?
HOOLIHAN : All gone now.
GRAINNE : Do you mean that the gentleman who . . .
HOOLIHAN (*rubbing the window in the downstage 'well'*): How does water soak through glass? You don't know? (*Going off right.*) He's another gobshite.
GRAINNE (*to Usheen*): Did you hear what he said? Fintan is gone. I'll just make sure. Shhh . . .

(*She tiptoes down to the door of the Emmet room. Within, Fintan suddenly stands up.*)

FINTAN : Shag him. Now he has *me* wanting to pee.
USHEEN : I refuse to set foot in that . . .

(*Grainne motions him to be silent. She puts her*

188

ar to the door, then opens it cautiously just as
Fintan disappears into the bathroom. She looks
nto the room, then turns to Usheen.)

GRAINNE : We're safe, he's gone.

USHEEN : I'm not going in there. I tell you there
was a dead woman in the wardrobe. She was
huddled on the floor, a shapeless lump . . . her
eyes were turned up. It was horrible. Funny thing
is, she looked familiar.

GRAINNE (*nastily*) : Are you sure she didn't have
a mole on her breast?

USHEEN : If you're going to be rude I'll go home.

GRAINNE : I'll tell you your trouble. You've been
watching too much television.

USHEEN : I never watch television . . . I still have
my pride.

GRAINNE : What you don't have are your trousers,
and they're in that wardrobe.

USHEEN (*craven*) : You get them.

GRAINNE : First I have a question. Out of common
Christianity, I offered to commit adultery with you
tonight. Now yes or no, James. Has rain stopped
play?

USHEEN : I knew there was something I was trying
to remember from twelve years ago. You're insane.

GRAINNE : Thank you.

USHEEN : Have you forgotten? . . . your husband's
partner is on these premises.

GRAINNE : He'll have gone home by now. And it
was Niamh he was after, not me—I can't think
why. Luckily for her, she's miles away.

Niamh comes crawling out of the wardrobe again.
She grabs the bedclothes and hoists herself on to
her knees.)

189

So are we or aren't we?

USHEEN: I know you'll think me hyper-sensitive, but with a corpse under the same roof I doubt if my performance would be at its peak.

GRAINNE (*icily*): Very well, James, there's no more to be said. I'll get your trousers—my husband's trousers. Would you kindly fetch my nightie and mink—they're in there. (*She half-opens the door of the Emmet room.*)

NIAMH (*seeing the door opening*): Oh shag. (*She wearily returns into the wardrobe.*)

GRAINNE: And, James . . . don't blame me if wherever you go from now on you keep seeing your precious Lucretia. (*She goes into the Emmet room, shutting the door, and stands trying to fight back tears of fury.*)

USHEEN (*to the closed door*): Her name is Venetia. And I do not suffer from hallucinations.

(*He opens the door of the Parnell room, just as Miss Manning comes from the bathroom dressed in the nightdress and mink coat.*

They see each other and scream. Usheen slams the door shut.)

MISS MANNING ⎱ (*together*): Oh, my God.
USHEEN ⎰

(*Grainne hurries out.*)

GRAINNE: Now, what? (*Looking at Usheen's stricken face.*) What is it?

USHEEN: Forgive me. You were right and I was wrong. It's all in my mind. I'll do anything you

190

say, only cure me, I'm sick. Where's the bed? (*He pushes past her into the bedroom.*)

GRAINNE : But what's happened?

USHEEN : I'm losing my sanity and she asks stupid questions. Are you coming to bed or aren't you?

GRAINNE : I'll get my nightie.

(*She stands for a moment, confused by his change of mind. Miss Manning is still reeling from shock in the Parnell room.*)

MISS MANNING : I shall never eat British Rail mushrooms again! (*She goes into the bathroom.*)

(*Grainne enters a moment later. Usheen, in the Emmet room, picks up his jacket and tie from the bed. He goes with them to the wardrobe and opens it.*)

NIAMH (*from within*) : Hello, Mr Usheen.

(*Usheen looks at her blankly, then writes her off as an hallucination. He makes a dismissive gesture, hangs his jacket over her head, and closes the door. He gets into bed. Grainne cannot find her nightdress. She attempts to enter the bathroom but is surprised to find that the door is bolted.*)

MISS MANNING (*off*) : Be patient, you impetuous man, I'll be out in a minute. And I've had rather a nasty shock, so you will be gentle with me, won't you, Mr Gibbon?

(*Grainne, facing downstage, is rigid with shock. She looks towards the audience and mouths: 'Mr Gibbon?' In the Emmet room, Usheen moves over*

in bed so that there is space for Grainne. He
plumps up her pillow. There is the sound of the
toilet being flushed. Usheen looks towards the bath-
room door, puzzled. Fintan comes out drying his
hands. He nods to Usheen.)

FINTAN : 'Evening.

(He sits on the edge of the bed, his back to Usheen.
Very slowly, he realizes that the bed has an occu-
pant. He stares at us with the same disbelief as is
manifested by Grainne in the other room. Emitting
a low animal growl, he turns slowly and points at
Usheen.)

Uhhh . . . hhh . . . hhh . . .
USHEEN *(clutching the bedclothes around him)* :
I'm the first of the English visitors.

(Fintan advances on him, Usheen gets out of the
bed on the far side.)

Is there anything I can do for you? Cup of sugar?
FINTAN *(in a terrible voice)* : Where is she?
USHEEN : She?
FINTAN : My adulterous trollop of a wife!
USHEEN *(avoiding him)* : I don't think I know the
lady, but if I see anyone answering that descrip-
tion I'll . . .
FINTAN : Whoremaster!
USHEEN : Who came in?
FINTAN : Tell me where she is, and I'll give you
the mercy of a swift death.
USHEEN : Keep away from me. I don't know where
she is or . . .
FINTAN : Stop! I know your face.

192

USHEEN (*seeing a way to safety*): Yes, most people do. And when you realize who I am, I think you'll change your tune, my man.

FINTAN: Wait . . . I know who you are!

USHEEN: I thought it would come to you.

FINTAN: You're Lester Piggott.

USHEEN: Try again.

FINTAN: Where was it? Where did I see you?

USHEEN (*confident now*): I presume you watch television?

(*A wild, drawn-out shriek from Fintan.*)

Oh, God, an Andrews fan.

FINTAN: You! The atheist, the adulterer. And my wife says she's mad about you.

USHEEN: Everybody is—don't take it personally.

(*Hoolihan appears in the corridor at a senile jog-trot, carrying another shillelagh. Meanwhile, Grainne is now pacing up and down the Parnell room like a tigress waiting for mealtime.*)

FINTAN: God! . . . God if you're in heaven, send me down a weapon to destroy him with.

USHEEN: Sir, if any harm comes to me, I have twelve million devoted fans who will . . .

(*As Fintan raises his hands as if in prayer, Hooli-han enters behind him and slides the shillelagh into his fist. Fintan makes a gesture of thanks towards heaven.*)

FINTAN: A time-honoured Irish weapon!

G

USHEEN (*wearily*) : Why did I ever come back?
FINTAN : *Now!*

(*He raises the shillelagh on high. This one does not break. Instead, it droops like a withered flower. All three men look at it.*)

Never mind. I'll kill him with my bare hands. And no one will hear your screams—there's not a soul within five miles.

(*Dermod appears in the corridor, singing loudly to himself, and carrying Miss Manning's vanity case.*)

DERMOD (*singing*) :
'There's a small motel,
And a wishing well,
I wish that we were there
Togeth-er . . .''

(*Fintan and Grainne both react in their respective rooms. Fintan goes to the door in time to see Dermod entering the Parnell room. Grainne, hearing him approaching, stands against the wall so that the opening door will conceal her.*)

(*Entering*) : I'm ba-ack!

(*At once, Miss Manning appears from the bathroom, every inch the man-eater in mink and nylon.*)

MISS MANNING (*archly*) : Well, Mr Gibbon?
DERMOD (*stunned*) : Miss Manning, you're . . .

MISS MANNING : I'm what?

DERMOD : You're beautiful.

MISS MANNING (*modestly*) : You're blind.

GRAINNE (*appearing from behind the door*) : You're banjaxed !

DERMOD (*thunderstruck*) : Grainne . . .

GRAINNE : Who is that faggot?

MISS MANNING : Oh, very nice.

DERMOD : Now don't jump to conclusions . . .

GRAINNE : I know—you can explain everything ! You, the man I trusted. I turn my back on you for an evening, and I find you here with that . . .

USHEEN (*from the other room*) : Grainne, save me !

GRAINNE : . . . Alone in a bedroom with that woman wearing my . . .

DERMOD : Who was *that*?

GRAINNE (*smiling brightly*) : No one, dear. (*Resuming her tirade.*) . . . Wearing my fur coat and my . . . my . . .

USHEEN (*yelling*) : Grainne !

DERMOD : No one, eh? Well, let's see what no one looks like !

(*He marches out and into the Emmet room. Grainne, now frantic, follows him.*)

GRAINNE : Wait . . . I can explain everything.

(*Dermod comes face to face with Fintan. Grainne comes in; Miss Manning straggles after them as far as the doorway.*)

DERMOD (*to Fintan*) : What are you doing here? (*He sees Usheen.*) And who is he?

GRAINNE : I never saw him before.

DERMOD (*a closer look*) : It's Mr Usheen.

USHEEN : Hello. Lovely to see you again.

MISS MANNING : It *wasn't* the mushrooms?

DERMOD (*hand outstretched*) : Forgive me . . . I didn't recognize you with your . . . (*He takes in Usheen's state of undress.*) You! You and my . . .

GRAINNE : Now don't jump to conclusions.

DERMOD : Him . . . the man you said you can't stand . . .

USHEEN (*to Grainne*) : Did you say that?

DERMOD : Yes . . . now I see it all.

GRAINNE : Never mind what *you* see. What about what *I* see? (*Pointing at Miss Manning.*)

USHEEN : What about what *I* see?

FINTAN : Yes, who the hell is that?

MISS MANNING (*explaining everything*) : I'm the new manageress.

HOOLIHAN : Hih-hih-hih-hih!

DERMOD ⎱ (*together*) : Shut up!
FINTAN ⎰

FINTAN : My God . . . you and her and her and him. Orgies under the Plough and the Stars . . . the Patrick Pearse Motel turned into a knocking shop. What sort of savages am I living with? And me— I'm the worst of the lot. I thought bad of the only decent, pure, honest woman left in the country. Niamh, Niamh . . . say you forgive me!

NIAMH (*coming out of the wardrobe*) : I do . . . I do!

(*Fintan looks at her and screams.*)

Blackout

Curtain

196

Scene 2

The same. Five minutes have passed.

Dermod, Grainne and Usheen—still without his trousers—are sitting on what transpires to be Fintan, spreadeagled on the bed. Hoolihan is sitting on the floor in a corner of the room with the brandy bottle, from which he helps himself during the scene. Niamh is standing as far away from Fintan as she can get.

Pause. In the Parnell room, Miss Manning comes out of the bathroom. She is dressed as in the previous scene. She picks up her vanity case and returns to the bathroom.

GRAINNE : We can't go on sitting on him all night.
USHEEN : If we get off he'll go berserk again.
DERMOD : He's been quiet for a while now. Should we chance it?
NIAMH : Don't. He's the same at home; not a stir out of him in bed, and when you think he's asleep, that's when he turns into a madman.
DERMOD : We've got to let him up some time. (*He lifts the pillow which he has been holding over Fintan's head.*) Fintan, are you all right?
FINTAN (*gasping*) : Get off me.
DERMOD : If we do, will you promise to be good? No more trying to strangle Niamh?
NIAMH : If you're going to let him up, at least give me a ten-minute head-start.
DERMOD : Fintan, we want your word that you'll behave.

197

FINTAN (*hoarsely*): Yes.

DERMOD: You swear as a gentleman?

FINTAN: I swear as a gentleman.

NIAMH (*hollowly*): Oh, Jay.

DERMOD: All right. (*To Grainne and Usheen.*) Slowly now . . .

(*They get up gingerly as if they were sitting on nitro-glycerine. Fintan arises like a whale surfacing. He bestows a baleful glance upon Niamh.*)

NIAMH: Watch him!

FINTAN (*with massive dignity*): I intend to prosecute everyone here for assault and being sat down on. (*Indicating Usheen.*) I intend to sue *him* for enticement and the loss of a housekeeper. (*Indicating Niamh.*) As for her, I intend to get a Papal annulment. You'll be hearing from my bishop in the morning.

NIAMH: And now for the *bad* news!

DERMOD: She won't be the only one who'll be hearing from a bishop.

GRAINNE: Meaning me?

DERMOD (*addressing the ceiling*): I'd say the Vatican is in for a profitable year.

USHEEN: That'll be a change! (*As Dermod glares at him.*) I suppose we should be thankful he doesn't intend to have us up for G.B.H.

FINTAN: What's G.B.H.?

DERMOD: It stands for Grainne Being Had.

GRAINNE: How dare you? You can accuse me after I saw you with that sex-mad rip wearing my . . . (*Amending.*) wearing a disgusting see-through nightdress.

USHEEN: That's unfair. Venetia is definitely not

198

sex-mad. I've known her to go without it for hours on end.

DERMOD : At least Miss Manning was here by right. She's the manageress.

GRAINNE : She certainly goes in for room service in a big way.

USHEEN : That's not bad.

DERMOD (*pointing at Usheen*) : Does *he* belong here? Look at him. He's in his underwear.

FINTAN (*scowling*) : Pansy.

USHEEN : There's a very simple explanation for that . . .

FINTAN
DERMOD } (*together*) : Yes?

(*Pause.*)

USHEEN (*to Grainne*) : Tell them.

GRAINNE : Certainly. Niamh, tell them.

NIAMH (*taking a deep breath*) : *Well* . . . when a ship is launched, it's always the owner's wife who—

GRAINNE (*panic-stricken*) : Don't listen to her. If you want the truth, James couldn't find a hotel room in town, so I brought him here.

DERMOD : You're lying.

GRAINNE : Ask James.

USHEEN : Ask me.

GRAINNE : James and I were good friends once. What more natural than that he should ring up and ask if I knew of a place where he could stay?

DERMOD (*almost convinced*) : I see.

GRAINNE : And Niamh came along as my chaperone. You know how people talk.

FINTAN (*to Niamh*) : Is this true?

NIAMH : May I drop down dead.

199

DERMOD (*to Fintan*): It sounds plausible.

GRAINNE: Do I offer him a room in our house, with you away? No, I bring him here, seven miles up a mountain road. I try to protect my good name, and this is the thanks I get.

DERMOD (*now contrite*): Grainne, I . . .

USHEEN (*heading for the door*): Well, now that's cleared up . . . !

FINTAN: Where are you going?

USHEEN: Back to my hotel. (*He comes to a shuddering standstill.*)

FINTAN ⎱ (*together, to Niamh*
DERMOD ⎰ *and Grainne respectively*): Liar!

USHEEN: No, no, what I mean is to *look* for a ho . . .

DERMOD (*coldly*): The best thing you can do at the moment is put your trousers on.

FINTAN: Yes, there are whores present.

GRAINNE (*to Fintan*): Are you calling me a . . .

NIAMH: Don't contradict him, it puts him in a bad humour.

GRAINNE (*to Dermod*): Are you going to let him insult your wife? (*As he turns his back on her.*) I swear on my mother's grave I'm innocent.

DERMOD: Your mother's alive.

GRAINNE (*snapping*): Her grave is paid for.

DERMOD (*losing his temper*): By me, more fool that I am. And may she never live to climb into it.

GRAINNE: That's it, now abuse my mother, a woman in constant pain.

DERMOD: She's worse than in constant pain, she's in a council house in Crumlin.

GRAINNE: How dare you throw Crumlin in my face, with your own parents slobbering in the shadow of a brewery! And if my mother's in Crumlin, *who left her there to rot*?

DERMOD : I wish I'd left more than your mother to rot in Crumlin. I wish I'd . . . Ha! Ha-ha!

(This is a derisory laugh directed at Usheen, who has taken his (Dermod's) trousers from the wardrobe and is putting them on. As before, he is having trouble with the zip.)

GRAINNE : What?
DERMOD : Your fancy-man's taste in trousers is well in keeping with his taste in women. Yech!

(Grainne emits a loud shrill laugh.)

What's so funny?
GRAINNE : I'll tell you after the annulment.
USHEEN *(struggling with the zip)* : Bugger it! Excuse me . . .
NIAMH : Can I help you with your fly, Mr Usheen?

(An anguished growl from Fintan.)

Now what?
FINTAN *(starting forward)* : I'll kill her, I'll kill her!
DERMOD : Fintan, you promised . . .
FINTAN *(picking up an easy chair)* : Only not to strangle her.
NIAMH : I only offered to—
FINTAN : I know what you are offering to do for him, I've seen you in action. You didn't learn that at your Ontario practice.
NIAMH : Learn what?
FINTAN : I curse that hour and a half we spent in the airport in Paris on our way to Lourdes.

201

NIAMH (*to the others, reasonably*) : His own mother told me not to marry him.

USHEEN (*who has been thinking*) : 'I'll kill her, I'll kill her!' (*The others look at him. To Fintan.*) I know where I've seen you before. The bastard in the Jensen.

FINTAN : The what in the what?

USHEEN : That face, that voice. Sir, allow me to inform you that you are without doubt the most wantonly irresponsible driver since Ben Hur. Where did you learn to drive, anyway—reform school? Do you know, I could have you prosecuted?

FINTAN : First he depraves my wife, now he criticizes my driving. Get him out of here.

DERMOD (*to Usheen*) : You'd better go.

(*Usheen points a denunciatory finger at Fintan. This involves him letting go of his trousers, which fall down. He picks them up, turning his attention to Dermod.*)

USHEEN (*to Dermod*) : You were in the car with him, weren't you? In which case you can whistle for your trousers. And furthermore . . . !

(*He kisses Niamh and goes out and into the Parnell room as Fintan roars with rage.*)

DERMOD : I wouldn't be seen dead in those . . . (*Staring at Grainne.*) He's wearing my . . .

GRAINNE : His got wet.

DERMOD : You gave him my good fifteen-guinea . . .

NIAMH : She had to.

DERMOD : *Had* to?

NIAMH : Fintan nearly ran over him. (*To Fintan.*) What if he does go to the police?

FINTAN : I can't be prosecuted. I'm out of that income group.

DERMOD (*to Grainne*) : You gave him my . . .

GRAINNE : Oh, shut up. And before you start throwing more sand in my eyes about your trousers, my semi-invalid mother and James Usheen, let me remind you that *I* was not the person who was caught red-handed with a nymphomaniac wearing a nightdress you could see the Hell-Fire Club through.

DERMOD : . . . Yes, *about* that nightdress . . . !

GRAINNE (*knowing what is coming*) : Don't change the subject.

DERMOD : When Miss Manning walked into that room, the nightdress was already there. So where did it come from?

GRAINNE : How do I know where it . . .

DERMOD : It was yours.

GRAINNE : Mine?

DERMOD : I bought it for you.

FINTAN : For *her*? (*An incredulous laugh.*) You madman.

GRAINNE : That nightdress was set fire to.

DERMOD : So you said. I remember I bought it at Chez Siobhan's. Why don't I go and get it, and we'll have a look at the label?

(*Grainne and Niamh look at each other in horror. Dermod starts towards the door.*)

Good idea, yes?

FINTAN (*magisterially*) : Wait just one minute?

(*In the Parnell room, Usheen taps on the door of the bathroom.*)

USHEEN : Venetia? My zip is stuck.

MISS MANNING (*off*) : I don't give a fig. Kindly go away.

DERMOD (*to Fintan*) : Well?

FINTAN : Man, are you so blind that you can't see the truth? That nightdress isn't hers . . .

GRAINNE : Of course it isn't.

FINTAN : It's *hers*, (*Niamh's*), and your wife is protecting her. Look at those two women, compare them. Now to hell with loyalty, own up. If you were a dirty anglicized renegade Irishman looking for his oats, which one of them would you go to bed with?

NIAMH : He's off.

(*Dermod looks numbly at Fintan.*)

FINTAN : I see by your face you agree with me. But don't think your wife is innocent. The ugly ones always encourage the good-looking ones.

GRAINNE (*indignantly*) : I beg your p . . .

FINTAN (*to Niamh, brokenly*) : How could you do it to me? Have I ever neglected you?

NIAMH : No, not once.

FINTAN : Was the sight of me raking in money not happiness enough for you? And if you had to commit adultery, why did you disgrace me by choosing *him*? Why couldn't you have picked a decent, good-living catholic? Why? Why?

(*By now he is on his knees before her. Niamh strokes his head.*)

NIAMH (*kindly*) : I will, next time.

FINTAN : A man who gets on the television and be-littles us in colour. He was the one who said that the Irish are under the influence of L.S.D.—laziness, slander and dirt. How dare he say that we're lazy? I'll get up early one of these days and kill him for that.

(*Still on his knees, he 'walks' to the door and shouts, for Usheen's benefit.*)

What's more, I'm going to sue him and expose him!

USHEEN : Venetia, he says he's going to sue me and expose me.

(*Miss Manning comes out of the bathroom, now dressed. She gets ready to leave.*)

MISS MANNING : High time, too.

DERMOD : Fintan, get up. (*He attempts to assist him.*)

FINTAN : Get your hands off me! You're as bad as they are . . . the first member of the staff to arrive, and you have her in her pelt before she has time to count the towels. You don't fool me.

GRAINNE : Nor me.

DERMOD : Fintan, I want a private word with you.

FINTAN : I have nothing to say to any of you.

DERMOD : This is about money.

FINTAN : I couldn't care less.

DERMOD : A lot of money.

FINTAN : I said I don't want to talk to you.

DERMOD (*curtly*) : Very well . . .

FINTAN : But if you're going to nag at me, I'll listen.

DERMOD : If the ladies would excuse us . . . ?

GRAINNE : Leave you? . . . with pleasure; excuse you? . . . not if you were to come begging on your hands and knees, and wearing a see-through night-dress! Come Niamh, now that we're free women again, we have plans to make.

NIAMH (*following her*) : Oh, Jay.

(*They go into the bathroom and shut the door. Dermod goes to the door and listens.*)

FINTAN : I'm done with you.

DERMOD : Shhhh . . . !

FINTAN : Don't you tell me to shush. Thanks to you, my marriage is in flitters, the motel is a mockery, and the cost of the Papal annulment will put me in the poorhouse.

DERMOD (*impatiently*) : Will you wait . . .

(*He listens. In the Parnell room, Miss Manning is ready to be off.*)

USHEEN : Venetia, where are you going?

MISS MANNING : Kensington High Street.

USHEEN : Good, I'll go with you.

MISS MANNING : I'll feel safer on my own . . . 'nk yow!

USHEEN : You silly cow, you'll drown in a boghole. Don't you know that it's pouring with rain and you're on top of a mountain?

MISS MANNING : Kindly move to one side.

USHEEN : At least help me get this fastened.

MISS MANNING : I've pulled up your last zip, James. And now I intend to give myself to the first gentleman farmer I meet on my way down the mountain.

USHEEN : If this is because of what happened to-night, I'm as innocent as you are.

MISS MANNING : How do you know I'm innocent?

USHEEN : Because this bloody country hasn't changed. They can't even commit adultery properly. Venetia, don't leave me alone with the one they call Fintan.

MISS MANNING : I won't say goodbye, James. You said it in London when you sent me out to buy my trousseau, and then changed the locks. (*She goes off, heading towards reception.*)

USHEEN : Venetia, wait. (*To his zip.*) Come up, come up . . .

(*In the Emmet room, Dermod comes away from the door of the bathroom.*)

DERMOD : I knew it. They're trying to think up a good story.

USHEEN (*in triumph*) : Got it !

DERMOD : Grainne is asking Niamh to . . .

(*Usheen emits a scream of agony. He doubles up, his arms folded across his thighs. The pain continues.*)

USHEEN : Aaaaaah . . .

DERMOD : My God, what was that?

FINTAN : Hah ! The decent man has cut his throat.

(*Usheen, still bent double, stumbles across the corridor and into the Emmet room. He stares at Fintan and Dermot, too agonized to speak.*)

USHEEN : Aaaaaah . . .

DERMOD : What do you want?

USHEEN (*begging for help*): Aaaaaah . . .

DERMOD: That's a bloody funny place to cut your throat.

FINTAN: Go away, we're not talking to you.

(*Usheen utters another 'Aaaaah . . .' and staggers across the room and into the bathroom.*)

Where's he going? Come back here!

(*There are loud screams from Grainne and Niamh, off.*

Usheen is thrown out of the bathroom. His first loud cry has brought Miss Manning hurrying back along the corridor. Grainne and Niamh reappear.)

GRAINNE: Filthy beast.

NIAMH: But thanks for the compliment.

(*They return into the bathroom and close the door. Usheen is as much in agony as ever. Miss Manning looks into the Parnell room.*)

DERMOD: You! Did you attack my wife?

FINTAN: Of course he did. The state he's in, he'd attack any old thing. Look at him . . . that's what television does.

DERMOD (*advancing on Usheen*): You animal . . . By God, I'll . . .

MISS MANNING (*coming in*): James!

USHEEN (*seeing her*): Aaaaaah . . .

MISS MANNING: Are you ill?

USHEEN (*negative*): Aaaaaah . . .

MISS MANNING : Is it your zip?

USHEEN (*affirmative*) : Aaaaaah . . .

MISS MANNING (*to the others*) : I'm afraid he's done himself a little mischief. Come with Venetia, dear.

(*She takes him by the hand and leads him, still bent double, into the Parnell room and towards the bathroom. On the way, Usheen attempts to speak to her.*)

USHEEN : Aaah . . . aaah . . . aaah.

MISS MANNING : I know, pet. That's why I'm glad I'm a girl.

(*They go into the bathroom. Fintan has been staring after them from the Emmet room. Dermod gets down to business.*)

DERMOD : Fintan, we must make it up with the girls.

FINTAN : To hell with them.

DERMOD : And with each other.

FINTAN : Get stitched.

DERMOD : If we don't make it up, there'll be a scandal.

FINTAN : Damn sure there'll be a scandal. If I've got to be the innocent party, I'll have something to show for it. I'll spread these goings-on all over town like jam on bread.

DERMOD : Right. Then you can say goodbye to the motel.

FINTAN : Don't threaten me, you pup.

DERMOD : Fintan, this is no ordinary enterprise. (*Mistily.*) Our motel is the fulfilment of the dreams of the men who died for this green island. Do you want to insult their memory? Do you want to make

their deaths meaningless? Do you want us to go
bankrupt?

FINTAN (*grabbing him*): You know something . . .
tell me.

DERMOD: I'm telling you that if there is one
whisper of scandal there'll be no grand opening
next week. Think of it, Fintan. No cabinet minister
to unveil the bust in the De Valera Snackery, no
bishop to bless our Kitchen-Garden of Remem-
brance, no guard of honour to fire a salute over
the swimming pool. Is that what you want?

FINTAN: Don't go on.

DERMOD: We may as well put a note in the
brochure: 'Unmarried Couples Welcome . . .
Fornicate in Comfort.'

FINTAN: Stop, stop . . .

DERMOD: 'Wine, Dine and Hate It Away by
Candlelight.'

FINTAN: Stop, or I'll kill you.

DERMOD: If you won't think of us, think of the
employment we're giving. What's going to happen
to the staff who'll be depending on us?

FINTAN: They'll all have to go back to Cyprus.

DERMOD: Exactly. Our wives are in there now,
going through hell to think up a tissue of lies.
Fintan, what kind of men are we that we won't
meet them halfway?

FINTAN: I'm a patriot: that means I'll believe anything.

(*Miss Manning and Usheen come out of the bathroom into the Parnell room. Usheen is visibly
shaken after his experience.*)

MISS MANNING: A little soreness won't harm you,

James. None of this would have happened if you'd married me.

USHEEN: I've already explained to you why I can't.

MISS MANNING: For religious reasons?

USHEEN: Yes.

MISS MANNING: What a bigot you are in this day and age. After all, it's the same God we all disbelieve in, isn't it?

USHEEN: There's another reason.

MISS MANNING: Might I know it?

USHEEN: I can't stand you.

MISS MANNING: You sillikins, that's not a reason. You've simply found out before marriage what other husbands and wives find out afterwards.

USHEEN: Venetia, there are two men in there who are prepared to sue me and cause a scandal.

MISS MANNING: They won't cause a scandal.

USHEEN: They're Irish-Catholic businessmen. They'd cut your head off and charge you for corkage.

MISS MANNING: They won't cause a scandal, because I can stop them.

USHEEN: How?

MISS MANNING: If I did, would you marry me?

USHEEN: No.

MISS MANNING: Not ever?

USHEEN (*firmly*): I'd sooner spend the rest of my life caught in a zip.

MISS MANNING: Oh. (*Then, with a strange smile.*) Never mind, perhaps I'll help you all the same. (*Tapping his cheek.*) I'm so fond of you.

USHEEN (*facing front*): Why do I suddenly feel frightened?

(*Niamh and Grainne come from the bathroom.*

Fintan and Dermod rise expectantly. Grainne has a coolly defiant look on her face; Niamh is downcast.)

FINTAN ⎞ *(together, with*
DERMOD ⎠ *welcoming smiles)* : Well?
GRAINNE : Perfectly.
NIAMH : We're grand, thanks.
DERMOD *(warmly)* : What Fintan and I mean is, have you anything to tell us?

(The women look at him blankly.)

We know you were both innocent, don't we, Fintan?
FINTAN *(non-commital)* : Uh.
DERMOD : We were just naturally wondering how you came to be up here with him. Not that we're the least bit suspicious.

(Silence.)

FINTAN *(appealingly)* : Niamh?
NIAMH : When a ship is launched, it's always the—
GRAINNE *(silencing her)* : Quiet Niamh! *(To the men.)* We have nothing to say.
DERMOD : Nothing?
FINTAN : Any old rubbish would do us.
DERMOD : Try us with anything.
GRAINNE *(turning on him)* : All right, then, you sarcastic devils. All right, if you want the truth you can have it!
FINTAN *(in dismay)* : The truth?
DERMOD : Who said anything about the truth?
FINTAN *(wheeling on Dermod)* : Now look what you've done!

212

GRAINNE : I *planned* to come up here with James Usheen. We were going to make . . .

(*Miss Manning is in the room, with Usheen in her wake.*)

MISS MANNING : . . . going to make this nice motel of yours famous !

(*She goes straight to Grainne, as if they were long-lost sisters.*)

You poor thing . . . having to keep silent for James's sake and mine. But I've spoken to James, and it's not a secret any more . . . (*To Usheen.*) is it, dear ?

(*Usheen looks at her, open-mouthed.*)

Now we can let it be known what a brave, good wife you are. Shall I tell them, or will you ?

(*Grainne and Niamh look at each other blankly, then at Miss Manning.*)

GRAINNE ⎱
NIAMH ⎰ (*together*) : You tell them.

MISS MANNING : Hem ! (*Indicating Grainne.*) This lady—may I call you Grainy ? Wrote to Mr Usheen some weeks ago, and asked if he would interview her husband and this charming gentleman (Fintan) on his programme. To publicize the motel, you know.

FINTAN : Us ? Him and me ? In colour ?

DERMOD : Grainne, is this true ?

213

GRAINNE (*staring dazedly at Miss Manning*) : Every word.

MISS MANNING : That was why Mr Usheen asked me to apply for the position of manageress. I haven't been honest with you, Mr Gibbon . . . I'm really here as a kind of spy . . . a snooper.

NIAMH (*to Grainne*) : She's very good.

MISS MANNING : Mind, what I've seen, I like. And to make doubly sure, Mr Usheen came up here this evening with Mrs Gibbon to inspect the premises for himself.

(*Usheen is oozing relief. He puts an arm around Miss Manning.*)

USHEEN : And I can't tell you how impressed I am.

FINTAN : Stop right there—I believe everything !

DERMOD : Grainne, can you forgive me?

GRAINNE ('*wounded*') : Not if I live to be thirty.

MISS MANNING : Hem ! Now you may ask, why should Mr Usheen and I visit the motel separately on the same night? Shall we tell them, Grainy?

GRAINNE (*being big about it*) : Yes, why keep it to ourselves !

MISS MANNING : James?

USHEEN (*squeezing her; lavishly*) : Tell them, everything !

MISS MANNING : I mean to. You might say that James and I are combining business with pleasure. After all, what better place than this for a quiet honeymoon?

USHEEN : Absolutely. It's peaceful, it's secluded . . . it's a lie.

MISS MANNING (*playfully*) : Now you did say I could tell them. You're the first to know. James and I were married yesterday.

USHEEN (*appalled*) : Venetia, you b . . .

(*A peal of hysterical laughter from Grainne.*)

MISS MANNING : We told Grainy, of course. As you can see, she's so happy for us.

NIAMH : Oh, Jay.

GRAINNE : I think I'm going to choke.

MISS MANNING : So, as we're newly-weds, James would hardly be interested in another lady, now would he? . . . nor I in another gentleman. Although I did rather flirt with Mr Gibbon, just to keep him from suspecting.

USHEEN (*feebly*) : Look, this is all a . . .

MISS MANNING : . . . A dead secret—until Sunday. That's when James is going to make it public on television. Aren't you, pet?

USHEEN : And if I don't . . . ?

MISS MANNING : Eamonn Andrews will.

DERMOD (*bounding forward*) : Mr Usheen . . . congratulations.

FINTAN (*hand outstretched*) : I always was a fan of yours. Put it there.

(*It is all too much for Usheen. His shoulders begin to heave.*)

MISS MANNING (*touched*) : Ahhh . . . he's so senti-mental deep down. (*She chucks him under the chin.*) Yes, he . . . is !

USHEEN : You . . .

(*His hands begin to reach for her throat, but Fintan wraps a massive arm around his shoulder.*)

FINTAN : Come here to me, old son. You won't forget about putting us on TV?

MISS MANNING : I'll remind him.

FINTAN : And you'll give us the full treatment? I mean, the few friendly little insults?

(*Usheen looks at him. At once his rage finds an outlet.*)

USHEEN : Yes! Yes, just to begin with, I think I'll call you an overstuffed upstart, who drives like a drunken Seminole Indian, and who combines the brains of a brontosaurus with the manners of a mongoose.

FINTAN (*wildly*) : I like it, I like it!

MISS MANNING : And now, who would like to kiss the bride? Mr Gibbon?

(*Dermod kisses her and is kissed back.*)

'Nk *yow*! (*She sees that Fintan is next in line.*) Oh, I like them big. Just a peck now!

(*Leaving Fintan gasping.*) 'Nk *yow*! Well now, who's next? Oh, no!

(*This is a reaction to the appearance of Hoolihan beside her. He has risen from the floor, and Miss Manning assumes that he wishes to kiss her.*)

HOOLIHAN : I only want to get past. I have to go to the lav . . . I have sudden kidneys. (*As she stands back.*) Thanks. (*He heads for the bathroom.*)

FINTAN : The outside lavatory!

HOOLIHAN : Oh, yis.

(*He goes out and off downstage right.*)

FINTAN (*good humoured*): You should have given him a kiss. It'd probably have been his last.

DERMOD: Fintan, the day we appear on English television we'll be set up for life.

GRAINNE: And all thanks to me.

DERMOD: No man ever had a better wife.

FINTAN: I told you all along the girls were innocent. Niamh, when we get home I'm going to make it up to you.

NIAMH: I think I'll slash my wrists.

(*They all come out in a group and go downstage centre, Fintan carrying the now empty brandy bottle.*)

MISS MANNING: Do try to smile, James. After all, marriage is only another form of entertainment tax.

(*Fintan holds up the bottle.*)

FINTAN: Will you look at this! The old get drank the lot.

DERMOD: We should get rid of him.

FINTAN: I'll give him the boot first thing in the morning. (*To Usheen.*) Now about this television lark . . .

MISS MANNING: Somebody's just gone past the window.

DERMOD: Where? (*He comes downstage and peers out.*) It's Hoolihan. He's gone off up the mountain.

FINTAN: There's so much brandy in him he can't see straight.

NIAMH (*to Fintan*): Maybe you ought to go after him.

217

FINTAN : Who, me?

NIAMH : It's as black as pitch out, and it's teeming.

GRAINNE (*not too concerned*) : He is nearly eighty.

DERMOD : If he goes over that rise he won't even see the lights of the motel.

USHEEN : He could die of exposure.

NIAMH : Or the wind could blow him over or he could get pneumonia or fall into a . . .

FINTAN : Nag, nag, nag! If we go out there, we could all get lost. I want to talk to James about this interview. (*To Usheen.*) Will we need dress suits?

NIAMH (*upset*) : Fintan !

FINTAN : All right! We'll give the old drunkard twenty minutes. If he's not back by then, I'll drive down to Foxrock, pick up a couple of flashlamps, Wellington boots and raincoats, and we'll go look for him. Fair?

DERMOD : More than fair.

NIAMH : But by then he could be . . .

FINTAN : Don't spoil the evening for us. We won't see him stuck. He was out in nineteen-sixteen . . . he's one of us.

(*Fintan, Usheen, Dermod and Niamh go off upstage right.*

The following is played very fast with speeches overlapping.)

FINTAN : Now about our other motel in Cork . . . The Michael Collins . . .

DERMOD : Hey, we might accept an investment.

USHEEN : Really?

FINTAN : If you're interested.

USHEEN : I could get my hands on twenty thousand.

FINTAN : You're in !

(*Grainne disengages herself from Dermod's arms and comes down to us, again with her warm hostessy smile.*)

GRAINNE : Hello, again. Please don't think we're not worried about Mr . . . I forget his name—because we really are. So, as you can see, money hasn't spoiled us one bit. We're still very humanitarian. And Dermod and I do hope you'll drop in on us—at the motel, that is, not at the house . . . I'm afraid we have so many close friends already. But—and we sincerely mean this—if you happen to be in town and you see our Jensen, do wave to us as you jump clear.

She blows us a kiss.

Curtain

TRELAWNY

A Musical Play

Adapted from A. W. Pinero's *Trelawny of the 'Wells'* by Aubrey Woods, George Rowell and Julian Slade.

Book by Aubrey Woods

Music and Lyrics by Julian Slade

The Bristol Old Vic Company staged *Trelawny* on 12 January 1972 with the following cast:

MR MOSSOP	*Timothy Kightley*
BARKER	*Graham Allum*
HERBERT	*Kenneth Shanley*
ARTHUR GOWER	*John Watts*
MRS MOSSOP	*Veronica Clifford*
TOM WRENCH	*Ian Richardson*
FERDINAND GADD	*Phillip Hinton*
AUGUSTUS COLPOYS	*John Parker*
JAMES TELFER	*Brendan Barry*
MRS TELFER	*Betty Benfield*
WELLS ACTORS	*Robert Lister, Jan Austen*

WELLS STAGE STAFF
Paul Spinetti, Kenneth Shanley, Graham Allum, David Rome, Jeanette Ranger, Carol Hall

MR ABLETT	*Nicholas Loukes*
AVONIA BUNN	*Elizabeth Power*
ROSE TRELAWNY	*Hayley Mills*
SIR WILLIAM GOWER	*Timothy West*

MISS TRAFALGAR GOWER
Rosamund Greenwood

CLARA DE FOENIX	*Jeanette Ranger*
CAPTAIN DE FOENIX	*Paul Spinetti*
CHARLES	*Robert Lister*

THREE LITTLE MAIDS
Jeanette Ranger, Carol Hall, Jan Austen

SIGNOR GIBOLINI	*Nicholas Loukes*
CALL-BOY	*Kenneth Shanley*
PRINCES STAGE MANAGER	*Robert Lister*
PRINCES A.S.M.	*David Rome*
MR HUNSTON	*Paul Spinetti*
MR DENZIL	*Nicholas Loukes*
MISS BREWSTER	*Carol Hall*

Directed by Val May

Assisted by Howard Davies

Musical Director : Neil Rhoden

Choreographer : Bob Stevenson

Designed by Alexander McPherson

Lighting by Jeremy Godden

Orchestration by Neil Rhoden

The production, with some changes in the cast, was staged at Sadler's Wells Theatre, London, on 27 June, 1972.

CHARACTERS

MR MOSSOP

BARKER

HERBERT

ARTHUR GOWER

MRS MOSSOP

TOM WRENCH

FERDINAND GADD

AUGUSTUS COLPOYS

JAMES TELFER

MRS TELFER

WELLS ACTORS

WELLS STAGE STAFF

MR ABLETT

AVONIA BUNN

ROSE TRELAWNY

SIR WILLIAM GOWER

MISS TRAFALGAR GOWER

CLARA DE FOENIX

CAPTAIN DE FOENIX

CHARLES

CAVENDISH SQUARE SERVANTS

LONDON STREET TYPES

THREE LITTLE MAIDS

SIGNOR GIBOLINI

H

CALL-BOY

PRINCES STAGE MANAGER

PRINCES A.S.M.

MR HUNSTON

MR DENZIL

MISS BREWSTER

PRINCES' ACTORS

SCENES

PART ONE

Scene 1. *The Wells Theatre, London*

Scene 2. *Tom Wrench's Letter*

Scene 3. *Cavendish Square*

Scene 4. *The Journey to the Wells*

PART TWO

Scene 1. *Wells Pantomime Prologue*

Scene 2. *Rose's Dressing-Room*

Scene 3. *The Wells Pantomime*

Scene 4. *Rose's Dressing-Room*

Scene 5. *To the Princes*

Scene 6. *The Princes Theatre*

THE SONGS

PART ONE

1. PULL YOURSELF TOGETHER   *The Company*

2. WALKING ON   *Tom and Avonia*

3. EVER OF THEE   *Rose and Arthur*

4. TRELAWNY OF THE WELLS
   Mr and Mrs Telfer and Company

5. QUITE OUT OF PLACE
   Sir William and Miss Gower

6. RULES   *Rose*

7. RULES (Reprise)
   Rose, Tom, Gadd, Colpoys and Avonia

8. BACK TO THE WELLS   *The Company*

PART TWO

9. TEA!   *Three Little Maids*

10. IT'S NOT THE SAME   *Rose*

11. WE CAN'T KEEP 'EM WAITING
    Gadd and Colpoys

12. THE TURN OF AVONIA BUNN   *Avonia*

13. LET'S PEEK IN AT OLD PEKIN   *Chorus*

14. ARTHUR'S LETTER   *Arthur*

15. TWO FOOLS   *Sir William and Rose*

16. 'LIFE'   *Tom*

17. EVER OF THEE (Reprise)   *Rose and Arthur*

18. TRELAWNY OF THE WELLS (Reprise)
    The Company

PART ONE

Scene 1

The Wells Theatre, London.

As the overture ends, the house-lights dim and the Front Curtain of the 'Wells' is revealed. Mr Mossop, the Stage Manager, pokes his head out through the centre opening and addresses the Musical Director in the pit.

MOSSOP : Thank you Mr Grayson. Gentlemen. (*He calls up to the circle.*) All out up there, Barker?

BARKER (*from above*) : All out, Mr Mossop.

MOSSOP (*calling to the back of the stalls*) : All out down there, Herbert?

HERBERT : All except the gent over there, Mr Mossop.

MOSSOP : Over where? (*He sees a figure in full evening-dress standing by the orchestra rail.*) Ah, good evening, Mr Gower, sir. (*Peering.*) It is Mr Gower, ain't it?

ARTHUR : Yes indeed, Mr Mossop, it is I.

MOSSOP : Come on up, sir. Up the steps there. Mind your footing, sir; 'andrail's a bit shaky . . .

ARTHUR (*clambering on to the stage*) : Thank you. Are you sure I shan't be in the way?

MOSSOP : God bless you no, sir. There wouldn't be no party if it weren't for you, Mr Gower. We don't lose a Rose Trelawny every night of the year. (*Calling up to the flies.*) Take your tabs out, Briggs. This way, sir . . .

(*The tabs are flown, revealing the set of* The Pedlar of Marseilles. *One or two stage hands are*

229

*quietly moving pieces of scenery or sweeping the
stage. The gas light is dim.*

Arthur gazes round in wonder.)

MOSSOP : Never been on the stage of the Wells
before, sir?
ARTHUR : No, never. It all appears very—different
—from down there.
MOSSOP (*with the air of one imparting an important
professional secret*) : The magic of the foot-
lights, Mr Gower.
ARTHUR : Ah, yes—of course. Er—Mr Mossop—I
—er—I realize that Mr Telfer may be persuaded
to make a brief speech after the supper tonight—
MOSSOP : Very little persuading needed there, sir.
ARTHUR : I was only hoping that I should not be
expected to follow his example—as Miss Rose's
future husband, I mean.
MOSSOP (*tapping the side of his nose and winking
heavily*) : You never can tell, sir !
ARTHUR : Oh, dear ! I fear I should be a laughing
stock . . .

PULL YOURSELF TOGETHER

*(Mossop, Mrs Mossop, Arthur, Tom, Gadd, Col-
poys, the Telfers and Members of the Wells
Company.)*

*For the first part of this song the accompaniment
creeps in unobtrusively and Mossop half sings,
half speaks his lines.)*

MOSSOP (*ad lib*) : Pull yourself together—sir—
ARTHUR (*speaks*) : I beg your pardon !

230

MOSSOP (*sings*):
Pull yourself together
Pull yourself together
For the Great Event
Now that Miss Trelawny
Is to leave these portals
Much preferring you, sir,
To us lesser mortals
You should have the confidence
To silence chortles
If you are called on
To speak this evening . . .
ARTHUR (*speaks*): Oh, I do hope I won't be—
MOSSOP (*speaks*): All I'm saying, sir, if it *should*
happen—you must
(*Sings.*)
Pull yourself together
Pull yourself together
Speaking should come easy
To a true blue gent—

(*Enter Mrs Mossop, somewhat tearful.*)

'Ere's my lady wife
Whom I believe you knows, sir—
MRS MOSSOP :
I'm the one that used to dress
Your lovely Rose, sir,
Now that the darling is leaving—
Well, that's how it goes, sir—
She really was a splendid pro . . .
MR and MRS MOSSOP :
But now it's our farewell show
For Rose.
ARTHUR :
It's all for Rose !

My darling Rose!

(*Enter Tom Wrench. He still wears part of his costume from* The Pedlar of Marseilles.)

TOM : Rebecca, my loved one!

MRS MOSSOP : Oh, go along with you, Mr Wrench.

TOM : My own, especial Rebecca!

(*He clasps her round the waist.*)

MRS MOSSOP : Now then, Mr Wrench, don't you be so forward. Not in front of Mr Gower here.

TOM : Then I shall reserve my protestations for later, Mossop mine.

MRS MOSSOP : I was just saying that Miss Rose will be sadly missed by us all—

TOM (*to Arthur*) : Oh she will—I assure you, she will. You were in front for *The Pedlar of Marseilles* tonight?

ARTHUR : Of course, Mr Wrench.

TOM : How many times does that make, Mr Gower?

ARTHUR : Fourteen. I am only sorry that I shall never be able to see her as Blanche again.

MRS MOSSOP : Oh don't, sir, don't say that. You'll have her at your side for the rest of your life, but we shall have lost her forever. Forever, Mr Wrench!

(*She bursts into floods of tears on Mossop's shoulder.*)

TOM and MOSSOP (*sing*) :
Pull yourself together!
Pull yourself together!

Quell your lamentations
Till the proper time.

TOM :
Everybody knows you have
A great big heart, dear

MOSSOP :
There's no need to sob it out
Before we start, dear

TOM :
Hecuba was charming, but
It's not your part, dear

BOTH :
Save all the sorrows
And sighs for later—

(*Enter Gadd and Colpoys, laden with provisions for the party, having lowered a glass or two along the way.*)

GADD :
Clear for us to enter !

COLPOYS :
In we move to centre !

GADD :
Loaded up with victuals—

COLPOYS :
And with wine sublime !

MOSSOP :
May I introduce you, sir,
To Gadd and Colpoys?

GADD :
Ever your obedient—

COLPOYS :
But who is this, boys?

MRS MOSSOP :
That's Mister Arthur Gower

233

COLPOYS:
Blow him a kiss, boys!
GADD:
How can the fellow sink so low?
ALL:
When this is our farewell show
For Rose!
ARTHUR:
It's all for Rose!
My darling Rose!

(*Music continues.*)

TOM (*speaks*): Mr Gadd is our leading juvenile man.
GADD: I'm hitting them hard this season, Mr Gower—tomorrow night, Sir Thomas Clifford! They're simply waiting for my Clifford . . .
COLPOYS (*to Arthur*): Kind sir, have you a strawberry mark
Upon one cheek or other?
If so, embrace me, no delay,
I am your long-lost mother!

(*Arthur stares at Colpoys in stark amazement.*)

GADD (*darkly*): Colpoys isn't nearly as funny as he was last year. Everybody's saying so. We want a low comedian badly.
ARTHUR (*breaking away from them*): What have I let myself in for? I could never make a speech to people like these!

(*Arthur now sings in counterpoint to Tom, Gadd, Colpoys, and the Mossops repeating the refrain*

234

sotto voce behind him. During this part of the music, other members of the Company enter to strike parts of the set, bring on tables, etc.)

ARTHUR :	TOM, GADD, etc :
Though near the stage	Pull yourself together
I've often been	Pull yourself together
Now I'm on it	Pull yourself together
I must say	For the Great Event
The stage presents	Now that Miss Trelawny
A diff'rent scene	Is to leave these portals
That's not at all	Much preferring you, sir,
Like any play	To us lesser mortals
It takes my breath !	You should have the confidence
I'm scared to death	To silence chortles
And, but for my Rose,	If you are called on
I would run away.	To speak this evening.

(The music changes to a grandiose march. The Company clear deferentially to allow a majestic entrance for Mr and Mrs Telfer who advance slowly downstage towards Arthur.)

TELFER (*recit.*) :
My friend ! Mr Gower !
I bid you welcome !
My wife—Miss Violet Sylvester—
God rest 'er—
I mean, God bless 'er—
Bids you welcome !
MR and MRS TELFER :
Our Theatre

Bids you welcome!

TELFER:
As you tread these 'allowed boards

MRS TELFER:
You'll realize the tradition

TELFER:
That Rose will leave be'ind 'er

MRS TELFER:
In her marital condition.
Betterton!

TELFER:
Garrick!

MRS TELFER:
Kean!

TELFER:
Macready!

MRS TELFER:
Telfer!

TELFER:
To name but a few—

BOTH:
Now hand over this precious pearl
To you, Mr Gower, to you.

(With deep emotion, he puts both hands on Arthur's shoulders. The Company heave a musical sigh.)

ALL: A-a-a-h!

(Telfer claps his hands with sudden managerial briskness.)

MR and MRS TELFER:
Pull yourselves together!

Pull yourselves together!
Get the tables ready
And the flats away!
Make the stage presentable
And in good order!
Clear the bits and pieces
And remove that border
Prove to Miss Trelawny
We can well afford a
Party that's worthy
Of such an actress!

*(The stage now becomes a hive of activity as the
set is completely cleared and the tables laid out.*

*Mr and Mrs Telfer march round, directing pro-
ceedings.*

*Arthur finds that wherever he stands he is in some-
body's way.)*

MRS TELFER:
Conquer all affliction!
TELFER:
Make this valediction
Something she'll remember
To 'er dying day!
MRS TELFER:
Let me see a happy smile
On all your faces
TELFER:
Please be'ave like gentlemen
And 'oist your braces
MRS TELFER:
Any of you who are ladies

Tighten your laces
BOTH :
And strive to make the party go
For this is our Farewell Show
For Rose !

(*Some of the stage staff take a counter-part, as the Company follows the Telfers bidding:*)

COMPANY :	A.S.M.'S :
Now the time has come for us to—	
Pull ourselves together !	Although we seldom
Pull ourselves together !	Take the stage
Get the tables ready	We often take
And the flats away !	The stage away
Make the stage presentable	While leading actors
And in good order	Rant and rage
Clear the bits and pieces	We work and work
And remove that border	That they may play
Prove to Miss Trelawny	Tonight at least
We can well afford a	At Rose's feast
Party that's worthy	We've just as important
Of such an actress	A part as they

ALL :
Conquer all affliction !
Make this valediction
Something she'll remember
To her dying day

We must put a happy smile
On all our faces
GIRLS :
Please behave like gentlemen
And hoist your braces
MEN :
Any of you who are ladies
Tighten your laces
ALL :
We have to make the party go
For this is our Farewell Show—
This is our Farewell Show—
This is our Farewell Show
For Rose !

TELFER : Ladies and gentlemen, your attention pray ! Let us mummers quit this scene and leave it in the 'ands of those who will transform it into a banqueting hall for our dear departing. When all is prepared, we shall descend from our tiring rooms and partake of the cold collation.

ALL : Bravo !

MOSSOP (*to Arthur*) : If you'll place yourself in my 'ands, Mr Gower, I'll find you somewhere to 'ide until (*He taps his nose.*)—the celebrations.

(*They all disperse, leaving the Stage Hands to complete the preparations for the supper. Tom and Mrs Mossop remain.*)

MRS MOSSOP : Aren't you off to change for the feast then, Mr Wrench.

TOM : No need, sweet Mossop, no need. I shall merely remove the trappings . . .

(*He rapidly takes the bandana from his head and*

239

*dons it as a necktie, removes his waistcoat, reverses
it, and puts it on again, takes off his curtain-ring
earrings and pulls his trouser legs out of his socks.)*

And don my 'one and only' . . .

(He puts on the coat he has over his arm.)

MRS MOSSOP : You look very nice, Mr Wrench.
TOM : False, dear Mossop . . . kind but false. I stand
desperately in need of a little skilful trimming at
your fair hands.
MRS MOSSOP *(produces scissors and sets about his
frayed cuffs)* : First it's patching a coat, and then
it's binding an Inverness—sometimes I wonder
where I find time for my duties in the wardrobe.
TOM : But what of your duties to me, heartless
Rebecca?
MRS MOSSOP : Do be quiet and hold still, Mr
Wrench. I can't stand 'ere all day, you know. I
'ave to go and keep cavey over Miss Rose, if she's
not to come rushing down, poor thing, and spoil
the surprise farewell.

*(Tom obediently proffers both cuffs, and stands
stock still.*

*Ablett, laden with groceries, appears through the
stage-door, and is nearly felled by a stage hand
carrying a cardboard tree.)*

ABLETT : 'Ave a care, there!
TOM : Aha! Provisions for the feast—borne aloft
by the eminent greengrocer himself!

MRS MOSSOP : Just put them on the table, if you'd be so kind, Mr Ablett.

TOM : Taking care to place the wizened apples behind the rosy ones as usual.

ABLETT : Presumpshus!

MRS MOSSOP : Didn't you see Miss Rose in her farewell then, Mr Ablett?

ABLETT : Wot do you take me for, Mrs Mossop? Hof course I did. Marrying a non-professional gentleman they give out, ma'am.

MRS MOSSOP : Yes.

ABLETT : Name of Glover.

TOM (*glowering*) : Gower.

MRS MOSSOP : Grandson of Vice-Chancellor Sir William Gower.

ABLETT : You don't say, Ma'am!

MRS MOSSOP : No father nor mother, and lives in Cavendish Square with the old judge and a great-aunt.

ABLETT : So Miss Trelawny quits the profession, ma'am, for good and all, I presoom?

MRS MOSSOP : Yes Ablett. She played tonight for the last time—the last time on any stage. (*She bursts into torrents of tears.*)

ABLETT (*embarrassed*) : Er—when is the weddin' to be, Mr Wrench?

TOM : Not yet decided. In point of fact, before the distinguished family give a positive seal of approval to the union, Miss Trelawny is to make her home with them for a short term—their own expression—to habituate herself to the rarified atmosphere of the West End; far from the rotting cabbage leaves we know so well!

ABLETT : Her leaving will make all the difference to the old Wells. The season'll terminate abrupt, then the company'll be hout, Mr Wrench—hout sir!

TOM : Which will lighten the demand for the spongy turnip and the watery marrow, my poor Ablett.

ABLETT (*with malice aforethought*): Wos you in the piece tonight, Mr Wrench?

TOM : As much as I am ever in any of the pieces in this theatre, yes, I was.

ABLETT : Ah, I must 'ave glanced away at that moment. Another small part, I take it, Mr Wrench?

TOM (*heavily*): You take it correctly, Mr Ablett.

MRS MOSSOP (*now recovered*): Ah well! Somebody must play the bad parts in this world, on and off the stage. There (*Putting away her scissors.*) there's no more edge left to fray; we've come to the soft.

(*Tom snatches the scissors from her and points them at his breast.*)

Ah! don't do that!

TOM : You are right, sweet Mossop, I won't perish on an empty stomach. But tell me (*Taking her aside.*) shall I disgrace the feast, eh? Is my appearance too scandalously seedy?

MRS MOSSOP : Not *it*, my dear.

TOM : Miss Trelawny, do you think she'll regard me as a blot on the banquet? Do you Beccy?

MRS MOSSOP : She? La! Don't distress yourself. She'll be far too excited to notice you.

TOM : H'm yes. Now I recollect, she has always been that. Thanks, Beccy.

(*Avonia bursts onto the stage from Rose's dressing room.*)

AVONIA : Tom Wrench, what do you think you're up to? Standing there as if tomorrow will do. There's Rose, poor dear, crying her eyes out, and the table's not even laid. Come along, now! Come along!

TOM : But whom do I see—can it be—surely not—but yes! Our one and only singing parlourmaid—*the* Miss Avonia Bunn! (*He bows low.*)

AVONIA : Oh, shut up, Tom Wrench.

(*She daps at her eyes with a handkerchief and turns to Mrs Mossop.*)

Rose will be down in about five minutes, Mrs Mossop : maybe you'd better go and keep your eye on her, and give the warning *when*.

MRS MOSSOP : Very well, dearie. Come along, Mr Ablett.

(*Mrs Mossop and Ablett go out.*)

TOM : Have you been crying, Vonia?

AVONIA : No, Tom Wrench, I haven't, and if I have I can't help it! Rose and I have chummed together all this season and part of last, and—oh it's a hateful profession! The moment you make a friend—(*She bursts into tears.*)

TOM : I hereby give due warning that if there's any more weeping I shall don my hat with the feathers.

AVONIA : Oh, Tom!

TOM : It never ceases to amuse the gallery boys, so why not you?

243

AVONIA : You can make fun—but I shall miss her terribly. It just won't be the same. Imagine the 'Pedlar' with a—stranger singing her song on the bridge . . .

TOM : No thank you Vonia—I'd rather not.

AVONIA : You're supposed to be a playwright, Tom —can't you say something to cheer me up?

TOM : My plays never cheer anyone up.

AVONIA : Well at least help me with the table. Bring those chairs over—and hurry up, she'll be here any minute . . .

TOM : Just a moment. (*Removing his coat.*) I don't want to get myself dishevelled—

AVONIA : Still anxious to make an impression— even down to the last?

TOM : Now, Vonia—

AVONIA (*kindly*) : Oh, Tom! It's no good your being sweet on her any longer, surely?

(*Pause.*)

TOM : Let us just say I shall miss her as much as you—

(*He brings the chairs to the table.*)

AVONIA : We're a fine pair, I must say. There's Rose, only nineteen years old, and soon she'll be ordering about her own powdered footmen and playing on her grand piano—and what will we be doing?

BOTH (*in chorus*) : General Utility !

AVONIA (*mock curtsey*) : Singing Parlourmaid—

TOM (*mock bow*) : Walking Gentleman. Oh, the frustration of it all . . . ! Still carrying a spear after ten years !

AVONIA : And in another ten years?
TOM : I'll be exactly where I am now.

WALKING ON

AVONIA :
Still no name in lights, Tom Wrench?
TOM :
    Still!
AVONIA :
Still darning your tights, Tom Wrench?
TOM :
    Still!
Still walking on in the same old wig—
AVONIA :
The one with the ringlets? Oh that's a pig!
TOM :
But still it's the time-honoured, much-loved rig
That my friends in the gallery
Recognize me by.
AVONIA :
But you will still write those plays you write?
TOM :
    Still!
AVONIA :
Well one of these days they might—
TOM :
    Oh yes they will!
    But until that day—until . . .
I'll be known to the public
As 'That Wrench man—
The one who played the courtier
Or was it the henchman?'
I'll be a walking gentleman
Walking still.
    Walking on

Walking on
This is the life
At the bottom of the bill
Years after Rose has gone
I shall be walking on
Walking, walking,
Listening to talking
Walking on
Still.

BOTH :
Walking on
Walking on
That's how it is
When you're runners-of-the-mill
Years after Rose has gone
We shall be walking on
Walking, walking
Listening to talking
Walking on
Still.

TOM (*speaks*): And what about you, Vonia? Will things be any better for you, in ten years time?

AVONIA : I don't expect so, Tom.

TOM :
Still playing the parlourmaid?

AVONIA :
    Still !

TOM :
Still getting the table laid?

AVONIA :
    Still !

Still walking on with my cap in place—

TOM :
A bright little smile lighting up your face

AVONIA :
To show I am 'naughty' and yet 'quaite naice'

246

And to make sure that I shall be
Seen if never heard

TOM :

But you will still have the pantomime

AVONIA :

    Still !

TOM :

That's always your chance to shine

AVONIA :

    And shine I will !
    But until that day—until . . .

I am doomed to be cast
As a humble servant
A nothing sort of mumble—
Grumble servant
I'll be a saucy parlourmaid
Saucing still.

BOTH :

Walking on
Walking on
This is the life
At the bottom of the bill
Years after Rose has gone
We shall be walking on
Walking, walking
Listening to talking
Walking on
Still.
Walking on
Walking on
Soldiering on
Going at it with a will
Years after Rose has gone
We shall be walking on

TOM :

Minding—

AVONIA :
Minding—
TOM :
The agony is blinding
BOTH :
But we shall be walking
Listening to talking
Walking, walking
Walking, walking
Walking on
Still.

(*As Tom and Avonia go out at the end of the number, the lights dim and the stage is empty for a moment. Then a dressing-room door at the back of the stage opens, casting a shaft of light down to where a bouquet of roses lies, left there since Arthur handed them up to Rose at the end of her farewell. Rose enters from the dressing room, and is framed in the door as she turns back to speak to someone inside.*)

ROSE : I must go and find my flowers, Mrs Mossop. I shan't be a minute.
MRS MOSSOP (*off*) : All right, Rose dear . . .

(*Rose's shadow is cast across the deserted stage, as she walks slowly down to where the bouquet is lying, and picks it up.*

She takes a long last look round the theatre—the stalls, the circle, the gallery, and after a long pause, turns abruptly, and makes for the stage door. At this, Arthur steps out into Rose's view, and she runs headlong into his arms, half laughing, half crying.)

248

ARTHUR : Rose!
ROSE : Oh, Arthur, my dearest, dearest Arthur! Where has everyone gone? I did say goodbye to them all, but I thought ...

(*Arthur hands her his handkerchief.*)

ARTHUR : The carriage will be here soon, Rose.
ROSE : We'd better wait at the stage door, then. (*She wipes her eyes.*) Forgive me, my love—but I did just want to see them all for the last time ...
ARTHUR : I know.

(*He gives her his arm and they turn and walk towards the stage door. Suddenly they are surrounded by a flickering circle of candles, as the entire cast appear from hiding with Telfer at the centre.*)

ALL (*singing quietly*) :
This is our Farewell Show—
This is our Farewell Show—
This is our Farewell Show
For Ro-o-ose!
ROSE (*breathless*) : Oh, I can't believe it!
TELFER : You surely didn't expect us to let you make your last appearance to an empty house, Rose!
ROSE : Oh, Arthur, you knew!

(*The stage is flooded with light and colour, as Rose is surrounded by all her friends. Everyone in turn greets her, except Tom, who just gazes.*)

TELFER (*embracing her*) : Blessings on you, my child!

249

MRS TELFER (*kissing her*) : Sweet lamb—be happy!
TELFER : Ladies and Gentlemen—fill your glasses
—let the festivities commence!

(*They move upstage to drink round the table, leaving Rose and Avonia together.*)

AVONIA : Well, Rose, the moment's come! Are
you nervous?
ROSE : No, Vonia—because I know this is my fate!
Mother often used to stare into my face when I
was little and whisper, 'Rosie, I wonder what is
to be your—fate.' Poor mother! I hope she
sees.
AVONIA (*admiringly*) : Your Arthur is lovely.
ROSE : Oh, he's a dear. Very young, of course—
but he'll grow manly in time, and have moustaches
and whiskers out to here, he says.
AVONIA : What luck he saw you in 'The Pedlar'.
ROSE : It was the song that sealed my destiny,
Arthur declares—
AVONIA (*singing quietly*) :
'Ever of thee I'm fondly dreaming . . .'
ROSE : Do you remember the flowers he sent the
next day . . . ?
AVONIA : And his first visit to the stage door—how
excited we were!
ROSE : Of course, I never spoke to him, never even
glanced at him. Poor mother brought me up that
way, not to speak to anybody, nor look.
AVONIA : Quite right.
ROSE : I do hope she sees.

(*Mrs Mossop and Ablett enter carrying trays of food.*)

250

MRS MOSSOP : Take your places please, Ladies and Gentlemen! Supper is served!

(*Colpoys takes the pigeon pie and puts it on his head.*)

ABLETT (*convulsed with laughter*): Oh, Mr Colpoys! Oh, really, sir! Ho, dear!

MRS TELFER : Yes, Augustus Colpoys, you are extremely humorous *off*.

COLPOYS (*stung*): Mrs Telfer!

MRS TELFER : *On* the stage, sir, you are enough to make a cat weep.

(*Colpoys retreats, muttering.*)

AVONIA : Well, God bless you, Rose. I'm afraid *I* couldn't give up the stage, not for all the Arthurs—

ROSE : Ah, but your mother wasn't an actress.

AVONIA : No.

ROSE : Mine was, and I remember her saying to me once, 'Rose, if ever a good man comes along, and offers to marry you and take you off the stage, seize the chance—get out of it.'

AVONIA : Your mother was never popular, was she?

ROSE : Yes, indeed she was—till she grew oldish and lost her looks.

TELFER : Ladies and Gentlemen, I beg you to be seated.

(*There is a general movement towards the table.*)

Miss Trelawny will sit 'ere, on my right. On my left, my friend Mr Gower will sit.

(The Company sit down, and the meal is eaten in a great atmosphere of confusion and hubbub.)

GADD *(to Avonia)*: Telfer takes the chair, you observe. Why he—more than myself, for instance.

AVONIA: He's the oldest man present.

GADD: True. And he's beginning to age in his acting too. His H's! Scarce as pearls!

AVONIA: Hush Ferdy.

GADD: And he's losing all his teeth. To act with him makes the house seem half empty.

TELFER: Mr Gower, sir, follow the advice of one who has sat at many a good man's feast—Have a little 'am.

ARTHUR: Thank you sir.

AVONIA *(throwing her wrap to Colpoys)*: Gus! Catch! Put it on the sofa, there's a good boy.

(Colpoys swathes himself in the wrap, and minces across to the wings. Ablett is convulsed with laughter.)

ABLETT: Oh don't, Mr Colpoys. I shan't easily forget this night, Mr Telfer. Ho, ho. Oh dear, oh dear!

(Telfer rises.)

TELFER *(banging the table for attention)*: Friends, Romans, fellow actors, lend me your ears. I 'ave devoted some time to the preparation of a list of toasts. I now 'old that list in my hand. I give you —*(To Colpoys.)* the ale is with you, Colpoys—

COLPOYS: Here you are, Telfer.

TELFER: I give you The Queen, coupled with the name of Miss Violet Sylvester—Mrs Telfer. Miss Sylvester has so frequently impersonated the various queens of tragedy that I cannot but feel she is a fitting person to acknowledge our expression of loyalty. The Queen and Miss Violet Sylvester.

(*All rise, except Mrs Telfer and drink the toast.*)

MRS TELFER (*heavily*) : Ladies and gentlemen, I have played fourteen or fifteen queens in my time . . .

TELFER : Thirteen, my love, to be exact. I was calculating this morning.

MRS TELFER : Very well, I have played thirteen of 'em. And as parts they are not worth a tinker's oath. I thank you for the favour with which you have received me.

TELFER : Ladies and gentlemen, Bumpers I charge ye ! I now give you what we may justly designate the toast of the evening. We are about to lose, to part with, one of our companions.

AVONIA (*with a sob*) : I detested her at first.

COLPOYS : Order.

TELFER : Miss Rose Trelawny—for I will no longer conceal from you that it is to 'er I refer—

(*Loud applause.*)

Rose is a good girl—(*More applause.*) a good girl—

MRS TELFER (*rising and clutching a knife*) : Yes, and I should like to hear anybody, man or woman—!

TELFER : She is a good girl, and will long be remembered by us. But now, what has happened to 'the expectancy and Rose of the fair state'?

GADD (*aside*) : Tsch, tsch, forced, forced !

TELFER : I will tell you—a man has crossed her path.

ABLETT : Shame !

ALL : Sssh !

TELFER : A man—ah, but also a gentleman. That gentleman, with the modesty of youth—for I may tell you at once that 'e is not an old man—comes to us and asks us to give him this girl to wife. And, friends, we have done so. May they—I can wish them no greater joy—be as happy in their married life—as Miss Sylvester and I 'ave been in ours ! Miss Rose Trelawny—Mr Arthur Gower !

THE COMPANY (*heartily*) : Miss Rose Trelawny ! (*Politely.*) Mr Arthur Gower.

(*Three cheers are asked for by Colpoys, and given.*)

TELFER : Miss Trelawny.

ROSE (*weeping*) : No, no, Mr Telfer.

MRS TELFER (*to Telfer, softly*) : Let her be for a minute, James.

TELFER : Mr Gower.

ARTHUR : Oh no—I—er—oh !

GADD : A reply there ! A reply !

TELFER : Be upstanding, Mr Gower.

AVONIA : Isn't he handsome ?

(*Gadd glowers.*)

ALL : Come now ! A speech ! Words from Mr Gower.

ABLETT (*resolving the situation*) : Silence for Mr Glover !

ARTHUR (*rises*) : Ladies and gentlemen, I—I would I were endowed with Mr Telfer's flow of—of—of splendid eloquence. But I am no orator, no

254

speaker, and therefore cannot tell you how highly
—how deeply I appreciate the—the compliment—

ABLETT : You deserve it, Mr Glover.

MRS MOSSOP : Hush!

ARTHUR : All I can say is that I regard Miss
Trelawny in the light of a—a solemn charge and
I—I trust that if I ever have the pleasure of—of
meeting any of you again, I shall be able to render
a good—a—a—satisfactory—satisfactory—

TOM (*in an audible whisper*) : Account.

ARTHUR : Account of the way in which—of the way
—in which—in which I—

(*Loud applause.*)

Before I bring these observations to a conclusion,
let me assure you that it has been a great privilege
to me to meet—to have been thrown with—a band
of artists—whose talents—whose striking talents—
whose talents—

TOM (*kindly, behind his hand*) : Sit down.

ARTHUR : Whose talents not only interest and
instruct the—the more refined residents of this
district, but whose talents—

AVONIA (*quietly to Colpoys*) : Get him to sit down.

ARTHUR : The fame of whose talents, I should say—

COLPOYS (*quietly to Mrs Mossop*) : He's to sit
down. Tell Mother Telfer.

ARTHUR : The fame of whose talents has spread to
—to regions—

MRS MOSSOP (*quietly to Mrs Telfer*) : They say he's
to sit down.

ARTHUR : To—to quarters of the town—to
quarters—

MRS TELFER (*to Arthur*) : Sit down.

ARTHUR : Eh?

MRS TELFER : You finished long ago. Sit down.
ARTHUR : Thank you. I'm exceedingly sorry. I knew! I knew! Great Heavens, how wretchedly I've done it! (*He sits. Vast applause.*)
TELFER : Rose, my child.

(*Rose rises to cheers and general excitement. Avonia runs to the piano and strikes up 'Ever of Thee'.*)

ROSE : Mr Telfer! Mrs Telfer! My friends! Boys! Ladies and Gentlemen . . .

(*Avonia stops playing.*)

No, don't stop, Vonia! Go on! Let it be my last memory of the Wells! My song in *The Pedlar of Marseilles* . . . (*Softly, looking at Arthur.*) The song which made Arthur fall in love with me . . .
ALL : Bravo! Encore! Encore!

(*They cheer her and thump the table, demanding the song.*)

EVER OF THEE

ROSE :
Ever of thee
I'm fondly dreaming
Dreaming of thee
My heart takes wing.
Under the moon
So palely gleaming
Ever of thee
I love to sing!
Singing of thee
I'm all-adoring

Suddenly Love
Has set me free
Far as the stars
My heart is soaring
Ever, my love,
To thee.

(*As she repeats the refrain, Arthur, more fluent in
song than in speech, sings to the assembled
Company—*)

ROSE :   ARTHUR :
Ever of thee
I'm fondly dreaming   The moment I heard
                                      her sing that song
Dreaming of thee   I knew
My heart takes wing   She'd be the only girl
                                      I'd ever love
Under the moon   And now we are
So palely gleaming   To be wed
Ever of thee   Ever with her
I love to sing   I shall be able to sing

(*He joins her, on the bridge, while the Company
hum quietly in the background.*)

ROSE and ARTHUR :
Singing of thee
I'm all adoring
Suddenly Love
Has set me free
Far as the stars
My heart is soaring
ALL :
Ever my love
To thee!

(*At the end, there is a pause, while Rose looks round at the Company in the flickering candlelight with tears in her eyes.*)

ROSE : I know I shall dream of you, of all of you, very often as the song says. Don't believe, (*Wiping away her tears.*) oh, don't believe that, because I shall have married a swell, you and the old Wells —the dear Old Wells !—

(*Cheers.*)

You and the old Wells will have become nothing to me. No, many and many a night you will see me in the house, looking down at you from the Circle, me and my husband—
ARTHUR : Yes, yes, certainly !
ROSE (*with open arms*) : And if you send for me I'll come behind the curtain to you, and sit with you and talk of bygone times, these times that end today. And shall I tell you the moments which will be the happiest to me in my life, however happy I may be with Arthur? Why, whenever I find that I'm recognized by people, and pointed out —people in the pit of a theatre, in the street, no matter where, and when I can fancy they're saying to each other, 'Look, that was Miss Trelawny! You remember Trelawny—Trelawny of the Wells !—'
ALL (*cheering and crying wildly*) : Trelawny ! Trelawny of the Wells !

TELFER :
Rose Trelawny !
Trelawny of the Wells !

The Wells wishes you well
In your new life
Among the swells.
MRS TELFER:
Now as you leave the Wells, Trelawny,
The lights begin to dim
BOTH:
But if you love the man
You are leaving us for
Then we wish you joy of him
TELFER:
Remembering the joy you gave us
When you were our Trelawny
BOTH:
Our one and only Rose Trelawny
Trelawny of the Wells!

(*Suddenly, Herbert, from the front of house, dashes down the aisle of the orchestra rail, wildly gesticulating.*

Music continues.)

HERBERT: Mr Telfer! The carriage is here, sir!
TELFER: If you have tears, prepare to shed them now. Rose, my dear, your carriage awaits.

(*Goodbyes and tears in profusion are showered upon Rose and Arthur as they go across the bridge into the stalls and up the aisle. The Company masses on the front of the stage and everybody from the Wardrobe Mistress to the Callboy takes up the refrain of—*

TRELAWNY OF THE WELLS (second time)

Rose and Arthur arrive at the back entrance to the stalls, and as they turn a large painted cloth descends from the flies on stage to wish them good luck, especially created by the Wells scene painters.)

ROSE *(calling)*: Thank you! Thank you, my dear friends! Goodbye!

(She takes Arthur's arm and they run out together as the Company waves a final farewell and the song comes to a finish. The Company now disperses, quietly singing:

TRELAWNY OF THE WELLS (third time)

Leaving Tom to finish the refrain alone, sadly watching the cloth as it flies out.)

Scene 2

TOM WRENCH'S LETTER

(As the cloth disappears, Tom turns, and walks slowly back to the centre of the stage, which is now a completely empty, dimly lit void. Empty, that is, save for a wooden chair with a pad of paper and a pen on it. He picks them up, sits down, opens the pad, and starts to write.)

TOM: March the sixteenth, eighteen sixty-four. My dear Rose. The two weeks since you left the Wells a sadder and an emptier place everything has managed to go on much as usual. Telfer's court-room exit as Shylock, achieved, on Wednesday last, the unprecedented length of two and a half minutes, timed by Mossop and his infallible hunter. Such malevolent glances and such snarls of defiance can, I am certain, never before have been witnessed. I heard Gadd remark to Colpoys that it was even longer than his death scene as Richard III, but, as Colpoys pointed out, not half as comic.

Apart from this ray of rather wintry sunshine, nothing of note has happened to brighten our lives . . . except that I have started yet another play— doomed, I am sure, to moulder with the rest of the rejected manuscripts in my already groaning cupboard . . . (*He looks up and gazes into space for a moment.*) But one of these days, dear Rose, one of these days, I'll show those timorous managers that they are wrong, and that those people out there—that great, faceless, hubbub we call the audience—will accept characters that behave like people, and scenery that looks like the real thing. I think (*He crosses this out.*) I *know* that when you read this letter, you will be sitting in just the kind of chamber that I want for the first act of my comedy. I won't have doors stuck here, there, and everywhere, nor windows in all sorts of impossible places . . .

(*As the speech proceeds, and as each item in Tom's letter is mentioned, it appears on the stage, just where he says, and as the light on each new piece of scenery grows, the stage gradually becomes the Gower's drawing room in Cavendish Square.*)

TOM : I'll have the windows in one wall and the doors in the others, just where they should be, architecturally. And locks on the doors—real locks, to work. And handles to turn. And the pillars in my room will look as if they support the ceiling, and are not there just to hide the gaslights. And the sky outside will look like a sky, not like a painted backcloth.

(*Light grows on the cyclorama.*)

And the light will come in through the windows, not from where the lime-lights just happen to be.

(*Sunlight streams in through the windows.*)

And when evening falls, my room will be lit by a chandelier that works—

(*Chandelier comes in and glows with light.*)

And at night, there will be a real moon in my sky, and real moonlight will cast its shadows across my stage.

(*Lights fade to a dim, moonlit sky, with the stage in darkness. He breaks down to the pros. arch.*)

And the words I have written will not be declaimed —will not be ranted—will not be sobbed out for the sake of squeezing meaningless applause from an audience that has lived far too long with the cardboard heroes of the Wells. Because above all Rose—oh! my dearest Rose—the people in my plays will be ALIVE!

(*Tom storms offstage, leaving his creation of Cavendish Square behind him.*

Scene 3

CAVENDISH SQUARE

*Immediately after Tom's exit the lights come up
to reveal Sir William Gower asleep under a newspaper, Miss Trafalgar Gower asleep under a handkerchief, Captain de Foenix asleep leaning against
the wall, Clara engaged, but very quietly, upon
some crochet work, Arthur sitting, gazing at his
boots, his hands in his pockets, and Rose, hands
clenched, sitting on a stool, staring despairingly at
nothing. As Tom's cry of 'ALIVE!' rings out, the
music which has built throughout the transformation stops dead, and all we hear is the slow tick-
ing of a grandfather clock. After a moment or
two, Arthur rises and tiptoes down to Rose.*

ARTHUR : Quiet, isn't it?

ROSE : Quiet! Arthur—Oh, this dreadful half
hour after dinner, every, *every* evening.

ARTHUR : Grandfather and Aunt Trafalgar must
wake up soon : they're longer than usual tonight.

ROSE : Your sister Clara over there and Captain
de Foenix—When they were courting, did they
have to go through this?

ARTHUR : Yes.

ROSE : And now that they are married they still
endure it?

ARTHUR : Yes.

ROSE : And we, when *we* are married, Arthur, shall
we . . .

ARTHUR : Yes, I suppose so.

ROSE : Phew!

263

(*De Foenix, fast asleep, is in danger of toppling over. Clara rescues him just in time.*)

CLARA : Ah! Frederick, no, no, no!
DE FOENIX : Oh! Who—What?
CLARA : Frederick dear, awake.
DE FOENIX (*dazed*) : How did this occur?
CLARA : You were tottering, and I caught you.
DE FOENIX : I wemember. I placed myself in an upwight position my deawest, to pwevent myself dozing.
CLARA : How you alarmed me!

(*Rose laughs, quietly.*)

DE FOENIX : Might have been a vewy sewious accident, Miss Twelawny.
ROSE : Never mind. (*Sitting on a footstool.*) Sit down and talk.

(*De Foenix looks at the old people and shakes his head.*)

Oh! do, do, do sit down and let us all have a jolly whisper.

(*A barrel organ can be heard in the square below, and the tune is now distinguishable as 'Ever of Thee'.*)

Hark! (*Excitedly.*) Hark!
CLARA
ARTHUR } (*together*) : Hush!
DE FOENIX
ROSE : That's the song I sang in the 'Pedlar'—

The Pedlar of Marseilles. The song that used to make you cry, Arthur—!

(*They try to hush her down, but she goes on in hoarse, dramatic whispers.*)

And then Raphael enters—comes on to the bridge. The music continues, softly. 'Raphael, why have you kept me waiting? Man, do you wish to break my heart—(*Thumping her breast.*) a woman's hear-r-rt, Raphael?'

(*The old people awake violently.*)

SIR WILLIAM : What a hideous riot, Trafalgar.

MISS GOWER : Rose dear, I hope I have been mistaken—but through my sleep I fancied I could hear you shrieking at the top of your voice.

SIR WILLIAM : Trafalgar, it is becoming impossible for you and me to obtain repose. Ha! Is that not a street organ?

MISS GOWER : Undoubtedly. An organ in the square at this hour of the evening—singularly out of place!

SIR WILLIAM : Well, well, well, does no one stir?

ROSE (*under her breath*) : Oh don't stop it.

(*Clara goes out*)

SIR WILLIAM (*to Rose*) : What are ye upon the floor for, my dear? Have we no cheers? Do we lack cheers here, Trafalgar?

MISS GOWER : My dear Rose, come, come, come, this is quite out of place! Young ladies do not crouch and huddle upon the ground, do they William?

SIR WILLIAM (*taking snuff*): A moment ago I should have hazarded the opinion that they did not.

(*Clara returns.*)

CLARA : Charles was just running out to stop the organ when I reached the hall, Grand-pa.

SIR WILLIAM : Ye'd surely no intention, Clara, of venturing yourself into the public street—the open Square—?

CLARA (*faintly*): I meant only to wave at the man from the door—

MISS GOWER : Oh, Clara, that would hardly have been in place!

SIR WILLIAM : In mercy's name, Trafalgar, what is befalling my household?

MISS GOWER (*bursting into tears*): Oh William!

SIR WILLIAM : Tut, tut, tut, tut.

MISS GOWER (*aside to him*): I—I—I—know what is in your mind.

SIR WILLIAM : Ah-h-h-h!

MISS GOWER : But do not despond already! I feel sure there are good ingredients in Rose's character. In time, William, we shall shape her to be a fitting wife for our rash and unfortunate Arthur—in time, William, in time!

SIR WILLIAM : Well, well, well. There, there, there. At least, my dear sister, I am perfectly aweer that I possess in you the woman above all others whose example should compel such a transformation.

MISS GOWER : Oh brother, what a compliment.

SIR WILLIAM : Even though my hopes for Rose's translation from her gypsy upbringing to our own sphere are sadly dwindling.

ROSE : I do wish you wouldn't all talk about me as if I were not here !

MISS GOWER : Oh Rose, that remark was very out of place.

SIR WILLIAM : Miss Trelawny, have no fear that we are—any of us—unaweer of your presence in this house. Be seated !

QUITE OUT OF PLACE

SIR WILLIAM (*recit.*) :
Now Rose, I fear, I must perform
A disagreeable duty
We know you have a heart that's warm
And some degree of beauty
But when it comes to Modes and Codes
And Rules of Good Behaviour
It will not do
To muddle through
Relying on what God gave 'yer—
(*Refrain*) :
When you speak to a servant
Pray be careful
To guard the expression on your face
To address a menial
With a countenance too genial
Is Quite—Out—Of—Place
(*To Trafalgar.*)
Is it not?

TRAFALGAR :
Quite distressingly Out of Place !

(*Rose laughs.*)

SIR WILLIAM :
You may think you charm us

With your laughter
But that, Rose, I fear is not the case
To express hilarity
With an unconfined vulgarity
Is Quite—Out—Of—Place
(*To Trafalgar.*)
Don't ye think?

TRAFALGAR :
Quite depressingly Out of Place !

(*Rose slumps.*)

(*To Sir William.*)
She ought to pay attention
To her posture
Her carriage is often a disgrace
And her strange capacity (*Rose rises suddenly.*)
For unwarranted vivacity
Can come as quite a shock
And is so *very* out of place—

SIR WILLIAM :
In short, Rose, we realize
You're a gypsy
With most of the instincts of your race
But to one who's your superior
Vagabond hysteria
Seems Quite—(*To Trafalgar.*) wouldn't ye say?—

TRAFALGAR :
Oh I would !

SIR WILLIAM :
Am I right?

TRAFALGAR :
Indeed you're right—

BOTH :
It is Quite
Out of Place.

(*Music continues under dialogue.*)

ARTHUR : Grandfather, perhaps Rose does not fully understand—

SIR WILLIAM : Then it is up to ye to instruct her.

ARTHUR : But, sir—Since you have thought it proper for me to lodge with Clara and Captain de Foenix during Rose's stay in Cavendish Square—

SIR WILLIAM : The only decorous course to pursue under the peculiar circumstances.

ARTHUR : But I do feel I might be allowed ocassionally to see Rose alone as we now have no opportunity for confidential conversation.

SIR WILLIAM (*to Arthur*) : No?—
They tell me you come
A-troubadouring
Well sir, be you tenor, be you bass,
These nocturnal frolickings
These merry midnight rollickings
Are Quite—Out—of—Place
(*To Trafalgar.*)
Are they not?

TRAFALGAR :
Irretrievably (I fear) Out of Place !

ROSE (*in defiance*) :
What of it if he stands there
By the railings
To sing—

ARTHUR :
and to glimpse her lovely face?

SIR WILLIAM (*to Rose*) :
If you think he's Romeo
Then, Juliet, I'd have you know
Your balcony appearances
Are scarcely quite in place.
(*To Arthur.*)

269

As for you, sir, your moonlight
Serenadings
Make *this* fiery steed gallop apace !
And I tell you categoric'lly—
Rhetoric'lly—(*Pause, then with heavy sarcasm at Rose.*)
Alas poor Yorick'lly—
These trysts in the night
Are a blight
And are Quite—(*To Clara.*)
Wouldn't ye say ?

CLARA :
Oh I would !

SIR WILLIAM (*to de Foenix*) :
Am I right ?

DE FOENIX :
Indeed you're wight !

ALL :
They are Quite—
Out of Place !

(*Charles enters.*)

CHARLES : The card table, Sir William ?
MISS GOWER : Yes, yes, by all means, Charles, the card table as usual. (*To Sir William.*) A rubber will comfort you, soothe you—

(*Rose draws Arthur aside.*)

ROSE (*in undertones*) : Infamous ! Infamous !
ARTHUR : Be calm, Rose dear, be calm.
ROSE : Tyrannical ! Diabolical ! I cannot endure it !
ARTHUR : They mean well, dearest—
ROSE (*hysterically*) : Well ! ! Ha, ha, ha !

270

ARTHUR: But they are rather old fashioned people—

ROSE: Old fashioned!—they belong to the time when men and women were put to the torture. I am being tortured—mentally tortured—

ARTHUR: They have not many more years in this world—

ROSE: Nor I, at this rate, many more months. They are killing me—like Agnes in *The Spectre of St Ives*. She expires in the fourth act, as I shall die in Cavendish Square, painfully, of no recognized disorder—

ARTHUR: And anything we can do to make them happy—

ROSE: To make the Vice Chancellor happy! I won't try. I will not! He's a fiend—a vampire—

ARTHUR: Oh hush!

ROSE (*snatching up Sir William's snuff box*): His snuff box. I wish I could poison his snuff, as Lucrezia Borgia would have done. *She* would have removed him within two hours of my arrival—I mean her arrival. And here he sits and dictates to me—to Miss Trelawny! (*Taking snuff.*) Have we no cheers? Do we lack cheers here Trafalgar? (*Suddenly.*) Oh—!

ARTHUR: What have you done?

ROSE (*in suspense*): The snuff—!

MISS GOWER: The table is prepared, William. Arthur, I assume you would prefer to sit and contemplate Rose.

ARTHUR: Thank you, Aunt.

(*Rose sneezes violently.*)

MISS GOWER: Oh, my dear child! Where are Frederick and Clara?

CLARA and DE FOENIX (*together*) : Here.
ARTHUR (*to Rose*) : Are you in pain, dearest?
ROSE : Agony.
ARTHUR : Pinch your upper lip.

(*She sneezes twice, loudly.*)

SIR WILLIAM : Sssh! This is to be whist, I hope.
MISS GOWER : Rose, Rose! Young ladies do not sneeze quite so continuously.
SIR WILLIAM : I will thank you, Captain de Foenix, to exercise your intelligence this evening to its furthest limit.
DE FOENIX : I'll twy sir.
SIR WILLIAM : Last night, sir—
CLARA : Poor Frederick had toothache last night, Grand-pa.
SIR WILLIAM : Whist is whist, Clara, and toothache is toothache. We will endeavour to keep the two things distinct, if you please.
MISS GOWER : Your interruption was hardly in place, Clara dear—oh . . .
DE FOENIX : Hey! What?
MISS GOWER : A misdeal.
CLARA (*faintly*) : Oh, Frederick!
SIR WILLIAM : Captain de Foenix!
DE FOENIX : I—I'm fwightfully gwieved, sir—

(*Rose gives way to a violent paroxysm of sneezing.*)

SIR WILLIAM : Is this whist, may I ask? Miss Trelawny—
ROSE : I think I had better—what d'ye call it—withdraw for a few moments.
SIR WILLIAM : Do so.

272

(*Rose leaves.*)

My snuff box Arthur, be so obleeging as to search for it.

ARTHUR : I'll bring it to you sir. It's on the—

SIR WILLIAM : Keep your voice down, sir. We are playing (*Triumphantly trumping.*) whist ! Mine.

MISS GOWER : No William.

SIR WILLIAM : No !

MISS GOWER : I played a trump.

DE FOENIX : Yes sir, Aunt Trafalgar played a trump —the . . .

SIR WILLIAM : I will not trouble you, Captain de Foenix, to echo Miss Gower's information.

DE FOENIX : Vewy sowwy sir.

MISS GOWER : It was a *little* out of place, Frederick.

SIR WILLIAM : Ssssh ! Whist.

(*The sound of Rose playing the piano and singing 'Ever of Thee' can be heard from the next room. Arthur moves towards the door.*)

SIR WILLIAM : No, no, let her go on, I beg. We will suspend our game while this young lady performs her operas.

MISS GOWER : Oh, William.

SIR WILLIAM : I fear this is no longer a comfortable home for ye, Trafalgar—no longer the home for a gentlewoman, I apprehend that in these days my house approaches somewhat closely to a Pandemonium. And this is whist—WHIST !

(*Sir William has a remarkably powerful voice for one of his years, and the din brings Rose dashing to the door in wide-eyed, happy expectation of mayhem.*)

ROSE : Did anyone call?

ARTHUR : You have upset my grandfather.

MISS GOWER : Miss Trelawny, how dare you do anything so—so out of place?

ROSE : There's a piano in there, Miss Gower.

MISS GOWER : You are acquainted with the rule of this house-hold—no music when the Vice Chancellor is within doors.

ROSE : But there are so many rules. One of them is that you may not sneeze.

MISS GOWER : Ha! You must never answer . . .

ROSE : No, that's another rule.

MISS GOWER : Oh, for shame!

ARTHUR : You see, Aunt, Rose is young, and—and —you make no allowance for her, give her no chance . . .

MISS GOWER : Great Heaven, what is this you are charging me with?

ARTHUR : I don't think the rules of this house are fair to Rose. Oh, I must say it—they are horribly unfair!

MISS GOWER (*clinging to Sir William*): Oh, brother!

SIR WILLIAM : Trafalgar! (*To Arthur.*) Oh, indeed sir. And so you deliberately accuse your great-aunt of acting towards ye and Miss Trelawny *mala fide*?

ARTHUR : Grandfather, what I intended to . . .

SIR WILLIAM : I will afford ye the opportunity of explaining what ye intended to convey downstairs, at once, in the library. Obleege me by following me sir. Captain de Foenix—I see no prospect of any further social relaxation this evening. You and Clara will do me the favour of attending in the hall, in readiness to take this young man back to Holles Street. (*Giving his arm to Trafalgar.*) My dear sister—

274

(*Arthur goes to Rose.*)

ARTHUR : Goodnight, dearest. Oh, Rose . . .
SIR WILLIAM (*outside the door*) : Mr Arthur
Gower !
ARTHUR : I am coming sir.
DE FOENIX (*to Rose*) : Haw—I weally—haw—
CLARA (*to Rose*) : Never mind ! We will let your
Troubadour out tonight as usual. I am a married
woman, and a married woman will turn if you
tread on her often enough—!

(*De Foenix and Clara leave. Rose is alone.*)

RULES !

ROSE :
Oh-h-h ! Ah-h-h !
Rules ! Rules ! Rules !

I may not cough !
I may not sneeze !
I may not move !
I have to freeze !
But they'll not beat
Me to my knees
They'll find I'm
More than a match for them !

I may not stoop !
I may not bend !
I may not even
See a friend !
But I shall show
That I intend
To do what—
Ever the Rules condemn !

275

On these restrictions
These rubs and these frictions
I pour maledictions
And seethe!
They won't let me dance!
They won't let me sing!
And soon—they won't let me breathe!

(*Mimicking over music.*)

'What a hideous riot, Trafalgar!'—'Rose dear, I
hope I have been mistaken, but through my sleep I
thought I could hear you shrieking at the top of
your voice!'

I may not laugh!
I may not joke!
I may not speak
Above a croak!
And when I eat
I almost choke
To think I'm
Watched by that pair of Ghouls!

If I'm a gypsy
Then let me get tipsy
And show these cantankerous fools
What I think of their
Old, out-moded,
Cold, corroded,
RULES!

(*Charles appears.*)

CHARLES (*mysteriously*): Miss Rose . . .
ROSE: What?

CHARLES : I see Sir William h'and the rest descend the stairs. I 'ave been awaitin' the chance of 'andin' you this Miss Rose. (*He produces a damp scrap of paper.*)

ROSE : Oh, it's damp !

CHARLES : Yes Miss. A gentle shower 'ave been takin' place h'outside. 'Eat spots, cook says.

ROSE : It's from some of my friends.

CHARLES : Perfesshunnal, Miss Rose?

ROSE (*reading*) : Yes—yes—

CHARLES : I was reprimandin' the organ Miss, when I observed them lollin' against the square railins examinin' h'our premises, and then ventured for to beckon me. An egstremely h'affable party, miss. One of them caused me to laugh !

ROSE : They want to speak to me—to 'impart something to me of an important nature'. Oh, Charles—when Sir William and Miss Gower have retired, do you think you could let me go forth, and wait at the front door while I run across and grant my friends a hurried interview?

CHARLES : Suttingly, miss.

ROSE : If it reached the ears of Sir William or Miss Gower, you would lose your place, Charles.

CHARLES : I'm aweer, miss, but Sir William was egstremely rood to me dooring dinner, over that mis'ap to the ontray—

(*Lightning.*)

ROSE : Oh, my friends, my poor friends !

CHARLES : Reely, I should 'ardly advise you to venture h'out, miss.

ROSE : Out. No ! Oh, but get them in !

CHARLES : In Miss Rose? H'indoors?

ROSE : Under cover—

(*Thunder.*)

Oh! They are my friends! Is it a rule that I mayn't even give a friend shelter in a violent storm? (*To Charles.*) Are you the only one up?
CHARLES : I b'lieve so miss. Any'ow the wimming-servants is quite h'under my control.
ROSE : Then tell my friends to be deathly quiet, and to creep—to tiptoe!

(*Lightning.*)

Make haste! I'll draw the curtains.

(*Charles goes out.*)

Oh my friends!

(*Thunder.*)

Oh! I'm not to sneeze in this house! or to sing! or breathe next! Oh, wretches! (*Singing wildly, under her breath.*) Ever of Thee . . . Have we no Cheers here, Trafalgar? Do we lack cheers . . . ?

(*Charles appears in the doorway, with the bedraggled quartet of Avonia, Tom, Gadd, Colpoys behind him.*)

CHARLES : I discovered 'em clustered in the doorway. (*He turns and beckons to them.*) Ssssh!

ACTORS' ENTRANCE

(*Avonia, Gadd, Colpoys, Tom, Charles, Rose.*

*This is entirely in mime, to a mysterioso 'hush'
version of the 'Rules' theme. The Actors creep in,
bedraggled and soaked to the skin. Charles and
Rose are on tenterhooks in case they make any
noise. Avonia gives her umbrella to Charles, Colpoys removes his coat and shakes it vigorously,
drenching everybody, Gadd scrapes his shoes on
the chair-rail, produces his pipe and clouds of
smoke, and Tom is deathly embarrassed. They all
finally sink, exhausted by the strain of keeping quiet,
onto chairs and the floor. Charles goes out. They
all look at each other. Suddenly Rose can restrain
herself no longer and rushes to embrace Avonia.)*

ROSE : Vonia !

AVONIA : Oh, ducky, ducky, ducky ! Oh, but what
a storm !

ROSE : Hush ! How wet you are ! (*She shakes
hands with the others.*) Ferdinand—Augustus—
Tom Wrench—

COLPOYS : My love ! My life !

ROSE : Hush !

COLPOYS : She speaks—she hears me !

TOM : It's a shame to come down on you in this
way. But they would do it, and I thought I'd better
stick to 'em.

GADD : Ha ! I shall remember this accursed
evening—

ROSE : Hush ! you must be quiet. Everybody has
gone to bed, and I—I'm not sure I'm allowed to
receive visitors—

AVONIA : Oh !

GADD : Then we are intruders ?

ROSE : I mean, such late visitors.

AVONIA : Yes, it is latish, but I so wanted to tell
you—

GADD : Vonia!

AVONIA (*meekly, which amazes Rose*) : Yes Ferdy?

GADD : Allow me.

AVONIA : Of course, Ferdy.

GADD : Miss Trelawny. (*Rising unsteadily to his feet.*) As you know, the clamour of my public has, in the past, engaged my wholehearted devotion, but even the tumultuous reception I received for my Orlando could not prevail against the . . .

AVONIA (*unable to contain herself any longer*) : Look! (*Tears off her left glove, revealing a wedding ring.*)

ROSE : Oh! Vonia!

AVONIA : Allow me to introduce—my husband!

ROSE : Oh! Ferdinand! How wonderful! Oh, you are lucky—when was it?

GADD (*sings*) : At St Michael's church at ten of the clock, I did her the honour!

AVONIA (*laughing delightedly*) : Yes! ha, ha, ha!

ROSE : Sssh!

AVONIA : And so I said to Ferdy over tea, 'let's spend a bit of our honeymoon in doing the West End thoroughly, and going and seeing where Rose Trelawny lives'. And we thought it only nice and polite to invite Tom Wrench and Gussy—

GADD : Vonia, much less of the Gussy!

AVONIA : Jealous boy! (*Her arm through his.*) Oh gracious, you're positively soaked—I'm sure you'll catch your death, my darling—

ROSE : I think I can get some wine. Will you take some wine, Ferdinand?

GADD : I thank you—anything, anything!

AVONIA (*to Rose*) : Anything, that goes with stout, dear.

ROSE (*at the sideboard*) : Sherry?

COLPOYS (*crashing from his chair, and crawling*

across the carpet as if it were the Sahara) : Water!
Water! Give me water! (*Reaching the sideboard.*)
Ah, port! Well—any port in a storm!

(*Rose pours wine and they all cluster round except
Tom.*)

ROSE : Tom, won't you—?

TOM (*watching Gadd anxiously*) : No, thank you.
The fact is, we—we have already partaken of
refreshments, once or twice during the evening—

GADD (*singing*) : 'At St Michael's church at ten of
the clock, I did her the honour!'

COLPOYS (*singing*) : 'He did her the honour!'

ROSE : Sssh!

COLPOYS (*in a whisper—raising his glass*) : The
Bride!

TOM and ROSE (*quietly together*) : The Bride!

GADD (*loudly*) : My Bride!

ALL : Sssh!

AVONIA : Well Rose, my darling, we've been talking about nothing but ourselves, how are you getting along here?

ROSE : Getting along? Oh, I—I don't fancy I'm
getting along very well, thank you!

COLPOYS and AVONIA (*together*) : No—!

ROSE : Oh no—Poor Arthur is a dear. But the
Gowers! The old Gowers! The Gowers! The
Gowers! The ancient Gowers! The venerable
Gowers!

AVONIA : You mean the Grandfather—?

ROSE : And the aunt—the great aunt—the great
bore of a great-aunt! The very mention of 'em
makes something go 'tap, tap, tap' at the top of
my head!

ROSE : Vonia, boys, you'll never believe it—

281

RULES (reprise)

I may not cough!
I may not sneeze!
I may not move!
I have to freeze!
But they'll not beat
Me to my knees
They'll find I'm
More than a match for them!

I may not stoop!
I may not bend!
I may not even
See a friend!
But I shall show
That I intend
To do what—
Ever the Rules condemn!

AVONIA:
Oh my poor darling!

TOM: With Grandfather snarling—

COLPOYS:
And Aunt going 'tap'
In your brain—

ALL:
How could you be dumb?
We're *so* glad we've come!
Besides—we're out of that beastly rain!

(Music changes to a slower, gentler tempo as the Actors gather round Rose sympathetically.)

TOM:
You're with your friends—

ROSE:
My dear, dear friends!

AVONIA :
We'll cheer you up !
TOM :
We'll make amends !
COLPOYS :
It's Class Dismissed !
GADD :
The Lesson ends—
TOM :
In what is surely the worst of schools—

(*Music suddenly reverts to wild 'gypsy' tempo.*)

ACTORS :
Come on, you gypsy,
Let's help you get tipsy
And show these cantankerous fools
What we think of their—
GADD :
Beg—Your—Pardy—
COLPOYS :
Lah—di—Dahdy—
ALL :
Ru—u—ules
Ru—u—ules
La la la la etc.

(*The singing builds to a rowdy crescendo and the
Actors get carried away into a wild 'gypsy' dance,
suddenly interrupted by the entrance of Sir William
and Miss Gower in night attire and slippers, and
carrying candles.*)

SIR WILLIAM : Miss Trelawny !
MISS GOWER : Rose ! (*Seeing the actors, and rushing behind a screen.*) MEN ! !

SIR WILLIAM : Who are these persons?

ROSE : Some friends of mine who used to be at the Wells with me have called to enquire how I am getting on.

(*Arthur enters, quickly.*)

ARTHUR (*looking round*) : Oh, Rose!

SIR WILLIAM : Ah! How come you here?

ARTHUR : I was outside the house. Charles let me in, knowing something was wrong.

SIR WILLIAM : Troubadouring?

ARTHUR : Troubadouring, yes sir. Rose, what is this?

SIR WILLIAM : No, sir, this is my affair. Stand aside!

MISS GOWER (*from behind the screen*) : William!

SIR WILLIAM : Hey?

MISS GOWER : Your ankles—

SIR WILLIAM (*adjusting his dressing gown*) : I beg your pardon. (*To Arthur.*) I can answer your question. Some friends of that young woman's connected with the—the playhouse, have favoured us with a visit, for the purpose of ascertaining how she is—getting on. (*Seeing Gadd's pipe on the floor.*) A filthy tobacco pipe. To whom does this belong?

ROSE (*picking it up and passing it to Gadd*) : It belongs to one of my friends.

SIR WILLIAM : Yes! In brief, a drunken debauch! So you see, gentlemen, (*To Avonia.*) and you madam, (*To Arthur.*) and you sir, you see, all of ye, exactly how Miss Trelawny is getting on.

MISS GOWER : William—

SIR WILLIAM : What is it?

MISS GOWER : Your ankles—

SIR WILLIAM : Bah!

MISS GOWER : Oh, they seem so out of place.

SIR WILLIAM (*flourishing his stick at the actors*):
Begone! A set of garish, dissolute gipsies! Begone!

AVONIA : Where's my umbrella?

GADD : A hand with my coat here.

COLPOYS : 'Pon my soul, London artists—!

AVONIA : We don't want to remain where we're
not heartily welcome, I can assure everybody.

SIR WILLIAM : Open windows! Let in the air!

AVONIA (*to Rose*): Goodbye, my dear—

ROSE : No, no, Vonia. Oh don't leave me behind
you!

ARTHUR : Rose!

ROSE : I'm very sorry, Arthur. Indeed, I am very
sorry, Sir William. But you are right—gipsies—
gipsies! Yes, Arthur, if you were a gipsy, as I am,
as these friends of mine are, we might be happy
together. But I've seen enough of your life, my
dear boy, to know that I'm no wife for you. I
should only be wretched, and make you wretched,
and the end, when it arrived, as it very soon would,
would be much as it is tonight—

ARTHUR : You'll let me see you, talk to you
tomorrow, Rose?

ROSE : No, never!

SIR WILLIAM : You mean that?

ROSE : Oh don't be afraid. I give you my word.

SIR WILLIAM : Thank ye. Thank ye.

TOM (*aside, to Arthur*): Mr Gower, come and see
me tomorrow—

ROSE (*to her friends*): I'm ready—

MISS GOWER : Not tonight, child! not tonight!
where will you go?

ROSE : Back to the Wells, Miss Gower. Back to
the Wells!

BACK TO THE WELLS!

COLPOYS (*ad lib*):
Roll out the carpet!
GADD:
Ring out the bells!
BOTH:
Trelawny is returning
AVONIA:
Home to the dear old Wells!
ALL (*tempo*):
Order your morning papers!
Every headline tells
That Rose is going back
Back to the dear old Wells!

(*The Actors gather round Rose and sweep her out into the Square.*

The set transforms as they go.)

Back to the Wells
Goes Rose!
She's going
Back to the Wells
With those
Dear old chums who appreciate her
She's going home to her own theatre
Book your seats and she'll see you later
Back at the dear old Wells!

(*As they start their journey, Arthur watches them, alone at the side of the stage.*)

Scene 4

THE JOURNEY TO THE WELLS

(With their umbrellas aloft against the rain, the Actors, with Rose, circle round the railings of Cavendish Square—while under a gas lamp in the foreground Arthur sadly sings:)

BACK TO THE WELLS (second time)

ARTHUR :
Rose have I lost you?
Oh my dearest!
Did I really mean
So little to you?
I believe that you loved me
But now you've left me
Where shall I go?
What shall I do?

(He turns up his coat-collar and crosses the stage, with the Actors crossing the other way behind him. This time they quietly sing their refrain as a counterpoint to his.)

ARTHUR :	THE ACTORS :
I shall be lonely	Roll out the carpet!
Oh so lonely!	Ring out the bells!
Living only on my	Trelawny is returning
Mem'ries of you	Home to the dear old Wells!
I believed that you loved me	Order your morning papers

But now you've left me	Every headline tells
Where shall I go?	That Rose is going back
What shall I do?	Back to the dear old Wells!

(Arthur goes out. The Actors sweep Rose down-stage, closing their umbrellas under a clearing sky, as they sing full voice :)

ACTORS :
Back to the Wells
Goes Rose!
She's going
Back to the Wells
With those
Dear old chums who appreciate her
She's going home to her own theatre
Book your seats and she'll see you later
Back at the dear old Wells!

(The set now changes to the streets of London, with the quintet of Actors making a merry progress through them.)

BACK TO THE WELLS (third time)

(As they go, anyone and everyone they meet is swept up in the mood. A Chorus of Window-Watchers sings a counterpart to the refrain.)

THE ACTORS :	CHORUS :
Roll out the carpet!	Quick, or you'll miss her,
Ring out the bells!	Rose Trelawny—

Trelawny is returning
Home to the dear old
  Wells!

Order your morning
  papers!
Every headline tells
That Rose is going
  back
Back to the dear old
  Wells!

She's returning to her
Happy old home

For she knows how to
  please here
She feels at ease here,
  Never to roam!

Rose, welcome
home!

(*The Street Scene opens to reveal the Stage Door of the Wells. The Telfers, the Mossops and the rest of the Wells Company are gathered outside to welcome Rose, amid great jubilation.*)

THE COMPANY:
Back to the Wells
Goes Rose!
She's going
Back to the Wells
With those
Dear old chums who appreciate her
She's going home to her own theatre
Book your seats and she'll see you later
Back at the dear old Wells!

All raise their arms in welcome. Tom moves forward to escort Rose inside—but she has turned away from the Company and is suddenly in tears. He stares at her, the only one to know, as the last joyful note of the refrain rings out, and the Curtain Falls.

PART TWO

(*Towards the end of the Entr'acte the curtain rises to reveal a front-cloth replica of the Wells programme for Aladdin.*)

Scene 1

WELLS PANTOMIME PROLOGUE

(*As the houselights fade, Mr Telfer, resplendent in the robes of The Emperor, enters before the dropcloth, and hobbles, Richard III–wise, to centre stage. The lights are not quite full.*)

TELFER : Now is the Winter of our Discontent— but no! I do not offer you . . . (*He glares at the prompt corner.*)
Mossop!
MOSSOP (*poking his head round the flat*): Yes, Mr Telfer.
TELFER : What is amiss with the lights? Am I to conduct this entire dress rehearsal in a gloom more fitting the Tomb of the Capulets?
MOSSOP : My apologies, Mr Telfer. The new man on the gas table is a little inexperienced. (*He disappears into the prompt-corner, and a muffled exchange takes place.*)
TELFER (*to the M.D.*): We are in the hands of amateurs, Mr Grayson, amateurs.

(*The lights come up to full. Telfer turns to the prompt-corner with heavy sarcasm.*)

Thank you. (*Peering round the house.*) It would have been the same had there been an audience present. Once again gentlemen.

290

(Telfer retires offstage, and immediately re-enters.)

TELFER :
Now is the Winter of our Discontent—but no !
I do not offer you Shakespearean show.
Each year at Christmastide, the Wells affords
The finest Pantomime upon the boards !

(He silences imaginary applause.)

But hush. *(To the Orchestra.)*
Good minstrels play—at once begin—
Transport us—one and all—to old Pekin !

(He goes out, as the orchestra strikes up and three exotically clothed Chinese Maidens enter.)

TEA !

(Enter 1st Maid.)

1st MAID :
The Tea ! The Tea !
    Refreshing Tea !
The green, the fresh, the ever free
    From all impurity
    From all impurity
The Tea ! The Tea ! The Tea !

(Enter 2nd and 3rd Maids.)

2nd and 3rd MAIDS :
The Tea ! The Tea !
Refreshing Tea !
The green, the fresh, the ever free

From all impurity
From all impurity
The Tea! The Tea! The Tea!

1st MAID :
I may remark that I'll be bound—

2nd MAID :
Full shillings six was this the pound—

3rd MAID :
I'm on for Tea!

ALL :
We're on for Tea!
The Tea! The Tea!
Refreshing Tea!
The green, the fresh, the ever free
From all impurity
From all impurity
The Tea! The Tea! The Tea!
For the savour sweet that doth belong
To the curly leaf of the rough Souchong—

1st MAID :
Is like Nectar to me!

2nd MAID :
Nectar to me!

3rd MAID :
Nectar to me!

ALL :
The Tea! The Tea!
Refreshing Tea!
The green, the fresh, the ever free!
Let others delight in their *Eau De Vie*—

1st MAID :
What matter?

2nd MAID :
What matter?

3rd MAID :
What matter?

ALL:
What matter?
I'm On—I'm On—I'm On
For Tea!

(*As they finish there is a roll of thunder and a flash of magnesium. Signor Gibolini appears as the Demon of Discontent in a vast pall of smoke and steps forward with a dramatic 'Aha!' but, blinded by smoke and fire, and with a cry of 'A—a—a—hhh!', falls headlong down the trap. The Three Little Maids, who have been cowering in feigned fear, dash forward, and peer into the depths. Telfer reappears.*)

TELFER: What is amiss? Stand aside! (*He peers into the abyss.*) Tragedy! The finest Demon in England, quite, quite down. Mossop!
MOSSOP (*his head appearing from the trap*): Yes, Mr Telfer?
TELFER: What's the damage?
MOSSOP: 'E says he's broken 'is leg, Mr Telfer, which I take leave to doubt, but the witches' cauldron will take a deal of repairing.
TELFER: Help him hence! (*For once, and with effort, he manages all the aitches, then turns to the three little maids, who are giggling amongst themselves.*) Let not your teardrops fall, he bears all like a soldier.

(*An agonized cry from below stage.*)

Call-boy! (*To the orchestra leader.*) I think our meetest plan is to proceed from Miss Trelawny's song in the Palace yard in—shall we say ten minutes?

(*The Call-boy arrives.*)

Ah! Call Miss Trelawny on stage ten minutes hence, and then come to my dressing-room. I shall require you to summon the immediate services of a substitute Demon. (*Calls.*) Fly the front-cloth, Mossop!

(*The cloth is flown, and the Call-boy circles the stage, calling, and knocking on various doors.*)

CALL-BOY : Princess's song in ten minutes, please! (*Knocks.*) Ten minutes please. (*He passes Avonia.*) From the Princess's song in ten minutes, Miss.

(*As he passes the stage-door, George gives him Rose's small prop basket.*)

GEORGE : For Miss Trelawny.
CALL-BOY : Right you are, George! (*Calls to a dressing room on fly level.*) You won't be needed for half an hour, Mr Wrench!
TOM (*miles away*) : Thank you . . .

(*During this, Rose and Avonia's dressing-room has been revealed. The lights now build on it and the orchestra begins the introduction to Rose's song.*)

Scene 2

ROSE'S DRESSING ROOM

(*Rose is standing in the middle of the room, while Mrs Mossop fastens the last of the hooks at the back of her costume.*)

MRS MOSSOP : There, Miss Rose—and a prettier Princess I never wish to see. (*She makes final adjustments to the dress.*) Now, I've put your last act change under the covers. There always was a lot of dust about this dressing-room, and it's even worse now with them three girls changing above our heads. Sweet pretty things they are to be sure, but remarkable heavy-footed for dancers.

ROSE : I'm sorry, Mrs Mossop. I'm afraid I wasn't really listening. What did you say?

MRS MOSSOP : Never you mind about me. I was just chattering on, same as usual.

ROSE : Yes . . . (*Managing a brave smile.*) Same as usual . . .

(*She wanders away to the dressing table, staring round the room. Mrs Mossop watches her anxiously.*)

MRS MOSSOP : Don't you worry your head about anything. It'll all come out right in the end.

ROSE : Thank you, dear Mrs Mossop. (*She sinks onto the dressing table stool.*) I'm afraid I've not been a very jolly person since I returned to the Wells . . .

MRS MOSSOP : There, there, dearie, you're back in your old room now, with all your old friends around you, and old Mossop to look after you! (*She has taken an exotic head-dress from the costume skip, and is staring at it in disbelief.*) Just look there! I've given you Mr Telfer's hat and him yours—and he'll probably put it on and never notice the difference! Back in a minute, dearie.

(*Mrs Mossop dashes out, leaving Rose alone. She starts to put the finishing touches to her make-up, sees the room reflected in the mirror, and looks about her, puzzled and uneasy.)*

IT'S NOT THE SAME

ROSE :
Everything
Around me
Is the same
But not the same
I'd know this chair
Anywhere
And those curtains were there
When I first came
But everything
Around me
Is somehow different
Am I to blame
If the life I'd have sworn
I was born for
Seems now—not the same?

(Music continues. There is a knock on the door.)

CALL-BOY *(off)* : Miss Trelawny.
ROSE : Come in.
CALL-BOY : Your prop basket, Miss Trelawny.
ROSE : Thank you, Albert. Put it over there, will you?
CALL-BOY : Right Miss. *(Puts it down.)* There! Nice to 'ave you back at the Wells, Miss Rose— wasn't the same without you. *(As he goes.)* Your song in ten minutes, please.

(Rose now unpacks Kean's insignia from the basket, and her mother's prop crown, which she puts in its usual place on her wig-block.)

ROSE:
Everything
I see here
Seems a reproach to me
And to my shame
I am finding the world
I believed in
Is now—not the same.
This world
Isn't *the* world
It's merely *a* world
And half unreal
And I'm like a doll
Like a marionette
Attempting to feel
What I can no longer feel
For everything
Around me
That once excited me
Seems now so lame
And the world that I once
Was in love with
May stay the same
But all the same
Without my Arthur beside me
It's not the same.

(*At the end of the number, Avonia pokes her head round the door. She is wearing a dressing-gown over her Principal Boy's costume.*)

AVONIA: Miss Rose Trelawny! May I have the inestimable pleasure of introducing to you—Mr Thomas Wrench in his latest role—Fearless, the Dragon!

297

(*Tom, dressed in the top half of his Dragon's costume, and a monstrous head, blunders in.*)

Isn't it priceless, Rose? They've made it with eyes to look through, but they are so low down that all you can see is your feet.

TOM : It's impossible, Vonia. Quite impossible. I shall tell Telfer that unless I can have my eyes in a reasonable place, I shall refuse to appear ! And I can't breathe ! This thing isn't a costume—it's a mediaeval torture ! It's like putting your head up a chimney with the fire lit !

ROSE : Oh Tom, I am sorry !

TOM (*struggling to get the head off*) : It's the final indignity, Rose ! (*Staring at his hands.*) Look ! The paint isn't even dry ! (*He looks at himself in Rose's mirror.*) I shall spend the rest of my days as green as Ablett's cabbages !

ROSE : Sit down here, Tom, and I'll clean it off for you.

TOM : Ah ! Rose, I knew I missed something all those weeks you were away from us. Sympathy, Vonia ! The helping hand stretched out—

ROSE : Do keep still, Tom—

AVONIA : Rose, I was wondering whether you'd lend me that belt you bought for Ophelia to wear during the first two or three weeks of the pantomime—

ROSE : Certainly, Vonia, to wear throughout—

AVONIA (*embracing her*) : No, it's too good. I'd rather fake one for the rest of the time. (*Looking into her face.*) What's the matter?

ROSE : I will make you a present of the belt, Vonia, if you will accept it. I bought it when I came back to the Wells, thinking everything would go on as before. But—it's of no use—they tell me I cannot act effectively any longer—

TOM : Effectively!

ROSE : First, as you know, they reduce my salary—

AVONIA (*lowering her eyes*): Yes—

ROSE : And now, this morning, they cut down my part.

TOM : Oh!

ROSE : Poor mother—I hope she doesn't see . . . I was running through it when Mr Telfer spoke to me. It is true I was doing it tamely, but—it is such nonsense.

TOM : Hear, hear!

ROSE : I am left with almost nothing but that poor little song I used to sing on the bridge—

AVONIA (*singing softly*): 'Ever of thee I'm fondly dreaming—'

ROSE : And it's hard even to do that properly in the middle of a pantomime—

AVONIA : But a few months ago you l-liked your work.

ROSE : That was before I went to Cavendish Square —when I was no more than a gypsy. How badly I behaved there—how unlike a young lady! There was a chance for me—to be patient, and womanly, and I proved to them that I was nothing but—an actress.

AVONIA : It doesn't follow, because one is a—

ROSE (*facing* AVONIA): Yes, Vonia, it does! Our heads are stuffed with sayings out of rubbishy plays. I was only a few weeks in Cavendish Square, and very few people came there, but they were real people—real! I didn't realize at the time the change that was going on in me. I didn't realize it till I came back. But now, every time I am called on stage, even to rehearse, I feel frightened, Tom, sick with fright, and I know that one day I just shan't be able to go on—ever again. Oh, Vonia! (*She lays her head on Avonia's shoulder.*)

(*After a moment a great hullaballoo is heard approaching along the corridor.*)

AVONIA : That sounds like Ferdy. (*Opens the dressing-room door, and calls.*) Ferdy! 'Aint you well, darling? (*To Rose and Tom.*) Now, what's put Ferdy out?

(*Gadd enters with a wild look.*)

Ferdinand!

TOM : Anything wrong, Gadd?

GADD : Wrong! Wrong! What d'you think?

AVONIA : Tell us!

GADD : I have been asked to appear in the pantomime.

AVONIA : Oh, Ferdy, you!

GADD : I, a serious actor if ever there was one, a poetic actor—!

AVONIA (*fearing the worst*) : What part, Ferdy?

GADD : The insult, the bitter insult! The gross indignity! I have not been seen in pantomime for years—not since I shook the dust of the T. R. Stockton from my feet! I simply looked at Telfer when he preferred his request, and swept from the stage.

AVONIA : What part, Ferdy?

GADD : A part too, which is seen for a moment at the opening of the pantomime, and not again 'till its close.

AVONIA : Ferdy!

GADD : Eh?

AVONIA : What part?

GADD : A character called—the Demon of Discontent.

(*Tom curls up on the top of a skip, and is seen to shake with laughter.*)

AVONIA : Oh, no! It's a rotten part! You won't play it, darling?

GADD : Play it? I would see the Wells in ashes first!

AVONIA : We shall lose our engagements, Ferdy. We shall be out, both of us.

GADD : Of course we shall. D'you think I have not counted the cost?

(*A knock at the door.*)

ROSE : Who is it?

COLPOYS (*without*) : Is Gadd there, Miss Trelawny?

ROSE : Yes.

COLPOYS : I want to see him.

GADD : Wrench, I'll trouble you. Ask Mr Colpoys whether he approaches me as a friend, an acquaintance, or the tool of Telfer.

TOM (*at the door, solemnly*) : Colpoys, are you here as Gadd's bosom friend, or as a mere tool of Telfer?

(*An inaudible colloquy follows between Tom and Colpoys. Tom's legs are seen to move convulsively, and the sound of suppressed laughter is heard.*)

GADD : Well—well?

TOM : He is here as the tool of Telfer.

GADD : I will receive him.

(*Enter Colpoys, carrying a small part and a letter.*)

COLPOYS : Ah, Gadd. Mr Telfer instructs me to offer you this part in the pantomime. (*Hands him the part.*) The Demon of Discontent.

(*Gadd takes the part and flings it to the ground. Avonia picks it up and reads it.*)

COLPOYS : You refuse it?
GADD : I do. Acquaint Mr Telfer with my decision, and add that I hope his pantomime will prove an utterly mirthless one. May Boxing Night, to those unfortunate enough to find themselves in the theatre, long remain a dismal memory, and may succeeding audiences, scanty and dissatisfied—

(*Colpoys now gives him the letter, which he reads.*)

I leave. The Romeo—the Orlando—the Clifford —leaves !
AVONIA : Ferdy, this ain't so bad.

(*Reads.*)

'I'm Discontent ! from Orkney's isle to Dover
To make men's bile bile-over I endover—'
GADD : Vonia ! (*Taking the part.*) Ho, ho ! no, that's not bad.

(*Reading.*)

'Tempers, though sweet, I whip up to a lather,
Make wives hate husbands, sons wish fathers farther.'
Vonia, there's something to lay hold of here ! I'll

302

think this over. (*To Colpoys.*) Gus, I have thought
this over. I play it!

AVONIA: Oh Ferdy! (*She implants a kiss on his
cheek, and turns to Rose.*) There, Rose, you see, if
Ferdy can go on in the pantomime, I'm sure you
can.

ROSE: Oh Ferdinand, I wish I had your courage.

GADD: Courage?

AVONIA: She's got the most awful stage-fright.

COLPOYS: Rose? Never!

ROSE: It's true, Augustus

GADD: Nonsense! Never let it be said that a Wells
artiste would disappoint the public! Follow Ferdy's
example, my dear.

WE CAN'T KEEP 'EM WAITING

GADD (*grandioso*):
They're waiting for my Demon—
I shall give it—for Them!
COLPOYS (*mimicking*):
They're waiting for my Twankey—
I shall give it—for Them!
BOTH:
For us poor fools who once decide
To enter this profession
However we may feel inside
There's no room for depression.
So be we actor—juggler—clown—
Magician—singer—dancer—
We cannot let our public down
And when it Calls—we Answer!
We can't keep 'em waiting!
We can't keep 'em waiting!
They're sitting there expectantly
With hearts a-palpitating

303

GADD :

They're dying for my Demon
The one they love to hiss

COLPOYS :

They're crying for my Twankey
To blow them all a kiss

BOTH :

They're waiting for the moment
When we—hit—town—
And we can't let our Public down !

BOTH :

We can't keep 'em waiting !
We can't keep 'em waiting !
It's mighty gratifying that they're
So discriminating

GADD :

They're stamping for my Demon
To enter through the smoke

COLPOYS :

They're champing for my Twankey
To crack an ancient joke

BOTH :

They're waiting for the moment
When we—hit—town—
And we can't let our Public down !
There's none to compare
With the old 'Wells' lot

COLPOYS :

With them Fair's Fair

GADD :

And they know What's What

BOTH :

So you get out there
And you Give All You've Got—

GADD (*rall.*) :

You *caress* every word

And you *stress* every pause
COLPOYS (*at him*):
Then you *mess* up your exit
And muff your applause!
GADD:
Well, that's better than getting it
By dropping your drawers!
BOTH:
We can't keep 'em waiting!
We can't keep 'em waiting!
It's selfish to withhold ourselves
When we're so fascinating
GADD:
They're screaming for my Demon
To scare them till it hurts
COLPOYS:
They're dreaming of my Twankey
Removing thirty skirts
BOTH:
They're waiting for the moment
When we—hit—town—
And we can't let our Public down!

(*Importantly to Rose.*)

BOTH:
And so, dear Rose,
In this Life you chose
COLPOYS:
You must Go It—
GADD:
Well you know it—
COLPOYS:
Or Begone!
GADD:
Gallantly concealing

305

COLPOYS :
The make-up that is peeling
GADD :
Though your blood is near congealing
At the fraud and double-dealing
COLPOYS :
And you'd like to hit the ceiling
Over somebody scene-stealing
GADD :
You must rise above the Nitter-Natter—
COLPOYS :
Chitter-Chatter—
BOTH :
It's a matter
Of Feeling That Feeling
COLPOYS :
When the Call-Boy comes—
GADD :
The Great Call comes—
BOTH :
To tell you
YOU'RE ON !
Then—
You can't keep 'em waiting !
You can't keep 'em waiting !
Your name is on the programme
In the boldest copper-plating
They're waiting for your Princess
To don her golden crown
GADD :
Agitating for my Demon
To flash his fearful frown
COLPOYS :
Supplicating for my Twankey
To hoist her gingham gown

306

ALL :
Waiting for the moment
When we—hit—town—
And we can't let our Public down—
GADD and COLPOYS (*forward*) :
They—*Want*—Us
And we can't let our Public down !

(*At the end of the number they sweep Rose off towards the stage. Tom and Avonia are left alone.*)

TOM : Thank heavens for Ferdy and Gus ! Now Rose will be able to show them that it isn't true.
AVONIA : What—?
TOM : That she is no longer up to her work. These fools at the Wells ! Can't act, can't she ! No, she can no longer spout, she can no longer ladle, the vapid trash, the turgid rodomontade—
AVONIA (*doubtfully*) : You'd better watch your language, Wrench.
TOM (*twinkling*) : You're a married woman, Vonia.
AVONIA : I know, but still—
TOM : Yes, deep down in the well of that girl's nature there had been lying a little, bright, clear pool of genuine refinement. Why, her broken engagement to poor young Gower has really been the making of her ! It has transformed her ! Can't act can't she ! How she would play Dora in my comedy !
AVONIA : Ho, that comedy !
TOM : D'you know, Vonia, I had Rose in my mind when I imagined Dora—?
AVONIA : You astonish me !
TOM : And Arthur Gower when I wrote the character of Gerald, Dora's lover. Gerald and Dora

307

—Rose and Arthur—Gerald and Dora. (*Suddenly.*)
Vonia—!

(*Avonia jumps and lets out a little scream.*)

I wish you could keep a secret.

AVONIA : A secret, Tom?

TOM : I should like to share it with you because—
you are fond of her too.

AVONIA : Ah—

TOM : But there, I can't trust you—

AVONIA : Mr Wrench!

TOM : No, you're a warm-hearted woman, Vonia,
but you're a sieve.

AVONIA : I swear! By all my hopes, Tom Wrench,
of hitting 'em as Aladdin in the coming Pantomime, I swear I will not divulge, let alone tell a
living soul, any secret you may entrust to me, or
let me know of, concerning Rose Trelawny of the
Wells. Amen!

TOM : Vonia, I know where Arthur Gower is.

AVONIA : *Is?* Isn't he still in London?

TOM : No. Mind, not a word—!

AVONIA : By all my hopes—!

TOM : All right, all right. (*Reading a letter.*)
'Theatre Royal, Bristol, Friday—'

AVONIA : Theatre Royal Br—!

TOM : Be quiet! 'My dear Mr Wrench : A whole
week and not a line from you, to tell me how Miss
Trelawny is. When you are silent I am sleepless at
night, and a haggard wretch during the day.
Young Mr Kirby, our Walking Gentleman, has
been unwell, and the management has given me
temporarily, some of his business to play.'

AVONIA : Arthur Gower—!

TOM : Will you—? 'Miss Mason, our leading lady

complimented me, but the men said I lacked vigour' . . . the old cry . . . 'and so this morning I am greatly depressed. But I will still persevere, as long as you can assure me that no presuming fellow is paying attention to Miss Trelawny. Oh, how badly she treated me—'

AVONIA : 'How badly she treated me—'

TOM : 'I will never forgive her, only love her—'

AVONIA : 'Only love her—'

TOM : 'And hope that some day I may become a great actor, and, like herself, a gipsy. Yours very gratefully, Arthur Gordon.'

AVONIA : In the Profession !

TOM : Bolted from Cavendish Square, went down to Bristol—

AVONIA : How did he manage it all?

(*Tom taps his breast proudly.*)

But when is Rose to be told?

TOM : When he begins to make strides.

AVONIA : Well, I hope he makes them quickly, I don't know how long Rose can carry on without him . . .

CALL-BOY (*off*) : Stand by for the first Palace scene —everyone on stage please !

AVONIA : Now do go away and leave me alone, Tom. I'll be off if you go on gossiping like this.

TOM (*turning to go*) : Sorry.

AVONIA : And don't you let her see that long face of yours—she'll need all the smiles around her we can find if she's going to get through this Panto-mime, you mark my words.

TOM : Fear not, Vonia. (*Picking up the dragon's head.*) I have my smile ready—what about you?

AVONIA : Don't you worry about me—I'm always

stark mad when the Pantomime comes round. I
often think my year must start at a different time
from everybody else's. I only really wake up in the
winter!

THE TURN OF AVONIA BUNN

AVONIA :

When the Spring has gone
And the Summer's gone
And the Autumn's half-way through
And the Winter is approaching.
I say to myself Ooo-hoo!
Now is the hour
Now is the time
When I'm in my element
I'm in my prime
And the boring 'straights'
Must find other dates
And recognize that I'm
The one who's *really* needed
For the Christmas Pantomime—
Then comes my turn
For which I yearn
When I justify
What little I earn.
When the serious work
Of the year is done
And the season has come
For a bit of fun
Why then—it's—the Tur-r-r-rn
Of Avonia Bunn—
Of Avonia Bunn!
And as I pin
The last sequin
I sincerely bless

310

The business I'm in.
As I get myself ready
To punch each pun
And to shine like the rays
Of the morning sun
I'm ripe—for—the Tur-r-r-rn
Of Avonia Bunn—
Of Avonia Bunn!
Then it's on with the spangles!
On with the bangles!
On with the feathers
At curious angles!
Finally my walk-down
In shades of begonia
Cut so low
That I risk pneumonia
But when I hear them
Shout 'Avonia!'
I can't help but churn—
So grateful it's My Turn!

(*She throws off her wrap and moves downstage out of the dressing room. The Aladdin Front cloth comes in behind her.*)

When Christmas comes
This theatre hums
And you won't catch people
Twiddling their thumbs
For they know there is one
Who is bound to stun
And they say to themselves
As they pay their mon.
'At last—it's—the Tur-r-r-rn
Of Avonia Bunn—
Of Avonia Bunn!'

She goes out with a high kick at the Pros and the cloth rises to reveal the full set for the Pantomime.

Scene 3

THE WELLS PANTOMIME

(A street in old Pekin.

A chorus line of assorted Pekin types crosses and recrosses the stage.)

LET'S PEEK IN AT PEKIN

CHORUS :
Let's peek in at old Pekin
It's a great old, grand old city we're in
Every Chinaman's proud of this ancient town
And we might run you through if you run us down
So come and enjoy the bustle and din
In the streets of Pekin
In the streets of Pekin
If it's pleasure you're seekin'
You can't do better than peek in
At the thousand and one delightful treats
You'll find if you wander through the streets
Of old Pekin !

(The last time they cross, Colpoys as Widow Twankey has joined the end of the line.)

TWANKEY :
A widow's lot's a wretched one, forsooth,

Ah where! Ah where's Aladdin, Truant youth?
To cry 'Ah Where' is very well for me,
But I am not a—ware where he can be.
Hark! *(She shades her eyes and looks off.)* Who is
   this approaching?

ALADDIN:
Hello Ma!

TWANKEY:
My child returned and safe. Ha! Ha! Ha! Ha!
He is a—lad—in every way.

ALADDIN:
Hallo!
What's that?

TWANKEY: The princess to her bath doth go,
As is her daily sanitary custom.
People must keep in doors and not look.

ALADDIN:
Must 'em?

TWANKEY:
When going to her bath 'tis law that none peep.

ALADDIN:
You go to Bath yourself, I will have one peep. *(He
peeps.)*
Oh, there she is! I madly love her!

TWANKEY:
Oh!

ALADDIN:
She must and shall be mine!

*(Mrs Telfer as the Spirit of the Lamp shoots up
through one trap.)*

SPIRIT:
Aha!

(*Gadd as the Demon of Discontent shoots up through the other.*)

DEMON : Oho !

(*Twankey and Aladdin cower.*)

I'm Discontent, from Orkney's Isle to Dover,
To make men's bile bile over I endover !
FAIRY :
But I, the Gracious Spirit of the Lamp
Your evil ways will soon frustrate and cramp.
DEMON :
A thousand curses !

(*Spirit waves her wand at him.*)

Ow ! I'll disappear,
Her fairy ways have made me feel quite queer. (*He disappears.*)
SPIRIT :
Fear not, Aladdin, all your worries banish,
Your future's in safe hands. I too must vanish. (*She vanishes.*)

(*The Pekin Types rush once more across the stage, two of them bearing a rather delapidated palanquin, in which is Rose as the Princess. Telfer as the Emperor enters with his Guard.*)

PRINCESS (*descending from the palanquin*) :
Good Morning, dear Papa.
EMPEROR :
Good morning, dear.

PRINCESS :
I do not find you very well, I fear.
There's something on your mind.
EMPEROR :
A trifle. We
Are simply in a state of beggary.
But if the Grand Vizier your hand you'll give—
PRINCESS :
Ah, no ! Alas ! Alack ! Not while I live !
Do hearken to my pleas, oh Father dear—
EMPEROR :
Enough, my daughter.

(A mighty dragon roar off.)

What is this I hear?
GUARD :
The Dragon, Sire !
EMPEROR :
Betake you to your heel,
Or else of us he'll make his midday meal,

(All leave the stage, save the Princess, who now faces the Dragon, who enters in the person of Tom.)

PRINCESS :
The Dragon fierce !

(The Dragon, who is smoking a pipe inside his mask to simulate nostril-fire, is choking slowly to death.)

Perhaps a lullaby

315

Will soothe his savage breast. I can but try.

EVER OF THEE (Reprise)

(Rose struggles to put feeling into the song, but after only a few bars, very weakly sung, she breaks down.

Telfer comes long-sufferingly forward from the wings.)

TELFER: Stop! All Right! (*To the Orchestra.*) Thank you Mr Grayson. Your indulgence for a moment, gentlemen. Now, what is the matter, Rose?

ROSE: It's—it's the song, Mr Telfer.

TELFER: It has been—'the song'—ever since we started rehearsals.

ROSE: But it really is so inappropriate; couldn't we please cut it out of the scene?

TELFER: Rose. I have had a very trying rehearsal, and I have little time—or patience—left. Ever since Mr Phelps' day, the princess has sung a love song at this particular juncture in the pantomime.

ROSE: But I feel so ridiculous singing this lovely song to a dragon—it is so stupid—it's not lifelike.

TELFER: I don't understand you young people—I really don't. This isn't meant to be life—this is the Theatre.

TOM: But, Mr Telfer, surely the theatre—even the pantomime—should try to be like life in some . . .

TELFER: I am not aware of having begged your opinion, Wrench!

TOM: Perhaps not, Mr Telfer, but Rose is right.

TELFER: And I am wrong?!

TOM: Yes, Mr Telfer—I believe you are. The

theatre should 'hold, as 'twere, the mirror up to nature', as Hamlet—

TELFER : I know my Bard, thank you, Wrench!

TOM : Well, of course, but can't you see that Rose is miserable?

ROSE : Tom, please! Mr Telfer, I—I can't sing that song, whatever you say. You must let me change it.

TELFER : Miss Trelawny. Will you, or will you not, rehearse and perform this pantomime as I direct you?

ROSE : It is not that I will not, Mr Telfer—I cannot.

TELFER : Then there is no longer a place for you here at the Wells.

TOM : Mr Telfer, you can't mean to—

TELFER : And I would remind you, Wrench, that your services are by no means indispensable! (*To Rose.*) You will hand over your part to Miss Pellatt forthwith. Perhaps she will treat the theatre with the respect and devotion you seem unwilling to accord it.

(*Rose bursts into tears and runs off. As the cast begin to disperse, whispering among themselves, Mrs Telfer comes down to her husband, and takes his arm.*)

Ah, Violet. D'you think I was too hasty? Rose is a most popular performer, I know—worth fifty seats a performance in the right role—but—

MRS TELFER : You could not have done otherwise, James; you could not allow the child to dictate to you. Not on your own stage.

TELFER : I fear it may not be ours much longer, my dear.

MRS TELFER : James?

TELFER : Burroughs spoke to me on be'alf of the owners today. Unless we manage to show a greater profit, he threatens to put another actor-manager into the old Wells.

MRS TELFER : Have they no respect for your knowledge of the theatre?

TELFER : The Theatre—they don't know what the word means, Violet. Don't know what it means.

(They go out, leaving only Tom and Avonia on stage. Tom puts his dragon's head carefully down on the stage, and kicks it—hard.)

AVONIA : Oh Tom. I feel so awful. I ought to have stood up for her.

TOM : No, Vonia, it wasn't your battle.

AVONIA : It wasn't yours but you took her part. You didn't need to.

TOM : Oh yes I did. Not just for Rose's sake but for my own. For the sake of the sort of plays I believe in, and that Rose ought to act in.

AVONIA *(after a long pause)* : Tom.

TOM : Yes, Vonia.

AVONIA : Tom Wrench.

TOM : Yes, Avonia Bunn?

AVONIA *(after a long pause, then all of a rush)* : Do you really and truthfully believe that if Rose played what's-her-name in that play of yours that you're forever on about, that she would get back all the old Rose Trelawny that she had before and really would, really and truly would be able to act again?

TOM : Well, Avonia—

AVONIA : No, Tom, don't stop me !

318

TOM : I couldn't even try!

AVONIA : No, Tom, but are you sure, cross your heart and hope to die, because—

TOM : Because what, Vonia?

AVONIA : Don't laugh at me, Tom, but when mother died—*she* was never in the theatre, you know—well, there was no one else but me, see, and she left me all she'd ever saved to put by for a rainy day, she said. Five hundred pounds it was, and don't you dare tell Ferdy or I'll—(*She bites her knuckles in fear of having said too much.*)

TOM (*still mystified*) : I promise, Vonia.

AVONIA : Well—I put it by, it's in my skip now—in sovereigns—wrapped in an old pair of tights. That's just to remind me, if I ever did go to dip into it, that there may come a day when I can't wear tights any more, and I may need it. Not that that day *will* ever come, Tom Wrench. But just in case.

TOM : But—

AVONIA : Oh can't you keep quiet for a moment, Tom? I thought that if I lent you the money, you could put your play on, and Rose could play what's-her-name—

TOM : Dora—

AVONIA : Dora, and then she wouldn't have to leave the profession, and break her heart all over again.

TOM : But what about your rainy days, Vonia?

AVONIA : I've got Ferdy now, but Rose hasn't got anybody—not any more—and don't you dare laugh at me, Tom Wrench.

TOM : I'm not laughing, Vonia. I'm not laughing.

AVONIA : Well, that's that then.

TOM : But, Vonia—if by some mad, remote chance we should become partners in this venture—where could we put my play on? Every manager in London—in England—has said it won't do.

AVONIA : Well, when Ferdy and I were walking through the West End the other day, we passed the old Princes, and I thought . . .

TOM : The old Princes?!

AVONIA : Well, it is empty.

TOM : Yes, it's been that for the last twenty years.

AVONIA : Don't throw wet blankets, Tom.

TOM : It would take a deal more than wet blankets to clean that place. Two hundred pounds would only just about remove the top layer—then there'd be a deposit on account of rent—say another two hundred pounds, and with a hundred pounds balance for emergencies—

AVONIA : Do we have to have a balance for emergencies?

TOM : We've already got the emergencies without the balance—that's your five hundred pounds gone before we even start on the play. We need at least another eight hundred!

AVONIA : Oh Tom, how awful. How unfair! Who's got it?

TOM (*wildly*) : The Queen's got it! Rothschild's got it!

AVONIA (*suddenly*) : I know! Do you remember old Mr Morfew, of Duncan Terrace? He used to take great interest in us all at the Wells. You read him one of your plays once, and you told me he liked it. *He* has money.

TOM : He has gout. We don't see him now.

AVONIA : Gout!—how lucky! That means he's at home. Will you run round to Duncan Terrace—?

TOM (*looking down at his clothes*) : Like this?

AVONIA : Nonsense, Wrench, we're not asking him to advance money on your clothes.

320

TOM : The clothes are the man, Jenny.

AVONIA : Oh no they're not, Tom Wrench! (*She dashes across and kisses him on the cheek.*) Oh no they're not! Well, don't stand there all day. Away to Duncan Terrace!

(*Tom starts for the door, but Avonia calls to him.*)

AVONIA : Tom. Why didn't you think of Mr Morfew years ago?

TOM : I can't be expected to write plays and think, all at the same time, Vonia! I needed a manager —I needed you! (*He dashes across the stage and out of the stage door.*)

THE TURN OF AVONIA BUNN (Reprise)

(*As the scene changes back to Rose's dressing room, Avonia, left alone in a state of excitement begins to dance round the stage.*)

AVONIA :
I have to dance
For here's my chance
To assist our Rose
And greatly enhance
The position of one
Whom I dearly love
This is all that she needs—
A decisive shove!
This may—be—the one supremely Good Turn
Of Avonia Bunn!
Of Avonia Bunn!

Scene 4

ROSE'S DRESSING ROOM

(*Rose is alone, finishing her packing. Mrs Mossop comes scurrying across the stage, and knocks on Rose's door.*)

MRS MOSSOP : Miss Trelawny!

ROSE : Come in.

MRS MOSSOP (*entering, and closing the door behind her*): Oh, Miss Trelawny, come here, my dear.

ROSE (*mystified*): Eh?

MRS MOSSOP (*in a heavy stage whisper*): Sir William Gower!

ROSE : Sir William? Oh no!

MRS MOSSOP : It was no good, dear. George tried to stop him at the stage door. 'Miss Trelawny, fellow!' he says. George, thinking him a stage door johnnie, tells him he's a deal too old and decrepit for such a pretty young thing as you are, and gets a thump over the head from the old gentleman's walking stick for his pains. Then he spies me, and demands 'to be conducted to your 'tiring room', and now he's puffing his way over here, and I came on to tell you so you could—oh!

(*There are three distinct raps with a stick on the dressing room door.*)

ROSE (*weakly*): Open it.

(*Enter Sir William.*)

322

MRS MOSSOP : Ah, and a sweet young thing Miss Trelawny is to be—

SIR WILLIAM : Are ye a relative?

MRS MOSSOP : No, I am not a relative, but—

SIR WILLIAM : Go.

(*She departs.*)

My mind is not commonly a wavering one, Miss Trelawny, but it has taken me some time—months —to decide upon calling on ye.

ROSE : Won't you sit down?

SIR WILLIAM (*sitting on a skip*) : Ugh!

ROSE : Have we no cheers here, Sir William? Do we lack cheers?

SIR WILLIAM : My grandson! My grandson! Where is he?

ROSE : Arthur?

SIR WILLIAM : I had but one.

ROSE : Isn't he—in Cavendish Square—?

SIR WILLIAM : Isn't he in Cavendish Square! No, he is not in Cavendish Square. He made his escape during the night of the twenty-second of August last, as you know well.

ROSE : Sir William, I assure you—

SIR WILLIAM : Tsch! How often does he write to you?

ROSE : He does not write to me. He did write, two or three times a day, for about a week. That was in the autumn when I came back here. He never writes now.

SIR WILLIAM : Visits ye?

ROSE : No.

SIR WILLIAM : Comes troubadouring?

ROSE : No, no, no. I have not seen him since that night. I refused to see him. Why, he might be—

SIR WILLIAM : Ah, but he's not. He's alive! (*He produces a small packet of letters.*) Arthur's alive, and full of his tricks still. His Great-Aunt Trafalgar receives a letter from him once a fortnight, posted in London—

ROSE (*her hand out for the letters*) : Oh!

SIR WILLIAM (*withdrawing them*) : Hey!

ROSE (*faintly*) : I thought you wished me to read them. (*He hands them over.*) Ah, thank you. (*She kisses his hand.*)

SIR WILLIAM : What are ye doing, Madam? What are ye doing?

ROSE (*reading*) : 'To reassure you as to my well-being, I cause this to be posted in London—by a friend.'

SIR WILLIAM : A friend!

ROSE : He would never call *me* that.

(*As Rose reads on, Arthur is seen engaged in some 'walking-gentlemanlike' activity, and reading his letter to Aunt Trafalgar.*)

ARTHUR'S LETTER

ARTHUR :

I write to you, dear Great-Aunt
Knowing full well that I can't
Write to my love,
To my own dearest love,
Even to ask
If she is well.
So I write to you, dear Great-Aunt
Hoping perhaps you may plant
Some little seed
In my Grandfather's heart
How does he fare?
I beg you—tell.

No doubt
He may suppose
I think
Only of Rose
But tell him how
I think about him, too,
And want him so much
To love her as I do.
Well that's all for today, dear Aunt.
If I could say what enchanted me
About my Rose
I could compose
More of a letter
Oh; if only you and my Grandfather
Knew her better
I might yet be happy—
Meanwhile
Can I ever forget her?

SIR WILLIAM : Read no more! Return them to me!

(*She holds the letters to her breast.*)

Give them to me, ma'am!

(*Slowly rising, she holds them out meekly to him.*)

(*Peering up into her face.*) What's come to ye?
You are not so much of a vixen as you were.

ROSE (*shaking her head*) : No.

SIR WILLIAM (*suspiciously*) : Less of the devil—?

ROSE (*her eyes cast down*) : Sir William, I am sorry
for having been a vixen, and for all my unruly
conduct, in Cavendish Square. I humbly beg your,
and Miss Gower's, forgiveness.

SIR WILLIAM (*uncomfortably*) : Extraordinary
change.

ROSE : Aren't *you* changed, Sir William, now that you have lost him?

SIR WILLIAM : I?

ROSE : Don't you love him now, the more?

(*Avonia, who has now donned her principal-boy walk-down finery, bursts in through the door.*)

AVONIA : Rose, have you seen Tom?

SIR WILLIAM : A-a-a-ah!

ROSE : Oh, go away, Vonia!

AVONIA : Sir Gower! Good day! (*She withdraws.*)

SIR WILLIAM : Yes, and these are the associates you would have tempted my boy, my grandson, to herd with!

ROSE : That young lady doesn't live in that attire. She is preparing for the pantomime—

SIR WILLIAM : And now he's gone—lured away, I suspect, by one of ye— (*Pointing to the open door.*) By one of those harridans—!

AVONIA (*reappearing*): Now, look here, Sir Gower—

ROSE : Go, Vonia—

AVONIA : We've met before if you remember, in Cavendish Square—

ROSE (*helplessly*): Oh, Mrs Gadd!

SIR WILLIAM : Mistress? A married lady?

AVONIA : Yes, I spent some of my honeymoon at your house—

SIR WILLIAM : What! (*He gapes at her.*)

AVONIA : Now, there's nothing to stare at, Sir Gower. If you must look anywhere in particular, look at that poor thing. A nice predicament you've brought her to!

SIR WILLIAM : Sir—er—Madam—!

AVONIA : You've brought her to beggary amongst

you. You've broken her heart, and what's worse, you've made her genteel. She can't act since she left your mansion. She can only mope about the stage with her eyes fixed like a person in a dream— dreaming of him, I suppose, and of what it is to be a lady. And first she's put upon half salary, and then she gets the sack—the entire sack, Sir Gower! So there's nothing left for her but to starve, or to make artificial flowers. Miss Trelawny I'm speaking of! Our Rose! Our Trelawny! (*Going to Rose*.) Excuse me for interfering, ducky. Good-day, Sir Gower. (*She goes*.)

SIR WILLIAM (*after a pause*): Is this—the case?

ROSE (*in a low voice*): Yes. Fortune has turned against me, rather.

SIR WILLIAM: Miss Trelawny, if you cannot act, you cannot earn your living, and if you cannot earn your living, you must be provided for.

ROSE: Provided for?

SIR WILLIAM: Miss Gower was kind enough to bring me here in a cab. She and I will discuss plans for making provision for ye while driving home.

ROSE: I beg you will do no such thing, Sir William.

SIR WILLIAM: Hey?

ROSE: I could not accept any help from you or Miss Gower.

SIR WILLIAM: You must! You shall!

ROSE: I will not.

(*Pause*.)

SIR WILLIAM: I am sorry, ma'am. I—I believe ye've kept your word to us concerning Arthur, and I—I grieve for your ill fortune.

ROSE: My mother knew how fickle fortune could

be to us gipsies. One of the greatest actors that ever lived warned her of that.

SIR WILLIAM : Miss Gower will also feel extremely —extremely—

ROSE : Kean once warned her of that.

SIR WILLIAM : Kean?

ROSE : Edmund Kean. My mother acted with him when she was a girl.

SIR WILLIAM : With Kean?

ROSE : Yes.

SIR WILLIAM : My dear, I—I've seen Edmund Kean. A young man then, I was—quite different from the man I am now—impulsive—excitable. Kean! Ah, he was a *splendid* gipsy!

ROSE : I've a little crown in there that my mother wore as Cordelia to Kean's Lear.

SIR WILLIAM : I may have seen your mother also. I was somewhat different in those days—

ROSE (*rummaging in the skip*): And the Order and the sword he wore as Richard. He gave them to my father. I've always prized them! That's the Order—

SIR WILLIAM (*takes it*): Kean! God Bless Me!

ROSE : And my mother's crown—

SIR WILLIAM (*looking at it*): I may have seen her. (*Gazing in front of him.*) I was a young man then . . . Put it on, my dear.

(*She looks at him enquiringly, then goes to the mirror and puts on the crown.*)

Lord bless us! How he stirred me! How he—

(*Music begins.*)

ROSE (*turning*): There!

SIR WILLIAM : Cordelia ! Cordelia with Kean !
ROSE (*putting the Order upon him*) : This should
hang so.
SIR WILLIAM : Kean ! I tell ye, when I saw him as
Richard—he almost fired me with an ambition to
—to—I was young then, and a fool, but—

TWO FOOLS

SIR WILLIAM :
There's no fool
Like an old fool
When he forgets what it is
To be young
If he can't remember
How he used to feel
The mighty illusions
That seemed to him real
The actors he'd follow
With passionate zeal
The popular songs
That were sung—
If he can't remember
He's a fool.
ROSE :
There's no fool
Like a young fool
Who is unwilling to learn
From the old
If she cannot learn
That the old may be wise
And age isn't something
To fear and despize
And sometimes her elders
May open her eyes
To knowledge
As precious as gold—

If she cannot learn that
She's a fool.

BOTH :

It seems then
We are two fools
On that at least we appear
To agree

SIR WILLIAM :

Perhaps you can help me
Recapture the past

ROSE :

Perhaps you can teach me
Some wisdom at last

BOTH :

But simply by talking
We're learning so fast
I wonder what makes you and me
Draw closer together?
Is it because
We are fools?

TOM (*off*) : Rose !

SIR WILLIAM : Who's that? I must not—remove these !

(*He struggles with the chain, the door handle turns, and Sir William hastily conceals himself behind the costumes. Tom bursts in.*)

ROSE : Oh—er—yes, Tom. What did you—Oh Tom, what is the matter, you look awful.

TOM : Well, Rose. That is it. The final blow.

ROSE : Not—not the sack? Not you too?

TOM : Worse, Rose ! Worse !

AVONIA (*entering*) : Tom ! Oh, Tom what's happened? Old Mr Morfew, isn't he willing?

TOM : I don't know—he's dead.

AVONIA : No!

TOM : Three weeks ago.

AVONIA : Oh what a chance he has missed!

ROSE : What is it, Tom? Vonia, what is it?

TOM : My play—my comedy—my youngest born! We can find a theatre, Vonia has offered—to help, and you were to play the part of Dora. Wasn't she?

AVONIA : Oh yes, Rose. It's just you. But we need at least another £500 and we thought old Mr Morfew would help us in the speculation.

TOM : Speculation? It's a dead certainty!

AVONIA : *Dead?* Poor Mr Morfew!

TOM : And they'll expect me to rehearse that dragon tomorrow with enthusiasm.

(*Into this scene of sorrow and despair emerges the incongruous figure of Sir William. Over-heated from his sojourn among the costumes, but, as always, dignified.*)

AVONIA : Oh—!

TOM : Eh—?

ROSE : Sir William Gower, Tom Wrench.

SIR WILLIAM : I have been an unwitting party, it appears, to a consultation upon a matter of business. (*To Tom.*) Do I understand, sir, that you have been defeated in some project which would have served the interests of Miss Trelawny?

TOM : Y-y-yes, sir.

SIR WILLIAM : Mr Wicks—

TOM : Wrench—

SIR WILLIAM : Tsch! Sir, it would give me pleasure —it would give my grandson, Mr Arthur Gower pleasure—to be able to aid Miss Trelawny at the present moment.

TOM: S-s-sir William. W-would you like to hear my play?

SIR WILLIAM: Hey?

TOM: My comedy.

SIR WILLIAM: Ho! So ye think I might be induced to fill the office ye designed for the late Mr—Mr—

AVONIA: Morfew.

SIR WILLIAM: Morfew, eh?

TOM: N-n-no, sir.

AVONIA (*shrilly*): Yes!

SIR WILLIAM: Read your play, sir. (*To Rose and Avonia.*) Sit down.

(*Miss Gower is heard outside the door.*)

MISS GOWER: William!

(*Rose opens the door. Miss Gower enters.*)

Oh, William, what has become of you? Has anything dreadful happened?

SIR WILLIAM: Sit down Trafalgar. This gentleman is about to read us a comedy. A cheer! Are there no cheers here?

(*Tom brings one.*)

Sit down.

MISS GOWER: William, is all this quite—A-a-a-ahhh! (*She has caught her first sight of Avonia in her finery.*)

SIR WILLIAM: Quite in place, Trafalgar, quite in place!

(*Gadd and Colpoys burst in, deep in conversation.*)

GADD : Remove your skirts further off left, Gus, then I can enter in a puff of smoke and—(*He sees Sir William and stops dead.*) Great Heavens!

SIR WILLIAM (*to Tom*) : Friends of yours?

TOM : Yes, Sir William.

SIR WILLIAM (*to Gadd and Colpoys*) : Sit Down.

COLPOYS : 'Pon my soul—

SIR WILLIAM : Sit down and be silent! (*To Tom.*) Now, sir.

TOM (*reads*) : Life, a comedy by Thomas Wrench.

(*In the confusion of Gadd and Colpoys jockeying for seats, Tom's double has taken Tom's place, and is sitting with his back to the house, his semi-circle of listeners facing front. The reading of the play is recorded, and as the light on the group is lowered, and the reading fades slightly, Tom steps from the wings into a spot.*)

LIFE

TOM :

As I read my play
And imagine the things they'll say
I'm regretting that they
Said they'd hear me
If they knew me they'd find
Such a concept in my mind
But I'm sure they're too blind
To get near me—
    Ah Well!
    That's Life
    M-m-m-m.
    That's Life.
They won't understand
That the plot of the play I've planned

Isn't noble or grand
It's their own life
And I'm willing to bet
What I read them they'll forget
For most people are set
To disown life—
    Ah well!
    That's Life.
    M-m-m-m.
    That's Life.
They won't want to know
When the characters that I show
Seem to come and to go
As people do
And they'll fiercely resist
When Love that was once In-a-Mist
Is now out in the open
And true.
Life is my play
And I pray there will come a day
When the things that I say
Will excite them
But I'm armoured for strife
I would go, beneath the knife
For this play I've called Life.
And I'll fight them
And succeed—if only to spite them!
And if I fail—ah well—that's Life.

(*Sir William rises. All watch him anxiously. Music continues under dialogue.*)

SIR WILLIAM : Mr Wicks—if this piece of yours will serve to provide employment for Miss Trelawny, I am willing to shoulder the financial responsibility. But I want no communication with your gipsy crew. There is something in your play which disturbs me, and I wish no part of it. All I ask is that my family and myself be left alone, to pursue the remainder of our lives in peace.

TOM : But, Sir William, may we proceed?

SIR WILLIAM : Ye may. Come, Trafalgar. (*He stumps out with Trafalgar.*)

TOM (*grandly*) : Ladies and gentlemen : *Life* goes on !

Scene 5

TO THE PRINCES

(*The dressing-room and the old-fashioned scenery behind it move out of sight and Tom leads Rose and Avonia out of the Wells and into a bare open space surrounded only by the sky.*)

LIFE (second time)

TOM :
Dear friends, come with me,
Look around you and you will see
What I mean you to be
In my new play
For it's under the sky
In the people who pass by
That the secret will lie
To a true play.

(*The three of them are isolated figures against the sky. Rose and Avonia look around as if seeing the 'real world' for the first time.*)

ROSE :
Out here
Lies life !
TOM :
Look round !
ALL :
That's life !
ROSE and AVONIA :
If, out in the street,
Just by studying those we meet
We can learn to defeat
Old pretentions—
TOM, ROSE, AVONIA :
We'll be turning a page
We will sweep away an age
We will bring to the Stage
New dimensions.
If Life's
A Stage
The Stage
Is Life.

(*A forlorn group from the Wells enter, downstage, comprising Mr and Mrs Telfer, Gadd, Colpoys and Mr and Mrs Mossop.*)

THE MOSSOPS :
We don't understand
Why they suddenly seem so grand
GADD, COLPOYS :
Why should we lend a hand
To all this fuss ?
TELFER :
It's been our simple boast—
ALL :
That the Wells is sufficient for most !

MRS TELFER :
But now what is to happen
To us?

(*During this, cobwebs and tattered tabs have flown in, surrounding the proscenium downstage. Behind them, centre, a small flat of the stage-door of the Princes Theatre, has appeared, seen from within. Tom can be seen through the grimy panes as he pushes open the door, and stands in an overhead spot. An unlit bulls-eye lantern is in his hand.*)

TOM : Well, Thomas Wrench, this is it ! (*He strikes a match on the sole of his boot and lights the lantern, then moves slowly down to the front of the stage, peering about him.*)

(*Music continues.*)

The old Princes Theatre ! A hundred years of tradition, and twenty years of cobwebs, dust and—

(*The lantern beam hits the topmost corner of the tabs. There is a flurry, and he follows the erratic flight of a bat into the flies.*)

BATS ! I must have been mad to think that two hundred pounds would clean up this mausoleum —two thousand perhaps—two million ! Vonia, what have we done? (*Drawing himself up.*) Pull yourself together, Wrench—there's no going back now. (*He directs the beam of the lamp round the theatre.*)

TOM (*calling*) : Dora !—Gerald—are you there? I know you can't hear me—not yet—you only exist

337

here. (*He waves his script aloft.*) But wait! When the cobwebs have been swept from the flies—(*He swipes at the cobwebs with his script and they begin to fly out.*) and the dust shaken from the curtains—(*He shakes the curtain remains, and they also fly out.*) when the walls have been scrubbed clean—

(*The light starts to come up on the Princes set which is now in place, and on the New Actors, who are grouped in a semi-circle awaiting their author-director.*)

and those new actors—my actors—meet on this stage—then—oh then . . . !

(*Rose, Avonia and the New Actors advance down-stage, singing:*)

COMPANY:
'Life' is our play!
When this play sees the light of day
We shall pray what we say
Will excite them!
But we're armoured for strife
We could go beneath the knife
For this play that's called 'Life'
And we'll fight them!
And succeed—
Surprise and delight them!
TOM:
And if we fail . . . ? (*He glances at his script and drops it on a table.*)
Ah well!
That's Life.

Scene 6

THE PRINCES THEATRE

(*Tom turns upstage to face his cast.*)

TOM : Good morning, Ladies and Gentlemen. We shall start our first rehearsal in ten minutes time. There is a coffee-house in the street next to the stage door, but I shall want everyone on call in the green-room from a quarter past ten. Thank you.

(*The cast disperses. Tom crosses to talk with the stage management at a table at the side of the stage. An A.S.M. starts rearranging the chairs for the rehearsal. As Mr Denzil crosses the stage, he is talking to Miss Brewster.*)

MISS BREWSTER : I say, Mr Denzil, who plays Gerald?
DENZIL : Gerald?
MISS BREWSTER : The man I have my scene with in the third act—the hero.
DENZIL : Oh, the young man from the country, I understand.
MISS BREWSTER : From the country?
DENZIL : He's coming up by train this morning, Mrs Gadd tells me, from Bath or somewhere.
MISS BREWSTER : Well, whoever he is, if he can't play that scene with me decently, my part's not worth rags.

(*As they wander upstage, they pass Telfer, who is*

339

*standing in the shadows—the first time on any stage
that he has been placed anywhere but centre—as
Mrs Telfer walks across to him.)*

MRS TELFER : Have you read through your role,
James?
TELFER : Yes, Violet. It is confined to the latter
'alf of the second act, so I shall steal away until I
am needed.
MRS TELFER : It affords you no opportunity?
TELFER : A mere fragment.
MRS TELFER : Well, but a few good speeches to a
man of your stamp—
TELFER : Yes, but this is so line-y, Violet—so very
line-y. And what d'you think the character is
described as?
MRS TELFER : What?
TELFER : An old, stagey, out-of-date actor.

*(They stand looking at each other for a moment,
silently.)*

MRS TELFER : Will you—be able—to get near it,
James?
TELFER : I daresay.
MRS TELFER : That's all right then.
TELFER : And you—what have they called you for,
if you're not in the play? They 'ave not dared to
suggest understudy?
MRS TELFER : They don't ask me to act at all,
James.
TELFER : Don't ask you—
MRS TELFER : Mrs Gadd offers me the position of
wardrobe-mistress.
TELFER : Violet.
MRS TELFER : Hush !

340

TELFER : Let us both go home.

MRS TELFER : No, let us remain. We've been idle six months, and I can't bear to see you without your watch, and all your comforts about you.

TELFER : And so this new-fangled stuff, and these dandified people, are to push us, and such as us, from our stools!

MRS TELFER : Yes, James, just as some other new fashion will, in course of time, push them from their stools.

STAGE MANAGER (*calling out*) : Mr Belfer.

TOM : No, no. Telfer.

STAGE MANAGER : Look alive there, Mr Telfer!

(*As Telfer starts towards the Stage Manager, Tom crosses quickly to him.*)

TOM : Mr Telfer, I'm so glad you were able to join the company. I—er—I hope the little part of Poggs appeals to you. Only a sketch, of course, but there was nothing else—quite—in your—

TELFER : Nothing? To whose share does the Earl fall?

TOM : Oh, Mr Denzil plays Lord Parracourt.

TELFER : Denzil? I've never 'eard of 'im. Will you get to me today?

TOM : We—we expect to do so.

TELFER : Very well. Let me be called in the street.

(*He goes out.*)

MRS TELFER : Thank Heaven! I was afraid James would break out.

TOM : Mrs Telfer, I am so sorry there was no part I could offer you.

341

MRS TELFER : Mr Wrench—if we are set to scrub a floor—and we may come to that yet—let us make up our minds to scrub it legitimately—with dignity. (*She leaves.*)

(*Avonia joins Tom.*)

AVONIA : Tom !

TOM : Yes Vonia.

AVONIA : He's not here !

TOM : He will be—never fear. (*Calling to the Stage Manager.*) That door should be further downstage, Mr Palmer.

AVONIA : I don't know how you can be so calm, Tom Wrench. There's Rose down left, and we don't even know whether he'll appear up right, and you stand there as if you didn't care !

TOM (*to Stage Manager*) : Thank you Mr . . . (*Turning on Avonia.*) didn't care !

AVONIA : He might have missed the train, Tom.

TOM : Any other train, Vonia—not this one.

AVONIA : But what if he lost his nerve and turned back at the station.

PULL YOURSELF TOGETHER (Reprise)

TOM (*spoken*) :
Pull yourself together.

AVONIA (*spoken*) :
But he might have done !

TOM (*sings sotto voice*) :
Pull yourself together
Pull yourself together
Don't let them see you're worried—
He is on his way

DENZIL (*to Tom*):
Where's this Mr Gordon?
He's extremely late, sir.

ACTOR:
Slackness in the theatre
Is a thing I hate, sir

STAGE MANAGER:
Will you start rehearsal
Or d'you mean to wait, sir?

ACTORS (*to each other*):
How can the action
Proceed without him?

(*A short babel of conversation from the actors.
'I have a very important scene with him in the
third act . . .'
'First rehearsal and no leading juvenile!'
'Has anybody heard of this Mr Gordon?' etc. Tom
silences them.*)

TOM:
Pull yourselves together
Pull yourselves together
Pull yourselves together
And rehearse my play—
Nothing will be right
Unless you pay attention
Follow my direction
And your own invention
Use imagination
But avoid pretension—

(*Noticing Rose's absence.*)

Where's Miss Trelawny?

343

Will someone call her?
STAGE MANAGER :
Call for Miss Trelawny !
A.S.M
Call for Miss Trelawny !
DENZIL :
Here is not an Author
Who can brook delay !
ACTOR :
Words are what he's plenty of—
MISS BREWSTER :
And never minces !
ACTOR :
The clothes are undistinguished
ACTRESS :
But the *man* convinces
ALL :
Better be ready for entrance
Here at the Princes
And help his precious babe to grow
For this is the op'ning show
This is the op'ning show—
And who knows?
AVONIA (*to Tom*) :
This may be the show of shows
For Rose !
TOM (*to Avonia*) : It's all for Rose !
CALL-BOY : Your call, Miss Rose !
TOM (*aside*) : My darling Rose !
CALL-BOY : Your call, Miss Rose !
TOM (*aside*) : It's all for—

(*Rose enters.*)

ROSE : I'm sorry, Tom, I didn't realize you were ready for me.

344

TOM : We're just about to start from the first scene. Now—when the curtain rises, you are seated here on a garden chair, under an apple tree. You can see the . . .

(*The Stage Manager hurries in.*)

STAGE MANAGER : Oh, excuse me, Mr Wrench, there's a gentleman to see you.
TOM : Who is it, Mr Palmer?
STAGE MANAGER : Sir William Gower.
AVONIA : Sir William!

(*Rose moves as if to leave the stage.*)

TOM : Yes, Rose, Would you mind waiting in the green room?
ROSE : Of course, Tom. (*She goes out.*)
TOM (*to Stage Manager*) : Bring the gentleman onto the stage, please.
AVONIA : Not now, Tom!
TOM : The boy can't arrive for another twenty minutes. Besides, we must sooner or later accept responsibility for our act.
AVONIA : Tom Wrench, I feel sick.
TOM : I know.
AVONIA : What if he should take his money back?
TOM : At least that would enable me to write a melodrama.
AVONIA : Why?
TOM : I should then understand the motives and the springs of crime!

(*Across the stage comes Sir William, the Stage Manager in tow.*)

STAGE MANAGER (*to Tom*): Sir William Gower.

SIR WILLIAM (*to Stage Manager*): Thank ye, we are acqueented. Leave us.

(*Stage Manager withdraws to side of stage.*)

TOM : Good morning, Sir William—

AVONIA (*curtseying tentatively*): Sir William—

SIR WILLIAM : Give me a cheer. Have ye no cheers here?

TOM : Yes. (*He provides one.*)

SIR WILLIAM : Thank ye. You are astonished at seeing me here, I daresay?

AVONIA (*nervously bright*): Not at all!

SIR WILLIAM : Addressing the gentleman. (*To Tom.*) You are surprised to see me?

TOM : Very.

SIR WILLIAM : Ah! The truth is, I am beginning to regret my association with ye.

AVONIA (*faintly*): Oh! You're—you're not going to withdraw your support, Sir William.

SIR WILLIAM (*ignoring her*): I—I have been slightly indisposed since I made your acqueentance in Clerkenwell. I find myself unable to sleep at night. That comedy of yours—it buzzes continually in my head, sir.

TOM : It was written with such an intention, Sir William—to buzz in people's heads.

SIR WILLIAM : Ah, I'll take care ye don't read me another, Mr Wicks. I don't relish being reminded of late members of my family in this way, and being kept awake at night, thinking—turning over in my mind—

AVONIA (*soothingly*): Of course not.

SIR WILLIAM (*taking snuff*): Pa-a-ah! And there-

346

fore, upon receiving your letter last night, acqueening me with your intention to commence rehearsing your comedy—

AVONIA (*proudly*): *Our* comedy!

SIR WILLIAM: Ugh!—I determined to present myself here—

TOM: To—to watch the rehearsal?

SIR WILLIAM: The rehearsal of those episodes in your comedy which remind me of a member of my family. I wish to be assured that whosoever is to impersonate that—*late* member of my family, shall not—disgrace him.

TOM: I can guarantee, Sir William, that Mr Gordon will not disgrace any member of your family—or himself.

SIR WILLIAM: Hrumph! Well, I don't wish to be steered at by any of your—what d'ye call 'em—your gipsy crew—

TOM: Ladies and gentlemen of the company, we call them.

SIR WILLIAM: I don't care what ye call 'em. Put me into a curtained box, where I can hear and see, but not be seen, and when I have heard and seen enough, I'll return home.

AVONIA: And—if—you are satisfied with what you see this morning, will you—

SIR WILLIAM: My future support of this enterprise, ma'am, depends upon that 'if'. (*Rising.*) What do plays and players do, coming into my head, disturbing my repose? You call your comedy 'Life', Mr Wicks. It comes too near my life, sir—too near my family—too near my heart. What business has the theatre to do that?

TOM: Mrs Gadd, would you be so kind as to escort Sir William to his box, and then return to the rehearsal?

AVONIA : Certainly, Mr Wrench. (*Taking his arm.*)
Sir William—?

SIR WILLIAM (*withdrawing his arm sharply*) : I'll
thank ye not to repeat that action, ma'am. (*To the
Stage Manager.*) My box, sir—my box—

(*The Stage Manager leads him off. Tom and
Avonia look at each other apprehensively.*)

TOM : We shall start again from the opening scene.
Call Miss Trelawny, please.

(*Tom replaces the chair used by Sir William, looks
out front, takes a deep, deep breath as Rose enters.*)

Everything is all right, Rose. We are starting from
the opening.

ROSE : Very well. (*She sits on the garden chair.*)

TOM : That's right. Now—you can see the church
tower and the outlying houses of the village beyond
the garden. You've been knitting, but now you've
stopped. You turn to look into the house—the
doors are down there—and the ball of wool falls
from your lap, and rolls across the grass.

(*She drops the wool, and he stops it with his foot.*)

It stops there. Peggy now enters from the house—

(*Avonia enters.*)

That's right, Vonia—and crosses to Dora, notices
the ball of wool—

(*Avonia gives a rather Wellsian reaction.*)

348

No, Vonia, she just notices it—she doesn't—try the entrance again.

(*Avonia does—much better.*)

She crosses to the garden gate, and looks across the fields. She looks back at Dora, smiles, and shakes her head. Dora says—

ROSE : Surely he can't have forgotten.

TOM : Peggy turns—leans on the gate—and says—

AVONIA : No one would dare to forget one of your mama's invitations.

TOM : A pause.

ROSE : What is the—

TOM : But before she can finish the line, the church clock is heard over the fields—one—two—three—four. Dora gets up, puts her knitting into the box, and shuts the lid—very firmly.

ROSE : Well, I don't intend to wait here all day. Are you coming?

AVONIA : No, not yet.

TOM : Dora goes into the house, to play the piano, and she's perhaps singing to herself as she—

ROSE : What shall I be singing, Tom?

TOM : Oh anything—you are waiting for the man you have fallen in love with—anything—we'll settle it later.

(*Rose goes out.*)

Peggy watches her—wait, let her get out of ear-shot—Now. She turns, and waves to someone approaching across the fields.

(*The piano offstage starts the melody of 'Ever of Thee'. Tom looks off into the wings, then back at*

*Avonia, and shakes his head. Suddenly the doors
at the back of the stalls burst open, and Arthur
dashes down the gangway and onto the stage as
Tom leaps forward to greet him.)*

TOM (*loud enough for Rose to hear*): Are you
ready for your entrance, Mr Gordon?

(*Arthur nods, breathless.*)

Good. Now—you enter here. Peggy motions to you
to be quiet, and runs into the house.

(*Avonia crosses to the exit, and stands there.*)

All right?

(*Arthur nods.*)

Good. Now you see the ball of wool—Dora
dropped it earlier—cross and pick it up. (*Calls off.*)
Dora—this is where we hear you—Dora!

(*Rose begins to sing 'Ever of Thee'*)

And she enters—

(*Rose enters singing, sees Arthur, and stops dead.
Neither moves.*)

You hand her the ball of wool, Mr Gordon, and
she says—
ROSE : Arthur!
TOM : No—er—!
ROSE : Oh Arthur, why are you here?

350

(The orchestra takes up the melody from the beginning.)

ARTHUR : I am trying to be what you are.
ROSE : What I am?
ARTHUR : Yes. A gipsy.
ROSE : A gipsy—oh, Arthur. *(She falls into his arms.)*
ROSE, ARTHUR *(sing)* :
Singing of thee
I'm all-adoring
Suddenly love
Has set me free.

(All the members of the New Company together with Rose's old friends from the Wells, gather quietly in the shadows at the back of the stage and softly take up the melody.)

ALL :
Far as the stars
My heart is soaring
Ever, my love,
To thee.

(On the last note of the song, Sir William enters from the side of the stage and stands staring at Rose and Arthur. Pause.)

SIR WILLIAM : What is this—conspiracy?
TOM : I beg you to understand, Sir William, that Miss Trelawny was, till a moment ago, as ignorant as yourself of Mr Arthur Gower's doings, of his movements, of his whereabouts. Whatever conspiracy there has been, Sir William, is my own—to

bring these two young people together again, to make them happy.

(*Sir William turns slowly to Arthur, and, after a moment's hesitation, impulsively embraces him. He then crosses to Rose, takes her hand, and bends over it. As he straightens up, Rose smiles at him, and then crosses to kiss Tom on the cheek.*

The melody of 'Trelawny of the Wells' has started very softly, and the entire company now takes up the words.)

ALL (*sing*) :
In your bright new life
That is shining ahead
We sincerely wish you joy !
Remembering the joy you gave us
When you were our Trelawny
Our one and only Rose Trelawny

(*Tom joins Rose and Arthur's hands.*)

TOM (*spoken*) : Oh ! my dears, let us—get on with the rehearsal.
ALL (*sing*) : Trelawny of the Wells !

Curtain

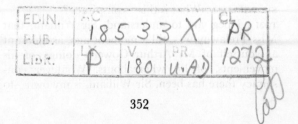

PLAYS OF THE YEAR

Plays of the Year was launched in 1949. So far forty-one volumes (and two Specials, *The Six Wives of Henry VIII* and *Elizabeth R*) have appeared chosen and edited by J. C. Trewin. It is regretted that volumes 1, 2, 3, 4, 5, 7, 8, 9, 10, 12, 13, 14, 15, 16, 17, 19, 21, and 22 are now out of print.

VOLUME 1 1948-49

COCKPIT by BRIDGET BOLAND

FAMILY PORTRAIT by LENORE COFFEE and W. JOYCE COWAN

THE HAPPIEST DAYS OF YOUR LIFE by JOHN DIGHTON

THE MISER by MOLIERE, adapted by MILES MALLESON

THE PARAGON by ROLAND and MICHAEL PERTWEE

DON'T LISTEN LADIES! by SACHA GUITRY, adapted by STEPHEN POWYS and GUY BOLTON

VOLUME 2 1949

ANN VERONICA by RONALD GOW, based on the novel by H. G. WELLS

DARK OF THE MOON by HOWARD RICHARDSON and WILLIAM BERNEY

BLACK CHIFFON by LESLEY STORM

THE LATE EDWINA BLACK by WILLIAM DINNER and WILLIAM MORUM

THE KING OF FRIDAY'S MEN by MICHAEL MOLLOY

BEFORE THE PARTY by RODNEY ACLAND, from a story by W. SOMERSET MAUGHAM

VOLUME 3 1949-50

THE HOLLY AND THE IVY by WYNYARD BROWNE

YOUNG WIVES' TALE by RONALD JEANS

BONAVENTURE by CHARLOTTE HASTINGS

CASTLE IN THE AIR by ALAN MELVILLE

*TARTUFFE by MOLIERE, adapted by MILES MALLESON

TOP OF THE LADDER by TYRONE GUTHRIE

VOLUME 4 1950

SEAGULLS OVER SORRENTO by HUGH HASTINGS

HIS EXCELLENCY by DOROTHY and CAMPBELL CHRISTIE

BACKGROUND by W. CHETHAM-STRODE

TO DOROTHY, A SON by ROGER MACDOUGALL

THE THISTLE AND THE ROSE by WILLIAM DOUGLAS HOME

VOLUME 5 1950-51

LACE ON HER PETTICOAT by AIMEE STUART

COUNT YOUR BLESSINGS by RONALD JEANS

DOCTOR'S DELIGHT by MOLIERE, adapted by SIR BARRY JACKSON

THE GENTLE GUNMAN by ROGER MACDOUGALL

THE CHILDREN'S HOUR by LILLIAN HELLMAN

VOLUME 6 1951

SAINT'S DAY by JOHN WHITING

THE PRODIGIOUS SNOB ("Le Bourgeois Gentilhomme") by MOLIERE, adapted by MILES MALLESON

THE SAME SKY by YVONNE MITCHELL

WHO GOES THERE! by JOHN DIGHTON

GUNPOWDER, TREASON AND PLOT by HUGH ROSS WILLIAMSON

VOLUME 7 1951-52

*THE YOUNG ELIZABETH by J. DOWLING and F. LETTON

NIGHTMARE ABBEY by ANTHONY SHARP, from THOMAS LOVE PEACOCK'S novel

UNDER THE SYCAMORE TREE by SAMUEL SPEWACK

THIRD PERSON by ANDREW ROSENTHAL

DIAMOND CUT DIAMOND by HUGH ROSS WILLIAMSON

* Plays marked thus are also available in single editions, cloth-bound and paper-bound.

Also available
A SWORD FOR A PRINCE and Other Plays for a Young Company, by J. C. Trewin 8s 6d